Ethiopia
Options for Rural Development

Ethiopia: Options for Rural Development

Edited by Siegfried Pausewang, Fantu Cheru, Stefan Brüne and Eshetu Chole

Zed Books Ltd
London and New Jersey

Ethiopia: Options for Rural Development was first published
by Zed Books Ltd., 57 Caledonian Rd, London N1 9BU, UK
and 171 First Avenue, Atlantic Highlands,
New Jersey 07716, USA in 1990

Cover design by Sophie Buchet
Cover pictures by Aase and Siegfried Pausewang

Printed and bound in the United Kingdom
by Billing and Sons Ltd, Worcester

British Library Cataloguing in Publication Data

Ethiopia: options for rural development.
  1. Ethiopia. Rural regions. Economic development
  I. Pausewang, Siegfried
  330.963
  ISBN 0-86232-958-2
  ISBN 0-86232-959-0 pbk

Library of Congress Cataloging-in-Publication Data

Ethiopia: options for rural development / edited by
Siegfried Pausewang.
    p.   cm.
  ISBN 0-86232-958-2. -- ISBN 0-86232-959-0 (pbk)
  1. Rural Development -- Ethiopia.   2.Agriculture
Economic aspects Ethiopia. I. Pausewang, Siegfried.
HN789. Z9C643   1990   90-39967
307.1'412'0963--dc20   CIP

Table of Contents

Foreword   1

Introduction   3

The Domestic and International Context 4
State Peasant Relations 6
Environment, Population and Resource Management 9
In Search of New Options 12

1 The Agricultural Sector *Stefan Brüne*   15

Agrarian Development in Peasant Societies: The Nature of the
Problem 17
The 1975 Land Reform 19
Agricultural Production (1974-88) 21
Producer Cooperatives and State Farms 21
New Land Use Policies: Resettlement and Villagization 26
Conclusion 27

**2 Urban-rural Relations in Agrarian Change. An Historical
Overview** *Taye Mengistae*   30

From Gult-lordship to Landlordship 30
Urbanization as a New Dimension of Agrarian Overlordship 32
A New Urban-rural Relationship 34
Concluding Remarks 35

3 Meret Le Arrashu   *Siegfried Pausewang*   38

Some Basic Principles in Relation to Land Rights 38
Land Tenure in Ethiopian History 40
Expansion of the Empire to the South 42
From Gult to Freehold 43
The Land Reform 45
Conclusion 46

4 The Evolution of Rural Development Policies *Dejene Aredo*   49

    National Economic Planning and the Agricultural Sector 49
    Concluding Remarks 55

5 Gender Relations in Mobilizing Human Resources *Hanna Kebede*   58

    Marriage, Education and the Family 59
    Economic Activity, Productivity, and Labour Compensation for
    Women. 61
    Property Ownership, Income Generation and Purchasing Power . . . 63
    Decision Making in the Household; Women's Political and
    Economic Participation2 64
    Conclusion 67

6 The International Context *Fantu Cheru*   69

    The Private vs. Public Debate 70
    Export-oriented Growth: A Way Out? 72
    Structural Adjustment: A New Orthodoxy? 75

7 Soviet-Ethiopian Cooperation in Agriculture *Grigori Polyakov*   79

    Agricultural Cooperation in the 1970s 79
    New Signals in Soviet-Ethiopian Cooperation 80
    Present Cooperation and Current Problems 81
    Glasnost, Perestroika, and Ethiopian Agriculture 83
    Toward a New Soviet-Ethiopian Economic Cooperation 84

8 Agriculture and Surplus Extraction *Eshetu Chole*   89

    The Problem 89
    Surplus Extraction through Agricultural Taxation 90
    Surplus Extraction through Grain Marketing and Pricing 93
    Surplus Extraction through Foreign Exchange Generation 97
    Other Forms of Surplus Extraction 98
    Postscript in Lieu of a Conclusion 98

9 Cooperatives, State Farms and Smallholder Production
Dessalegn Rahmato   **100**

The Policy Framework for Transition 100
Peasants, Cooperatives, State Farms: A Comparative Analysis 103
Whither Socialist Transition ? 107

10 The Marketing and Pricing of Agricultural Products
Befekadu Degefe and Tesfaye Tafesse   **111**

Introduction 111
Marketing and Pricing Policies 111
Domestic Market and Export Policies 112
The Peasant Viewpoint 117
Concluding Remarks 119

11 Resettlement: Policy and Practice *Alula Pankhurst*   **121**

Historical Background1 121
The Emergency Phase (1984-89) 122
Assessments 128
Policy Changes 131

12 Villagization: Policies and Prospects *Alemayehu Lirenso* **135**

The Emergence of Villagization as a National Programme 136
The Villagization Guidelines 139
Achievements and Shortcomings 141

13 What Change and for Whom? *Helen Pankhurst*   **144**

Introduction 144
Women and Production 144
Women and Modern Structures 147
Women and Reproduction 148
Women and Cultural Beliefs .150
Conclusions 151

14 Population Issues in Rural Development *Markos Ezra* **156**

Population Size and Growth Rate 156
Population Distribution and Density 156

Morbidity and Mortality 158
Fertility: Levels and Trends 159
Population Density and Land Availability 160
Growing Ecological Degradation 162
Conclusion 162

15 Environment and Mass Poverty *Daniel Gamachu*   164

Introduction: Developing Hunger? 164
Population Explosion: A Problem of Procreation ? 165
Exploitation: Policing the Policy Makers ? 166
The Rural Poor: Too Many or Too Weak? 166
Vulnerability: A Side-effect of Development? 168
The Good Old Days: How Bad Were They? 169
Post-Revolution: Proclamations and Disincentives? 170
Future Prospects: Central or Local Knowledge? 172

16 Peasants, Environment, Resettlement *Alemneh Dejene* 174

Peasant Views on Resettlement 176
Environmental Impact in Settlement Areas 178
Conclusion 184

17 Natural Resource Management and Rural Development in Ethiopia *Adrian P. Wood*   187

Introduction 187
Trends in Natural Resource Use .187
The Causes of Environmental Degradation 191
Experience of Recent Years 192
Towards a New Approach to Conservation for Sustained Agriculture 195
Prospects 197

18 Famine or Preparedness? *Dag Hareide*   199

The Need for Preparedness 199
A New Thinking in a Continuum .200
Preparedness: A Bridge between Development and Relief 201
Elements in a Famine Preparedness Plan in Ethiopia 201

19 Pastoral Nomadism and Rural Development *Fecadu Gadamu*   **205**

    The General Condition of Pastoral Nomads 205
    The Need for Development of Pastoral Nomads 206
    Ecological and Socio-economic Constraints upon Nomadic
    Development 208
    A Development Strategy for Pastoral Nomads 209
    A Minimum Package Programme .210

20 The Peasant Perspective *Siegfried Pausewang*   **213**

    The Land Reform 213
    Re-Establishing Central Control 214
    A Socialist Agriculture? 215
    Rural Alternatives? 215
    A Peasant Option 216
    The Market, AMC, and the Peasant 217
    Socialism and Democracy 218
    Mechanization 219
    Cooperation 219
    Central Control or Local Democracy? 220
    Urban - Rural Relations 221
    Is Rural Democracy Possible? 222
    New Alliances? 223
    Outlook 224

Bibliography   **227**

Glossary   **244**

Acronyms   **248**

Geographical Names   **250**

Index   **256**

Contributors

Alemayehu Lirenso, Research fellow, Institute of Development Research, and lecturer at the Department of Geography, Addis Ababa University. Research interest in rural development and agricultural policies. Author of several articles on grain marketing and pricing systems in Ethiopia, and other rural policy issues.

Alemneh Dejene Ph.D., was a research fellow, Energy and Environmental Policy Center, John F. Kennedy School of Government, Harvard University; at present working for the World Bank's Southern Africa Division (Agriculture). Author of: *Peasants, Agrarian Socialism, and Rural Development in Ethiopia* (1987), *Environment, Famine, and Politics in Ethiopia: A View from the Village* (1990).

Befecadu Degefe, Assistant Professor at the Institute of Development Research, University of Addis Ababa.

Stefan Brüne Ph.D., Assistant Professor, Department of Geography, University of Osnabrück, Germany. Author of: hiopien: Unterentwicklung und radikale Militrherrschaft, Hamburg 1986; several articles on political development in Ethiopia.

Daniel Gamachu, Associate Professor in the Department of Geography, Addis Ababa University.

Dejene Aredo, Lecturer in the Department of Economics, Addis Ababa University.

Dessalegn Rahmato, Senior research fellow, Institute of Development Research, Addis Ababa University. Research interest in rural development. Author of: Agrarian Reform in Ethiopia(1984); numerous publications on rural policies, local markets, famine prevention and resettlement.

Eshetu Chole Ph.D., Professor of Economics, University of Addis Ababa; currently at the Institute of Nationalities, Addis Ababa. Research interest in political economy, Ethiopian development, rural economy etc. Currently president of OSREA Author of numerous articles on economic development.

Fantu Cheru Ph.D., Assistant Professor of African Development Studies, American University, Washington, research interest in social and economic development in Africa. Author of: *The Silent Revolution in Africa: Debt, Development and Democracy* (1989).

Fecadu Gadamu Ph.D., Associate Professor, Department of Sociology, Addis Ababa University. Research interest in pastoralists, ethnicity; Study of pastoral nomads in Ethiopia. Author of: *State and Pastoralism* (forthcoming), *Ethnicity*, (forthcoming).

Hanna Kebede, 15 years of experience in rural development; served as consultant for UNDP, FAO, and other non-governmental organisations.

Dag Hareide, Sociologist, project "Alternative Future" in Norway; from 1984 to 1987 head of the United Nations famine relief cooordination office in Ethiopia, currently chairman of the Norwegian Association for the Conservation of Nature.

Markos Ezra, Research fellow, Demographic Training and Research Center of the Institute of Development Research, University of Addis Ababa.

Alula Pankhurst Ph.D., Manchester University; currently teaching at Addis Ababa University.

Helen Pankhurst, Edinburgh University, currently finishing a doctoral thesis based on fieldwork in Manz, Ethiopia.

Siegfried Pausewang Ph.D., Research Fellow, Chr. Michelsen Institute, Bergen, Norway; research interest in rural society and development. Author of: *Peasants, Land and Society. A Social History of Land Reform in Ethiopia* (1983); articles on rural development in Ethiopia.

Grigori Polyakov, Candidate of Science, consultant to the journal *International Affairs* and *Economics and Life*, Moscow, USSR.

Taye Mengistae, Lecturer in the Department of Economics, Addis Ababa University.

Tesfaye Tafesse, Lecturer, Department of Geography, and research fellow at the Institute of Development Research, Addis Ababa University.

Adrian P. Wood Ph.D., Senior lecturer, Department of Geographical Sciences, Huddersfield Politechnic. Co-author of: *Ethiopia. National Conservation Strategy*. Phase I report; author of numerous articles on rural development in Ethiopia and Africa.

Foreword

On the fifth of March, 1990, President Mengistu Haile Mariam announced in a speech to the central committee of the Workers' Party of Ethiopia new reforms for political and economic development. The speech was followed up by a central committee resolution enacting first steps towards "perestroika" in Ethiopia. It inaugurated a mixed economy with a combination of plan and market instruments in economic policies. In the field of agriculture, it declared the peasants the legal owners of the crops, plants and trees on their land, and made their usufructuary rights on farm land hereditary. Grain market restrictions and quota deliveries were abolished and AMC confined to the role of state marketing board competing on open markets. Cooperatives were given the right to dissolve themselves, while plans for a new policy designed to strengthen cooperatives was announced.

So far, no further major action has been taken to clarify the new policies. In the villages, all redistribution of land has been stopped, and no more quotas are being collected. Many cooperatives have dissolved or are in the process of dissolving. Peasant associations appear considerably weakened and reluctant to take any decisions knowing that any major change in the rural social order is bound to affect their power and position. Their leaders are deeply disturbed by insecurity about their future support from the state. State interference appears conspicuously absent from villages at present, the only exception being recruiting campaigns for the army, which are carried out with increasingly repressive methods. Peasant associations have to meet a quota of recruits, and this is enforced with military power. In some cases, members of the executive committees of peasant associations that failed to fulfil their quota were sent to the war themselves. Such campaigns inevitably antagonize peasants and peasant leaders alike , serving only to spread discontent and to turn the peasants against the state and its representatives.

Individual peasants are hesitantly beginning to assume their new rights, to test the strength of their new position. The net result is an unmistakeable decline in the authority of local administration, and a general feeling of insecurity, in the expectation of further changes to come. Everybody seems to be trying to consolidate and entrench their position, in view of an imminent period of struggle for a new rural order.

This book was conceived long before these latest changes, in August, 1988, at the International Conference of Ethiopian Studies, in Paris. A group of Ethiopian and European scholars felt that a more profound discussion of options and alternatives in rural development policies was needed. one that went behind the easy simplifications of "rural socialism" versus "market liberalization".

Some twenty contributors volunteered to write one chapter each on their respective field research in rural Ethiopia. Financial support from the Norwegian Foreign Ministry, the Norwegian Ministry for Development Cooperation, from NORAD and from the German non-governmental organization *Brot für die Welt* is gratefully acknowledged. In July 1989, the authors met at the Chr. Michelsen Institute in Norway to discuss the individual contributions with a view to integrating them into a book. Each author revised his or her text accordingly, then a group of four editors put together the chapters that make up this book.

Much time and space has been devoted to a discussion of rural society and agricultural policy as they were before the Central Committee introduced the recent changes. Nonetheless, we believe that the new developments have made this book all the more topical. The main motivation of the authors was to stimulate a debate, which is more necessary now than ever before. Flexible solutions do not simply flow from a change of ideology or political mentor. they can only be worked out in an open debate which involves all groups and interests.

Such a debate ought to concentrate on finding policies, conditions and institutions which allow the peasants to develop agriculture and rural society using their own resources and initiative, building on their existing base. For this, we believe peasants need at least three guarantees. They need long-term security on the land they till not necessarily private property, which carries the risk of being forced to sell through debt or economic pressure. They need local democracy, participation in local planning and influence over the decisions which affect their social situation. And they need institutionalized guarantees to safeguard their influence upon those central decisions that shape the context of their work, such as taxation levels. We believe these three guarantees would change the stifling social climate which has developed in Ethiopia over the last decade. It is our hope to stimulate discussion as to how such guarantees can be established and institutionalized.

A recent publication on rural Ethiopia is entitled *Agricultural Revolution and Peasant Emancipation in Ethiopia: A Missed Opportunity*. As recent world events demonstrate, history does sometimes offer a second chance to take up opportunities missed in the past; but when it does, public impatience has a fatal propensity to spoil them once again. We hope our book, and the debate it may stimulate, will contribute to making sure that the opportunities of the Ethiopian peasant revolution of 1975 are not squandered once again.

October 1990

Introduction

Agricultural development is at present a central issue in Ethiopia. Agriculture is the major source of employment, revenue and export earnings, and Ethiopia desperately needs to increase the productivity of the agricultural sector. Almost 90 per cent of the population depend on agriculture for their livelihood. Rural development is an indispensable prerequisite, not only for any improvements, but even for the maintenance of a minimum basic living standard for a growing population. However, production figures for the last ten years show alarming trends towards stagnation. The land reform of 1975 has so far not delivered the hoped-for increased output and productivity. The performance of collective agriculture, and particularly of state farms, has been disappointing, not to mention the high cost involved in this experiment. The productivity of smallholder agriculture has also not kept pace with the growth of population.

Since the land reform of 1975 the Ethiopian Government has embarked on a consistent policy of "socialist transformation of agriculture". It has formed peasant associations and service cooperatives, created a new marketing system, state farms, cooperative farms, launched a major resettlement programme, and instituted a programme of villagization. Despite official rhetoric regarding the role of peasants and their associations in "socialist reconstruction", the agricultural policy of the government concentrated on establishing large-scale mechanized farming patterned after East European models. Large-scale, capital intensive production was expected to enable the country to increase its food production in the shortest amount of time. The unquestioned assumption that modernization and mechanization would increase productivity was a critical mistake. Despite fifteen years of socialist development, Ethiopia is far from achieving food self-sufficiency, for numerous reasons discussed in this book.

The agrarian crisis in Ethiopia has prompted major international debates on the causes of the disaster. While drought and regional wars are partly to blame, both domestic and external critics of the regime attribute the crisis mainly to government policies. Consequently, Western donors have been urging the government to adopt "free market" policies, consistent with the overall development strategy of the World Bank and the IMF. Unfortunately, a proper debate on policies has seldom emerged. Rather, the issue has been simplified into a dichotomy between just two possible models: rural development through a "free market economy" alternatively termed a "smallholder model" or a "peasant strategy", versus a "collective agriculture" model within which socialism was without reservation identified with present government policies.

This book is an attempt to get away from this black-and-white interpretation of assumed antagonistic policies. The authors share the view that rural development is not just a question of choosing one or the other model, and that the "socialism" versus "capitalism" dichotomy has little relevance to Ethiopian rural society. Small peasants in rural communities have their own forms of organizing cooperation and equity. Instead of importing solutions from Western or Eastern models, it would be worth considering indigenous knowledge and experience, and building on local institutions with traditions of mutual aid and solidarity.

The reader should not look for a comprehensive programme or policy in the present text. The authors thought that attempting to develop one alternative option for agricultural policies would be both too ambitious, and at the same time too simplistic. Instead, it was considered more appropriate that each contributor should give a summary overview of current problems in her or his sub-field of specialization, and spell out which options currently exist and what their consequences might be, on the basis of research findings and discussion of facts. Against this background, the book attempts to stimulate a debate which addresses major issues in agricultural policies, and the choices open for government action.

The reader may thus distinguish varying political judgements in different contributions, and may find one author contradicting another. Such flexibility is fruitful, and intended. At the same time, this book aspires to be more than a mere collection of individual papers. Each of the issues dealt with by individual authors has to be seen in relation to the others, and in terms of a common concern for a renewed public debate.

The Domestic and International Context

Rural development cannot be planned in the abstract. The cultural background of different peoples, ecological conditions, available technology and manpower, health conditions and many other factors constitute a context within which planning measures attempt to stimulate growth. Existing legislation, local and international market relations, rural institutions, but also educational standards, the position of women, religious norms or agricultural practices can all have a limiting effect on political measures. But at the same time, and conversely, politics can also have a retarding effect on rural productivity, disrupting rural activities and inhibiting local initiatives. Rural society is a complicated web of human relations, where each link has an effect on the whole net, and on all the other individuals in it. Rural policies must influence a complicated pattern in a desired direction, with considerable caution and sensitivity, to achieve limited goals without disrupting wider peasant growth potentials.

Policies must find an optimal balance between collective democratic responsibility for local development which has substantial traditions in Ethiopia and the need for central control over abuses, corruption, or the re-emergence of elites with exploitative economic power. Moreover, macro-economic demands and developmental goals may occasionally conflict with human relations and with needs on a local level.

A balance, moreover, must be sought within a historically specific society with its own conditions, notably a cultural tradition and historical heritage which place more emphasis on secure stability than on growth, and an agriculture limited by a low technical level. In 1975, the new government of Ethiopia inherited huge problems of rural unrest, characterized by regional and ethnic differences, social conflicts, peasant exploitation, evictions, insecurity and discontent, and no doubt had to make major efforts to overcome this imperial heritage in the provinces. Our first contribution, by *Stefan Brüne*, offers a summary analysis of the agricultural sector after the revolution of 1974 and outlines the political developments which formed the context for present rural options.

Rural society is also defined through its twin counterpart, the urban society. Whether development based on the interest of peasants is possible at all, given the political strength of urban demands, is well worth critical reflection, as *Taye Mengistae* demonstrates in his essay. Urban-rural relations also dominate the history of land ownership, formed in the process of centralization of power and urbanization during the second half of the 19th century. *Siegfried Pausewang* highlights the change, during this process, from unique and complex local systems of collective responsibility for land distribution into a land tenure system which resembles feudal structures. This change radically redefined conditions of access to land for peasants, which up to today pre-occupy the minds of peasants and condition rural social life. An urbanizing nobility, and urban interests linked to the colonial powers, opened up the rural areas for foreign commercial interests, even without colonial rule. The strength of such links, more than the military power of the Ethiopian Emperor, may help to explain why Ethiopia remained the only African territory to maintain political independence.

Rural structures and institutions which regulated the relations between peasants, urban centres, and the government administration, created during this period of centralization of the Ethiopian Empire, were radically changed after the revolution of 1974. *Dejene Aredo* discusses agricultural policies after the land reform of 1975, identifying the major attempts of the government to structure rural development through its campaigns, plans and development programmes.

An issue long neglected in discussing the context for rural development is gender relations. Rural productivity may depend more on distribution of work than of land, more on relations within the family than between families. And yet these relations are seldom given sufficient attention as a major factor for rural productivity development. The chapter by *Hanna Kebede* takes up such issues. Gender relations in rural society cannot be improved with a few projects for women, or by strengthening women's associations: an integral part of rural development is to find ways of employing and expanding the human and economic potential of rural women, to give them access to social involvement. Encouraging more women's initiatives, engaging women in any field of rural activities, may well result in projects or rural institutions allowing more appropriate planning, more production, or more cultural activity, better food, more environmental quality, improved well-being, better health, more knowledge, more joy - in short, more development.

No country can escape the international economic climate. Neither can any country escape the need to import goods and services, without seriously disrupting essential infrastructures, cultural values, public health, and human life. Imports have to be financed through exports, and there is thus always a strong imperative to export. But African countries cannot, given existing international market relations, export their way out of debts, argues *Fantu Cheru*. Nor can they even expect to finance their social programmes of redistribution through exports. All exports contain a component of redistribution, in general from poor economies to the rich, from labour to technology, and from the working masses to elites on international and national levels. It is an important challenge for policies to minimize this component in foreign trade, and to protect domestic markets and labour relations as much as possible from adverse effects. Imports are expensive for a poor country. As a rule of thumb, which needs however to be moderated through sensitive and balanced policies, production for local needs should precede export production, and production with own resources should get preference over imports. Politicians should have good reasons to deviate from this rule.

While we thus see significant problems inherent in a free market model of development, *Grigori Polyakov* shows that the socialist alternative, binding rural development in Ethiopia to the Soviet economy, has its own problems and also exposes peasants to adverse influences from outside. Perestroika seems so far not to have been translated into a more flexible and adequate rural policy for Ethiopia. It offers no better prospects for peasants than the World Bank with its restructuring packages. Both together form the international context within which, one way or the other, rural development policies have to work. But none of the two major concepts can claim to solve the compounding problems. Ethiopian peasant societies must find their own solutions for their development and their relation with the state.

State – Peasant Relations

There is a lot of potential unutilized in Ethiopian agriculture. Investments to develop agriculture in its own right may offer much higher returns than is assumed in current expectations, and may compare much more favourably with growth potentials in other sectors. Any investment increasing agricultural production is a contribution to future growth in agriculture and in other sectors, while too strong taxation of agriculture may reduce its ability to produce the resources needed for its own and, in the long run, other sectors' development.

Investment in agriculture is just as much a question of peasant motivation and of local initiatives as it is one of physical production capacities. This is why rural development is intimately linked to local democracy. Local accumulation for local development, local decisions, utilizing resources where they are produced, can make the hardships of forsaking consumption more acceptable to peasants. Policies should consider not only the direct economic returns when comparing investments in different sectors, but the cultural context as well. State policies which stimulate local investments, and allow individual savings for the sake of future production, may well multiply the effects of investments, free local energies and initiatives for development, and as a non-economic by-product, greatly increase support for the government among peasants. Decentralization of investment decisions may thus be a multiplier of limited "seed money". Detailed regulation of rural investments by the state may prove to be expensive, inefficient, and unpopular. It requires extensive controls, which in themselves demand manpower and resources, increasing expenses unnecessarily. They may soon cost more than they gain, becoming counter-productive in the long run. Instead, the state could restrict itself to creating a legal framework for rural investments, the details of which could gainfully be left to collective decisions and local solutions.

Rural development thus boils down to the role of the state *vis-à-vis* that of the peasants. In different fields - be it rural institutions, like peasant associations, cooperatives or settlements, be it in taxation, environmental matters, promotion of agricultural techniques, health care or schooling - nothing can stimulate initiatives, activities, and a positive culture nurtured by local human involvement more than state support. But at the same time, nothing can disrupt peasant growth potential as much as insensitive state decisions.

There are good reasons to postulate a primacy of policies in controlling economic power. Where individual activities and personal gains threaten to seriously disturb social or ecological balances on which collective survival may depend, political intervention is necessary. But there are options also in policies; there are never just two alternatives. A policy to prevent exploitation and to redistribute the gains of common work may look quite different in different social contexts. Within a given tradition, there are ways to work together in solidarity, to make individual privileges at the expense of others impossible. Solidarity, common work, and redistribution for the well-being of all can only be achieved within a given cultural context, not against it. Ethiopia cannot simply copy foreign models, be they from the USSR or the USA, from Korea or Japan.

Certainly some kind of extraction of rural surplus is necessary. In a sense, the state is extractive in essence not only in Ethiopia, but anywhere. The historical base of the state, certainly in Ethiopia, is not a *contrat social*, but military power, based on extraction which is justified as protection. Today, extraction is justified by a complex balance of the interests and needs of all citizens; but however a *volonté générale* is constituted, the need for the state to control resources and extract a surplus from productive sectors for the common interest has certainly not decreased. In addition, it is quite clear that unrestricted market integration without taxation could not release agriculture from contributing its surpluses: in fact, international market forces may constitute the most forceful means of extraction, but not to the benefit of the

Ethiopian people. Sensitivity is essential in surplus appropriation from agriculture, a field full of misconception, needing discussion and clarification. *Eshetu Chole* analyses direct and hidden forms of extraction in Ethiopia.

The significance of surplus lies in the three interrelated needs for services, for redistribution, and investments. The Ethiopian economy is hardly in a position to subsidize agriculture. Without taxation, state services to agriculture could not be financed, nor could extension and marketing services, health and educational facilities be provided. For a long time to come, agriculture will remain the major sector in Ethiopia which can provide the necessary resources for expansion in such necessary service. But extraction is only possible on the basis of solid production. Nothing produced means nothing to distribute. Stimulation of production is the prerequisite for redistribution. Economic and social progress are closely interwoven, and depend on each other.

More complex is the social service function of surplus. Care for the needy is in Ethiopia still mainly functioning in the context of family or community services for the elderly and the sick, and in mutual help associations. Neighbour solidarity may offer the best prospects through consequent development of indigenous forms of cooperation, as opposed to introducing producer cooperatives and copying foreign models. Cooperatives which grow out of mutual aid organizations may be better equipped to mobilize the energies of the rural population, and may therefore also achieve better economic results.

Rural development is tied to the market. A clear distinction is necessary between local markets which have a function in a subsistence economy, and a wider market linked to the international economy. Local markets may be a form of mutual aid, as they allow peasants to improve their lives through some exchange of their produce. On the local market, the peasant faces another producer. In the open market he meets an abstract system, in which he is just one of many small bidders offering and demanding the same goods at the same time. From a national point of view, the international market may be of great importance. But the local market, on which peasants depend, needs some protection against the dominating forces of a stronger external system.

Comparing the advantages and disadvantages of state farms, cooperatives, and peasant agriculture, *Dessalegn Rahmato* argues that the advantages of each sector will be lost if preference is given to collective farming merely on grounds of doctrine.

Another form of redistribution tries to level out differences in natural and geographical chances. A properly functioning one-price system in agricultural marketing could be a good investment, giving the country a chance to rely not only on those natural resources which are favourably located, but also on the developing agricultural potential all over the country. However, such a system is difficult to administer, and may generate more costs than gains. As long as communications are not well developed, no redistribution may be better than one which makes services more expensive for all. If it is too inefficient to even out differences, and if it can be circumvented, such a system leads to dual markets, and necessarily discredits the state in the eyes of peasants prevented from securing better prices.

Pricing and marketing policies have a subjective significance besides their political and economic importance. The contribution by *Befekadu Degefe* and *Tesfaye Tafesse* analyses the significance of government marketing and pricing policies for peasants, and their reactions. They suggest a set of policy changes to achieve a better balance between the legitimate demands of the state and the needs and capacities of peasants.

State-peasant relations have also been central in the debate on the resettlement programme. *Alula Pankhurst* gives an overview of the programme, not doubting the environmental necessity to level out population pressure in the ;drought-ridden areas, but pointing at unnecessary rigidity in application, and restrictions upon settlers which have caused frustration and limited their initiatives.

The villagization programme was launched in order to give peasants more efficient access to rural services and help for development. *Alemayehu Lirenso's* description of the programme, its policies and practice exposes a critical lack of flexibility. Differences between central planning and local application raise the question whether state intervention has actually brought more help or more hardship to peasants, and whether the point of the exercise is better control or better services.

In describing, in a local example, the effect of state intervention on rural women, *Helen Pankhurst* comes to a paradoxical conclusion. To the extent that peasants experience state intervention as disruptive, women feel privileged because the state reaches them only marginally, or indirectly. But at the same time, she registers a need for more active help from the state to allow women a more active role in rural social life.

State intervention proves not to be unequivocal. It is needed for development, but it can do harm to rural society if it is not sensitive to rural needs. Nowhere, maybe, is this ambiguous relation more relevant than in the field of environmental issues, where local communities and the state compete as actors in the attempt to maximize the productive use of resources without disrupting a vulnerable balance in the natural environment.

Environment, Population and Resource Management

Ecological problems are not just a concern of specialists, nor a field for some secondary projects and activities. Without ecological balance, agriculture cannot produce, and without consideration for ecology in all areas of agricultural activity, there is little chance of maintaining such a balance. Famine is the most ravaging and deplorable expression of serious disturbances in the social and ecological balance.

A debate on rural development can therefore not be complete without thoroughly examining the relationship between demography, environmental degradation and mass poverty, and the need for the Ethiopian Government to develop appropriate measures for the management of natural resources.

The relationship between hunger, poverty, and environment is essentially based on an interplay between social and natural, political and economic factors. Solutions can only be found through determined and flexibly adjusted action in all these fields, but starting with local activity.

Markos Ezra discusses the need for a population policy to bring rural growth into a new balance with resource development. Two other contributions examine the impact of environmental degradation on mass poverty. *Daniel Gemechu* calls for the establishment of an "environmental watch-dog" to monitor environmental issues in planning. Poverty renders peasants vulnerable to famine, and forces them to over-exploit their environment and disregard long-term effects. Daniel argues that development efforts can increase vulnerability, if they are not finely tuned to an ecological equilibrium. The same effect is observed in the resettlement programme by *Alemneh Dejene*. Resettlement cannot be a panacea for dealing with environmental degradation, or famine victims. As it is presently implemented, he fears it may result in a rapid degradation of new land resources. Conservation and rehabilitation measures in the famine-prone highland regions are needed in addition to resettlement.

Adrian Wood documents the extent to which the Ethiopian highlands are already exposed to environmental degradation. Alarming figures show a need for rapid, decisive, and efficient conservation action. Wood shows that the only way to win the race against erosion and self-accelerating destruction of soil fertility and agricultural potential is to mobilize peasants' own interest in conservation as an integral part of farming.

But the paradox of rural hunger reminds us that urban-rural relations may prevent even such mobilization. Experience shows that famine was worst where food is produced, in the rural areas. The towns found ways to get access to rural produce even in drought years, because peasants have tax obligations, debts, and need money to pay for urban goods. Even in the worst drought years, peasants conscientiously delivered their taxes and quota to the state, sometimes for fear of being recruited for resettlement. A strict but artificial division between "normal" development planning and relief efforts has precluded food being left to be consumed where it was produced and using imported relief grain to feed the urban population. Even if production is not sufficient to feed the peasants through a drought year, a rebate on taxes and quotas would make it much easier to bring to the villages the additional supplies needed, through the existing infrastructure. A state plan combining foresight, flexible extraction and rural reserves would reduce vulnerability and enhance food security.

Rain is highly unpredictable and drought years re-occur more or less at cyclical intervals, but they need not develop into famine. *Dag Hareide* argues that appropriate action can prevent the destructive consequences of drought. Famine preparedness, as an integrated part of development planning, can save both human lives and the environmental balance, as well as safeguarding the continuity of development. But preparedness demands a thorough knowledge of vulnerability, at the local level, and flexible adjustment to the needs of each village and social group.

Particular environmental and social adaptations allow different ethnic groups to survive in separate niches and utilize the resources of marginal zones. Such adaptations may be in particular danger because of social processes, population growth, changing demands, pressure on land, and other developments. Without consideration for the particular needs of these groups, development efforts can reduce the possibilities for habitation in such zones, instead of improving living conditions. *Fecadu Gadamu* analyses this complex relationship for the nomadic pastoralists in Ethiopia, describing restraints and suggesting a series of recommendations for an adapted approach to development for this group.

However, such recommendations will meet little understanding as long as tremendous ignorance about the conditions of nomadic life prevails amongst administrators, who want to settle, civilize, and adjust nomads to supposedly superior life patterns. A great deal of work may be necessary to generate understanding, based on respect for the culture of nomads, their wealth of knowledge about natural cycles and human adaptation, and their own economy of survival in a poor and merciless environment. This may demand the kind of alliance between rural interests and urban intellectuals which is called for in the concluding paper.

Capitalizing on peasant knowledge and initiative may be the most efficient technique of adjusting measures optimally to local conditions. In a country with as much cultural, social, economic and climatic variation as Ethiopia, sensitive adjustment is an essential part of development. One of the pitfalls of modern development theory is its failure, by negligence or by intent, to recognize how much local knowledge matters. Development is not only a matter of what is technically possible, but also of what is locally practicable, what is suited to the varying natural and cultural conditions. Therefore, the real expert on local agriculture and natural conditions is not the agriculturalist trained abroad, but the peasant. Cooperation is only fruitful where the peasant can contribute his knowledge on equal terms.

Subsistence peasants know best for themselves what they need, and will be motivated most thoroughly to productive effort if they participate actively in decisions regarding their own development. But subsistence peasants have no macro-economic perspective, and cannot be expected to balance their interests against the concerns of others outside their local circles, or to political, ecological, social and economic conditions of wider relevance The state is needed to mediate such wider concerns. This demands a difficult, complex balance, a flexible development strategy which is responsive to the natural and social conditions of the country, a strategy which takes into account the local cultural and ecological variations as well as the international context. Such a balance, argues *Siegfried Pausewang*, can only be guaranteed if peasants consciously build up and expand their influence in state decision making. Only the state can add a dimension of social order to local decision making. State policies can balance economic stimulation with social needs. Only state intervention can ensure that local democracy takes care of the basic needs of all despite powerful local interests. But only strong public representation of peasant interests can safeguard the balance between local democracy and central authority.

In Search of New Options

One issue of utmost contextual importance is not discussed in these texts: the on-going war. It has been said so many times that Ethiopia cannot afford this war that it seemed pointless to repeat it. Ethiopia just cannot bear the costs, in deaths and human suffering, in material damages, in social destabilization, in sharp internal differences, not to mention the waste of resources and ecological destruction. Rather than seeing the war as a limiting condition for rural development, it seemed appropriate to discuss options for rural development without war. Significant peasant development simply cannot be expected before the war has been ended; the sooner the better.

Agriculture will remain the mainstay of the Ethiopian economy for some time to come. There is a need for policies aiming to develop agriculture in its own right rather than just as a surplus producer for other sectors. Agriculture employs by far the largest part of the Ethiopian population, and development in agriculture translates directly into improvements: better health, more wellbeing, and improved quality of life for the large majority. At a certain level of development, consumption is investment: a starving peasant cannot produce much. Even neglecting the welfare argument, the difference between keeping a starving or a well-fed farmer alive is certainly less than the difference in what they produce. One should not forget that there is a psychological side to investment: a frustrated farmer feels it hardly worth while making an effort to sell at disappointing prices, while an optimistic farmer will mobilize whatever resources he has to use his chances and improve his and his family's life.

Rural development creates an employment effect, which translates both into more consumption and more marketable production. Increased incomes transform the unfulfilled needs of the poor into buying power, creating a demand for industrial products as well. Rural development may thus be expected to put in motion a process of industrialization based not on export produce, but on internal demand. On the other hand, agriculture demands resources for its development, which the state cannot provide from the surplus of other sectors, given Ethiopia's economic structure. For some time to come, agriculture has to produce the resources for its own development, one way or the other.

Comparative studies have demonstrated that peasant agriculture under present Ethiopian conditions is relatively efficient. Neither cooperatives nor state farms can make better productive use of limited land and financial resources and relatively abundant labour. Only peasant agriculture can at present feed the rural majority and offer productive employment to all who need a livelihood. But this conclusion should not lead us to romanticize peasant life. Living conditions are, all in all, deplorable. Technical standards are unnecessarily low, forcing people to do back-breaking work which could be alleviated, thereby allowing peasants to devote their energies to more productive work. The problem is not a lack of work for all, but that much of the necessary work does not produce enough food and income. Therefore, technology which saves time and hardship should be welcome but not if it costs more resources than it generates. Living culture needs no protection against innovations: culture is always incorporating improvements which allow people a better life. But where culture is in danger of being overrun by a "progress" which destroys local adaptations and resources, without offering livable alternatives, people must be allowed to defend the culture and agriculture which allow them to survive.

Wherever peasants experience that more effort invites more control and more taxation, instead of improving their own living conditions, they try to withdraw altogether from the market. A trend of retreating into subsistence has been reported from many countries, not only in Africa. In Ethiopia before the revolution, the experience of increased land rents and peasant evictions in consequence of development projects made peasants try to escape into self-sufficiency, to avoid a progress which was not to their benefit. Today, there are signs of renewed attempts to retreat from taxation and political control.

The question of whether such an "exit option" really exists has been raised repeatedly. Every peasant needs some items from the market, such as salt, or tools, or blankets. Barter is no substitute for market participation. With few exceptions, all peasants in Ethiopia are members of peasant associations, and have to pay their taxes. In this sense, they have no way of opting out. It nonetheless makes a difference whether a peasant tries to get involved as little as possible, to rely as much as he can on his own production, to do no more than absolutely necessary for the marketing system or whether he works with optimism, expecting that increased effort will provide his family with a better standard of living. In this sense of minimal effort and involvement, an exit option into passivity, is certainly available.

In sum, the significance of policy may well be its ability to create democratic structures which release local initiative and individual energies. The release of such energies will in itself be a factor of agricultural development, initiating a process of rural-led growth and impinging upon other sectors as well.

The options discussed or implicitly suggested in each individual paper all point to the instrumental role of policies in supporting or disrupting rural development. Rural development appears to be not just a question of less state intervention. Rather, the critical issue is on whose behalf the state intervenes. State support remains essential; but policies need to be sensitive to the needs of agriculture. Agriculture ought to be developed in its own right, based on the resources it can produce and mobilize on its own. Increasingly, sensitivity to the needs of a local and world-wide natural environment will be fundamental to any long-term ability to maintain a productive management of natural resources. For both concerns, democratic participation of the involved local population is the key to sensitive adjustment.

The challenge of agricultural development is not a choice between a "free market economy" and a "socialist restructuring of agriculture". The real challenge is to develop sensitive policies, which are supportive and not disruptive to a process of agricultural development financed through peasant work, on the basis of their own natural, economic and human resources.

1 The Agricultural Sector: Structure, Performance and Issues (1974 - 1988)

Stefan Brüne

The Ethiopian Government, which claims to have a popular political orientation and a coherent development strategy, has gone to great lengths to overcome its imperial heritage. Since the overthrow of Emperor Haile Selassie in 1974, the country has witnessed a period of radical agrarian change. Following the 1975 land reform legislation, which nationalized rural land and established peasant associations, the new military administration introduced a wide range of reform measures with the aim of converting an agricultural system based on individual peasant farming into more modern and collective forms of production. Along with tax and investment policies which gave special privileges to service and producer cooperatives, the government has increasingly intervened in the rural economy. In support of its long-term aim - the development of "agrarian socialism" - measures have been taken such as the large-scale state purchase of main food crops, the fixing of agricultural prices, the expansion of state farms and the creation of state monopolies in crop exports. Moreover, two major programmes, both of which reflect a radical new land use policy, have been launched. Since 1984 Ethiopia has witnessed the largest government instigated resettlement programme ever carried out on the African continent. Within a few years several hundred thousand peasants were moved from the north into sparsely inhabited, but potentially fertile regions in the south-west. In addition the government has embarked upon an ambitious villagization programme. By mid 1987 some 8 million people had been villagized.

Given the magnitude and complexity of this agrarian transformation, this chapter can only serve as an introductory overview. It provides basic information on Ethiopia's agricultural sector and a summary of its performance since the revolution and touches upon central issues in post-1974 agricultural policy. What are the key variables and major constraints on Ethiopia's agricultural development? Can the dramatic decline in food production be attributed to government policies that persistently discriminate against smallholders? Could higher farm-gate prices and a stronger private sector stimulate agricultural production, as the IMF and World Bank contend ? And finally, what bearing does the government's ideology have on the issue? To what extent is the distinction between "capitalist" and "socialist" development strategies relevant to rural Ethiopia?

Ethiopia-Topography

Source: Le Monde   Cartography: Manfred Dlozcik
© Institute of Geography, University of Osnabrück

Agrarian Development in Peasant Societies: The Nature of the Problem

Like most of its sub-Saharan neighbours, Ethiopia is a pre-industrial, agrarian based society. Nearly 90 per cent of the country's population live in rural areas. The agricultural sector accounts for some 85 per cent of total employment and is still the backbone of the economy. Agriculture is dominated by smallholders who produce most of the country's food, largely for their own use. Ethiopia remains a country of subsistence agriculture. With the average farm size being close to one hectare, only a fraction of the annual harvest is marketed. Recent estimates suggest that peasants retain 80 per cent of their produce for home consumption and for seeds (Dessalegn 1984:67). Virtually all crop production and almost three quarters of livestock production take place in the highlands, which comprise some 50 million hectares, 40 per cent of the total land area. The main staple crops are grain (teff, maize, barley, sorghum, wheat), oilseeds (neug, flax, rapeseed, sesame, castor beans), sugar-cane, long-staple cotton and, of course, coffee - the country's most important cash crop. The importance of the latter as the country's principal export has risen steadily over the years and is still rising in comparison to other exports such as oilseeds, hides and skins. Coffee exports account for some 60-80 per cent of the country's foreign exchange earnings. Raising livestock is also important, providing draught power as well as dairy products, meat, hides, skins, and leather. Indeed, livestock accounts for about a third of the output value of the agricultural sector. Nomads move about in the less fertile lowlands and depend almost exclusively on cattle grazing.

Table 1
Population Growth and Available Grain Equivalent Per Capita

	75/76	79/80	80/81	81/82	82/83	83/84[1]	84/85[1]	85/86[1]
Population estimate (m)	33.4	37.5	38.6	39.7	40.8	42.0	43.2	44.5
Per Capita available grain equivalent[2]								
Kg	154	179	153	143	170	135	119	104
Index	100	114	100	92	111	88	78	67

1) Excludes Eritrea and Tigray
2) Excludes livestock products and food imports

Source: Faught (1987:2) as published in Cohen/Isaksson (1988:329)

With an estimated GNP of US $ 110 per capita, Ethiopia is one of the poorest countries in the world, with 28 million people, i.e. 60 per cent of the population, believed to be living below the absolute poverty line. Classified by the United Nations as a "least developed country",[1] Ethiopia's shows all the characteristics of an underdeveloped country. It relies heavily on foreign exchange and imported technology, modernization and

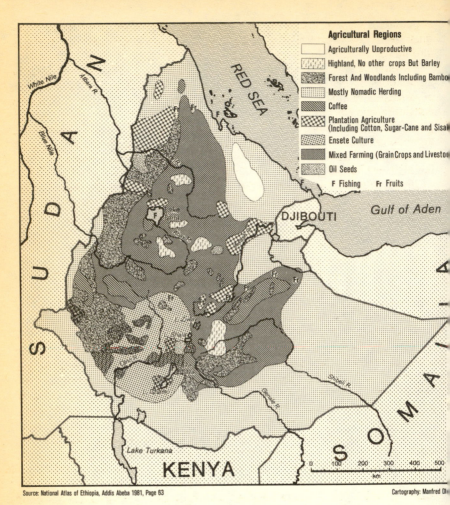

Agricultural Regions

Agriculturally Unproductive
Highland, No other crops But Barley
Forest And Woodlands Including Bamboo
Mostly Nomadic Herding
Coffee
Plantation Agriculture (Including Cotton, Sugar-Cane and Sisal)
Ensete Culture
Mixed Farming (Grain Crops and Livestock)
Oil Seeds
F Fishing   Fr Fruits

Source: National Atlas of Ethiopia, Addis Abeba 1981, Page 63

Cartography: Manfred Dl...

© **Institute of Geography, University of Osnabrück**

economic progress are hampered by a poor infrastructure,[2] a small industrial base, a shortage of skilled manpower, low agricultural productivity and heavy dependence on one export commodity.

Given this low level of development and the resulting importance of agriculture for the economy as a whole, Ethiopia's development planners face a variety of complex problems. Among the major issues to be taken into consideration are climatic and topographic constraints, alarming trends in population growth and rapid ecological degradation. In view of this and the agricultural sector's multi-faceted role within the national economy, agricultural and agrarian policies have to reconcile complex and sometimes conflicting aims and interests.

From a development perspective agriculture has to fulfil four main functions. It must (1) feed a steadily growing rural and urban population, (2) finance its own growth and structural change, (3) provide capital and raw materials for the country's long-term industrial development, and (4) provide cash crops for export.

Under prevailing circumstances, Ethiopia's agricultural sector is not even able to fulfil its most basic and important function: the provision of food for a large and fast-expanding population. Ethiopian agriculture has been in decline for nearly a quarter of a century, and post-revolution agrarian policies so far have not succeeded in improving the record.

As a result Ethiopia's dependence on food aid and commercial grain imports has increased considerably over the last years. Far from achieving self-sufficiency by the mid-1990s, as government planners had forecast, the country is likely to suffer serious food shortages all through the next decade.[3]

Prospects for a quick recovery are bleak. Current trends in population growth, land resource utilization and environmental degradation point to very serious problems in the near future and, most probably, a sharp increase in famine vulnerability over the next 10 to 30 years. By the year 2000 Ethiopia might have to sustain a population of 100 million (Bureau 1988:23), while current soil loss rates, which are highest in cultivated land, amount to 1.5 million tons a year. Hurni (1987) estimates that the current soil loss and the resulting water loss[4] - taken together with biological degradation and land degeneration - effectively mean an annual 2 - 3 per cent reduction in soil productivity.[5]

Agricultural output is presently barely adequate to sustain its own labour force. The country's planners will for years to come be faced with the dilemma of how to generate agricultural growth without further depriving the peasantry of essential food and basic consumer goods.

The 1975 Land Reform

Prior to the Ethiopian revolution, the most frequently cited reasons for Ethiopian agricultural underdevelopment were of a structural nature: a land tenure system that encouraged absentee landlordism and was characterized as feudal; the neglect of peasant agriculture to the advantage of the

landlords and the lack of political will on the part of the imperial government to bring about the profound political and economic change needed
to stimulate peasant agricultural production. As a consequence land reform
was considered a key issue for Ethiopia's future. Without any doubt the
Public Ownership of Rural Lands Proclamation No. 31/1975 eliminated
many of the basic problems inherent in the pre-revolutionary agricultural
system. All private ownership of land by individuals and organizations was
outlawed; the transfer of land by sale, lease or mortgage was declared illegal
and anyone willing to farm was to be given land. Tenancy was abolished and
peasants were freed from all obligations to landlords. The maximum plot
allocated to each household by the newly founded peasant associations was
to be 10 ha, this being the maximum an average peasant family could till
with standard farming equipment and oxen. In actual practice, plots were
much smaller. Average holdings vary greatly in different areas, but on a
national level are estimated to be slightly above or even below 1 ha.

The nationalization of rural lands liberated peasants from feudalistic
bonds and contributed towards a more equal distribution of wealth and land.
For a short while many peasant families were able to improve their nutritional
and living standards. The establishment of Peasants Associations and the fact
that peasants were guaranteed usufructuary rights by the state created an
important legal and institutional framework for accelerated rural development. Although an indispensable step in the right direction, it appears in
retrospect that the impact of the land reform has been overestimated. It would
appear that the leadership was primarily concerned with creating social jus-
tice without giving due consideration to the complex and long-term economic
implications of the reform. Considerations such as farm size and the choice
of technology were not thoroughly analysed. As in other developing countries,
the Ethiopian reform was first and foremost about land tenure, and not about
farming in general. The government's motives were in part political, part
social and part economic, and of the three the political factors were overriding. Rectifying obvious injustices in both land ownership and the allocation of
resources, the government - under the pressure of political events - had no
long-term strategy to improve agricultural productivity and raise the social
and economic status of peasant families. As Dessalegn put it, being "a
redistributive and levelling reform, its strength lay not so much in having
increased the resources and wealth of the rural community as in having
created equal, if modest, opportunities for everyone" (Dessalegn 1984:62/3).

By preventing further social divisions based on private ownership of rural
land, the 1975 reform legislation brought the peasants - the majority of rural
producers - into a direct relationship with the state. But it did not alter the
basic pattern of agricultural production. Ethiopia's agriculture was and is still
dominated by the peasant and smallholder sector.

Agricultural Production (1974-88)

In the early post-imperial years Ethiopia's agricultural sector did surprisingly well. Although food grain production often falls during the initial stages of an agrarian reform, this was not not the case in Ethiopia. Rainfall in the period was above average and smallholders in the major food-producing areas reacted favourably to a land reform which abolished rents, created the impression of securer tenure and also increased access to production inputs (Cohen 1980, Koehn 1980). But since the 1979/80 harvest the level of food grain production has fallen well below that achieved under Haile Selassie's government during its last decade in office. According to World Bank estimates the output value added in agriculture[6] grew at an average annual rate of 1.1 per cent between 1974/75 and 1983/84, resulting in a sharp decline in per capita output and a growing food deficit.

A period of stagnation was followed by a recovery in 1979/80. Since then the agricultural output has slowed considerably, except for the year 1982/83. Compared to the relatively high, but still inadequate production level of 7.3 million tons of cereals and pulses in 1982/83, production in the following year fell to just 6.2 million tons and in 1984/85 to about 5 million tons, the lowest level of the last decade. This - together with the armed conflicts - led to regional famines. According to government statements 10 million people were affected, the highest figure ever recorded for a famine. It led to an emergency operation, of a total value estimated at US$ 470 million. However, the international effort was overshadowed by the fact that it began several months too late. As the start of the famine coincided with preparations for the tenth anniversary of the revolution, the regime played down the scale of the problem for a considerable time. Although a further substantial recovery was made between 1985 and 1987, the production level remained well below its peak of 1982/83.

Producer Cooperatives and State Farms

In countries like Ethiopia, peasant farms have a relatively good productivity record. Although they employ traditional technology and hardly use modern inputs, their crop-yields are often comparatively high, as they make more efficient use of productive resources than cooperatives or state farms. However, small-scale agriculture is often considered an obstacle to long-term industrial development and the creation of more mechanized farms. Faced by the choice between a smallholder strategy and a "socialist" approach based on collective ownership, group and state farming and governmental control of the rural economy, the government chose the latter.

Nevertheless the process of collectivization is very much at an embryonic stage. In 1987 there were still 5.6 million hectares or 94 per cent of total farmland under cultivation by individual families. Another 2 per cent was tilled by producer cooperatives and the remaining 4 per cent by state farms.

Table 2
ETHIOPIA: Estimates of Area Production and Major Crops(1981/82-86/87) [7]
(Area in thousands of hectares and production in thousands of quintals)

Fiscal year ending July 7

Type of crop	1981/82 Area	1981/82 Prod.	1982/83 Area	1982/83 Prod.	1983/84 Area	1983/84 Prod.	1984/85 Area	1984/85 Prod.	1985/86 Area	1985/86 Prod.	1986/87 Area	1986/87 Prod.
Cereals	4,629.5	53,919.8	5,030.3	67,199.4	4,715.5	55,268.0	4,181.6	39,843.4	4,555.2	44,496.5	5,163.8	59,064.3
Pulses	793.5	8,204.5	798.9	9,654.6	760.3	7,123.3	694.3	4,737.5	642.0	4,420.0	656.0	5,784.3
Oilseeds	230.4	822.7	260.0	1,216.8	256.4	986.4	267.4	976.4	275.6	955.1	229.9	915.1
Others	37.2	922.5	39.3	848.9	43.1	947.2	46.5	1,230.1	50.2	1,321.9	50.5	1,495.1
Total	5,690.6	63,939.5	6,128.5	78,919.7	5,775.3	64,324.9	5,189.8	46,787.4	5,523.0	51,193.5	6,100.2	67,258.8

Annual percentage change
Fiscal year ending July 7

Type of crop	1981/82 Area	1981/82 Prod.	1982/83 Area	1982/83 Prod.	1983/84 Area	1983/84 Prod.	1984/85 Area	1984/85 Prod.	1985/86 Area	1985/86 Prod.	1986/87 Area	1986/87 Prod.
Cereals	-1.8	-4.0	8.7	24.6	-6.3	-17.8	-11.3	-27.9	8.9	11.7	13.4	32.7
Pulses	6.9	-3.3	0.7	17.7	-4.8	-26.2	-8.7	-33.5	-7.5	-6.7	2.2	30.9
Oilseeds	-1.4	-18.9	4.3	47.9	-1.4	-18.9	4.3	1.1	3.1	-2.2	-16.6	-4.2
Others	-7.2	1.2	5.6	-14.5	9.7	11.6	7.9	29.8	8.0	7.5	0.6	13.1
Total	-0.5	-4.1	7.7	23.4	-5.8	-18.5	-10.1	-27.3	6.4	9.4	10.5	31.4

Sources: 1981/82-1982/83 Central Statistical Office and Ministry of State Farms, as published in IMF (1987:46)

However, there were indications that the government was determined to speed up the process in the future. According to the original version of the 10-year plan, half of all farmland was due to be collectivized by 1994 - with a simultaneous increase from 2 per cent to 50 per cent in their share of the total output.

Table 3
Share of Cultivated Land by User (1983/4-93/4)
(Per cent)

	Actual 1983/84	Actual 1985/86	3-Yr. Plan 1988/89	10-Yr. Plan 1993/94
State Farms	3	3	4	6
Producer Coops	1	2	6	52
Individual Farms	95	94	91	40
Settlement Schemes	1	1	-	2

Source: World Bank (1988,46)

Although these targets no longer seem realistic and attainable, the government has largely channelled its agricultural resources towards state farms and producer cooperatives. Producer cooperatives enjoy guaranteed access to fertile land and priority in purchase of oxen, in distribution of fertilizer and improved seeds as well as in extension services. They receive higher farm gate prices from the Agricultural Marketing Corporation than smallholders.

Most state farms were privately owned commercial operations before 1975.[8] They cultivate primarily fertile soil in rain-fed and irrigated areas. When they were placed under state control in 1976 they covered some 70,000 ha of land. Since then the number of state farms has tripled and the production area has grown to over 200,000 ha. Being capital-intensive large-scale operations, they are expected to provide food for the urban areas and produce cotton and sugar for export. By 1986/87 they accounted for about 7 per cent of grain production and about 35 per cent of the agricultural surplus marketed through official channels.

So far the experience with state farms has not been encouraging and accordingly their share of the capital expenditure budget has been reduced to 12 - 15 per cent in recent years. Although yields are higher than the national average in some areas, so are their costs, thus rendering state farms unprofitable. The high cost of land-reclamation, ineffective management, an unmotivated workforce and problems with machinery have led to heavy losses - and this in spite of the fact that the Agricultural Marketing Corporation pays as much as 50 per cent more for their grain than it does to private farmers. Despite the rescheduling of state farm debts by the Agricultural and Industrial Development Bank in 1981/82 and the provision by the government of significant new capital, arrears on state farm debts were estimated to be close to 1 million birras of June 1987. Even if it proved possible in the near future to raise the standard of management and increase the yields substantially, a further basic economic problem would remain. Given their high level of

Table 4

Estimates of Area and Production of Major Crops by Farming Sectors, 1981/82-1986/87

(Area in thousands of hectares and production in thousands of quintals)
(for belg and meher seasons)

Fiscal year ending July 7 Farming sector	1981/82		1982/83		1983/84		1984/85		1985/86		1986/87*	
	Area	Prod.	Area	Prod.	Area	Prod.	Area	Prod.	Area	Prod.	Area	Prod.
Peasant (private sector)	5,341.1	59,321.1	5,801.9	74,559.4	5,390.5	60,095.5	4,838.2	42,241.1	5,104.1	45,508.5	5,508.5	59,363.1
State farms	231.0	3,824.0	212.7	3,410.9	179.1	2,981.7	182.0	3,490.5	200.8	4,147.6	203.2	4,806.7
Cooperatives	118.5	794.4	113.9	949.0	205.7	1,247.7	169.6	1,055.8	218.1	1,637.4	392.5	3,089.0
Total	5,690.6	63,939.5	6,128.5	78,919.3	5,775.3	64,324.9	5,189.8	46,787.4	5,523.0	51,193.5	6,100.2	67,258.8

Annual percentage change

Fiscal year ending July 7 Farming sector	1981/82		1982/83		1983/84		1984/85		1985/86		1986/87	
	Area	Prod.	Area	Prod.	Area	Prod.	Area	Prod.	Area	Prod.	Area	Prod.
Peasant (private sector)	-1.3	-5.0	8.6	25.7	-7.1	-19.4	-10.2	-29.7	5.5	7.5	7.9	30.7
State farms	3.2	8.5	-7.9	-10.8	-15.7	-12.6	1.6	17.1	10.3	18.8	1.2	15.9
Cooperatives	43.3	17.9	-3.9	19.5	80.6	31.5	-17.6	-15.4	28.6	55.1	80.0	88.7
Total	-0.5	-4.1	7.7	23.4	-5.8	-18.5	-10.1	-27.3	6.4	9.4	10.5	31.4

Sources: 1980/81-1986/87 Central Statistical Office; and Ministry of State Farms, as published in IMF (1987:47)

*Figures for 1986/87 crop product of the belg season are not included.

capital investment and the need to import foreign machinery, state farms cannot avoid consuming large amounts of foreign exchange.

Critics of the government's agrarian policies see the steady discrimination against smallholders as the major cause of the decline in food production since 1980. Although there is no unequivocal documentary evidence that peasant production is superior to collective forms of agriculture, most studies undertaken so far suggest that the smallholder approach has greater potential for Ethiopia's agrarian sector than producer cooperatives and state farms.[9] An ILO mission visiting the country in 1982 concluded that smallholders

Table 5
Crop Yield on Peasant, Cooperative and State Farms 1979/80-1985/86
(Quintals/hectare)

Peasant	79/80	80/81	81/82	82/83	83/84	84/85	85/86
Teff	9.5	9.7	8.2	9.9	8.3	6.8	7.5
Barley	11.7	13.3	12.0	13.3	10.9	10.7	10.0
Wheat	11.1	11.2	10.1	12.7	10.5	10.3	9.8
Maize	17.3	12.3	18.2	20.2	18.7	11.4	11.4
Sorghum	16.2	14.6	14.7	15.4	13.3	6.1	11.0
Pulse	12.1	11.7	10.6	12.3	9.5	6.9	7.1
Coop							
Teff	7.2	7.0	5.0	6.6	7.2	5.4	5.8
Barley	8.3	7.7	9.1	6.7	1.9	7.7	7.8
Wheat	7.4	6.0	8.2	9.5	8.5	6.4	9.3
Maize	20.2	14.6	7.7	10.5	13.4	9.6	8.9
Sorghum	3.8	6.0	8.5	14.3	11.4	8.3	11.0
Pulse	5.6	4.9	4.6	9.4	6.1	3.4	5.2
State							
Teff	5.8	5.2	5.6	4.7	4.2	2.8	5.6
Barley	13.5	19.8	18.7	23.5	12.1	12.8	16.4
Wheat	11.9	14.1	13.1	16.1	13.3	14.8	16.3
Maize	23.3	28.5	27.8	19.9	21.3	24.2	24.2
Sorghum	11.8	14.9	14.1	12.7	9.1	9.9	5.1
Pulse	4.6	3.2	3.4	3.8	3.5	3.6	3.0

Source: CSO 1984, 1986, 1987, for Peasant and Coop sector

are more successful at absorbing labour, raising yields and increasing income than producer cooperatives and state farms are. This is underscored by a MoA national survey, which shows that productivity in producer cooperatives was lower than in individual farms in almost all parts of the country in the 1983/84 crop year (MoA 1985). Similarly a SIDA report based on data taken during 1985 in Bale and Arssi sees no advantages for large scale agriculture, concluding that "the most efficient method of quickly stimulating agricultural production and increasing marketable grain surplus is by encouraging peasant agriculture" (SIDA1985:196-7).

New Land Use Policies: Resettlement and Villagization

Resettlement - the chief means of increasing agricultural production in developing countries until the late 1950s - can be traced back in Ethiopia to a World Bank report of 1973.[10] At the end of the imperial regime, with demographic pressure and soil erosion becoming a major concern in parts of the northern highlands, it was widely agreed that well prepared voluntary resettlement could well aid those regions where overgrazing and intensive soil use had reached crisis proportions. As a consequence, the World Bank and US-AID proposed resettlement programmes to relieve certain areas of Tigray and Wollo. By 1979, under the supervision of the Relief and Rehabilitation Commission (RRC), some 20,000 ha were under cultivation in 84 settlement sites. Until then the programme had involved 35,520 families or a total of 110,090 people.[11] With the projects underway costing millions of birr and with self-sufficiency not in prospect, the government suspended the resettlement programme in 1979 (Dawit 1989:287).[12] It was only in November 1984 - at the height of the famine - that the government resumed the programme and declared its intention to move 1.5 million people within nine months from Wollo and Tigray to south-western Ethiopia. During the first phase, which lasted from December 1985 until March 1986, efforts were concentrated in Shoa, Arssi and Hararghe. These three regions contain about a third of Ethiopia's farming population and produce about 40 per cent of the national cereals crop (Cohen / Issakson 1988:30).

Closely related to resettlement is the villagization programme, whose central aim is to move people into villages in order to provide them with essential services, including social and economic infrastructural facilities. During this first phase, which lasted from December 1985 to March 1986, 4.6 million people or 12 per cent of Ethiopia's rural population were rehoused in 4,500 villages. By July 1987 more than 180,000 dwelling units had been constructed and more than 8 million people villagized. Plans to villagize an additional three million people were announced in October 1987.

Both resettlement and villagization programmes have come under severe criticism from bilateral and multilateral donors. While some condemn the idea based on their general dislike of Marxist ideology, others - among them the EEC - admit that the programmes are difficult to criticize in principle. For them the conditions under which such operations are carried out is the major issue. SIDA, which supported similar programmes in Tanzania, viewed the villagization programme as an indefensible disruption of peasant production at a time when Ethiopia was desperately short of food. Dawit, the former head of the RRC, assumes that close to 20,000 out of the 700,000 people moved by the end of 1986, died either en route or at the new settlement sites - where malaria, bilharzia and tsetse flies were major problems. According to Dawit almost 500 people were executed while trying to escape, 10,000 managed to cross the border to Sudan and some 5,000 succeeded in getting back to their home areas. Again according to Dawit half of the 700,000 people

(250,000 families) resettled at that time were separated from one or more members of their family (Dawit 1989:304).

In the meantime, the Ethiopian Government acknowledged that the resettlement process was hastily conceived, poorly planned and executed, and resulted in considerable hardship for the population. In response to international criticism the government declared a temporary moratorium on resettlement in March 1986.

Conclusion

Although the 1975 land reform effectively destroyed the long-standing agricultural system, it has not created a coherent replacement. The landowners, it is true, were stripped of their power through radical new land tenure rules, and as such the measure was effective in ridding the country of its imperial legacy and preventing further social divisions based on private land ownership. But the basic problem - that of how to bring about profound structural changes needed for long-term agricultural growth - remained largely unsolved. Problems relating to farm size, agrarian technology and land use policy became more pressing and - in the absence of a landowning class and a strong private sector - government policies and intervention became more important. So far the government's attempts to stimulate agricultural production by extending its own control over the rural economy have not paid off. As a result a sharp increase in famine vulnerability is likely to go hand in hand with accelerated "agrarian involution", "a tendency already in evidence of peasants turning inwards, of being solely concerned with self sustenance rather than involvement in the general exchange process, in accumulation in innovative endeavour." (Dessalegn 1984:62)

There are two divergent interpretations of the failure of post-imperial Ethiopia's agricultural policies. Some critics of the government take the view that the "socialist" strategy - as opposed to a smallholder approach - is to blame for the disappointing agricultural performance. Whereas this analysis focuses on alternatives offered by differing political ideologies, the other views the make-up and structure of peasant society as the critical factor. In this latter theory, that of urban bias, the neglect of smallholder agriculture in Africa is similar under all regimes irrespective of ideological orientation. According to this theory, African governments desire industrialization and also want to preserve their political power. For these reasons they subsidize the politically sensitive urban food prices, tax agriculture and try to increase their political control in rural areas. In this view it is not so much the ideological orientation of political leaders but rather the need to produce quick results which seduces them into believing that complex agrarian problems can be solved swiftly through large and capital-intensive projects.

However, in any discussion and evaluation of these competing schools of thought it is vital to distinguish between structural constraints, political options and ideological perceptions. Only on the basis of these distinctions can a debate on agrarian strategies and development options be of practical relevance. However, it is possible to make one point in advance. Irrespective of which theory one prefers, all point to one fact: that the peasantry has difficulties in getting its interests taken seriously. Ethiopia must try to avoid the fate of those other developing countries which pronounce self-sufficiency as an important objective but adopt policies which increase dependence upon imported food.

NOTES

1 Least Developed Country

2 This applies particularly to the road system. Nearly three-quarters of Ethiopia's farms are at least half-a-day's walk away from all-weather roads. The lack of roads has been a major impediment to extension, input supply, output marketing and change in agricultural technology.

3 According to World Bank forecasts Ethiopia will require annual food aid totalling 3 million tons in the coming years (World Bank 1986:21). Indeed the prospects of achieving self-sufficiency by the turn of the century are slim and would require an annual increase in agricultural productivity that few countries in the developing world have attained. Accordingly the World Bank thinks that "a policy of food security rather than food-self sufficiency would be a more efficient objective" (World Bank 1988:124).

4 Degraded soil and vegetation lead to direct run-off rates of up to 80 per cent of rainfall, while well-covered soils (long grasses, trees) will retain more than 90 per cent.

5 Given an average of 60cm of cropland soil depth and assuming a loss of 4mm per annum, Ethiopia's current cropland soil will have eroded within 150 years.

6 At constant prices.

7 The data given here are as accurate as can currently be compiled. Data vary between different sources, methodologies for computing have been changed and census data are unreliable (especially for the war-affected northern regions). The table can only claim to show general and underlying trends.

8 An early draft of the land reform legislation had exempted these farms from nationalization. Experts feared that the government would not be able to successfully manage these farms, and that premature nationalization would destroy their productivity at a time when it would be needed most.

9 A study commissioned for the Ethiopian Government tried to measure the comparative advantages of the three sectors, but the criteria employed were unconvincing. It gave 3 high ratings out of 5 to the peasant sector, while the state sector got 2 (ILO 1982:42).

10 North-south migrations are traditional in Ethiopia. As early as the last century - during the great famine of 1888-92 - sections of the Amharic and Tigrean populations moved to the south of the country. The provision of southern land for settlers and soldiers from the north was one way in which the Emperor attempted to buy loyalty.

11 On average, one settlement unit is designed to accommodate 500 families on some 1,000 ha of land.

12 At the beginning of 1986 the RRC initiated a reunification programme. Social workers went around to all the camps, trying to locate people who had been separated from their families.

2 Urban-rural Relations in Agrarian Change. An Historical Overview

Taye Mengistae

From *Gult*-lordship to Landlordship

The last quarter of the 19th century saw the expansion of the "Abyssinian Kingdom" southwards through conquest, which eventually led to the rise of the modern day Ethiopian state by the 1930s. This process marked the beginning of the dissolution of the *gult* system - the particular Abyssinian system of government through a local nobility that depended on a share in the production of all peasants in their *gult* area.[1]

Although the conquest initially meant the spread of *gult* to the newly incorporated regions, it eventually led to the conversion of the conquering *gult*-lords from the north and some co-opted indigenous *balabat*, into the landlords of one third to one half of the peasantry in the South. The new landlords were at the same time integrated into a newly emergent bureaucracy, or they were soldiers and officers of a standing army in the process of becoming a modern military force. The regional seats of the evolving state power were the nuclei for an urbanization of the army and the bureaucracy. The same urbanization and bureaucratization of *gult*-lordship was taking place in the North as well. But as the *rist* system gave peasants a stronger position to defend their rights, this development did not give rise to private property in land or landlordship to any significant degree in the north.

Such developments would have been impossible without the fast growth of trade as well as the European presence in Africa and its diplomatic and military relations with the institution of *gult*-lordship. The brief conquest of the country by the Italians accelerated the centralization of power and the urbanization of agrarian overlordship. The two decades that followed the expulsion of the Italians completed the same process, with the eventual juridical separation of landlordship and official capacity in the new bureaucracy. The period saw the formal granting of property rights in land to all former *gult*-lords, the official abolition of labour service obligations of peasants to overlords, the introduction of land tax payments directly to the central treasury, and the conversion of all land that had not been claimed by officially recognized proprietors, into state property (Mahetme Selassie, 1957).

The *rist* system was originally a communal institution of definition and realization of usufructuary rights over some share of a genealogically defined agrarian territory. The village, in which a peasant household operated a farm in exercise of its *rist* right, was always a part of the *gult* estate of some *gult*-lord.[2] The *gult*-lord "kept law and order" in the territory and, in return, extracted tribute from the inhabitants, mostly in kind or in labour, in the name of overlords higher up in the regional hierarchy of political power. The exercise of *rist* right by a cultivator was conditional on his meeting tribute obligations to the *gult*-lord.

By the late 1950s, the *gult* institution had almost disappeared, although many of its elements, such as labour rent and political rights over tenants, continued to be features of the newly emerging landlordship in the south. By the mid-1960s a distinct geographical pattern had emerged, whereby the *rist* institution was the dominant system of tenure over agricultural land in the northern provinces, while land was mainly the private property of individuals and the property of the state in the south.[3] Cutting across this spatial pattern of legal titles to land were two forms of agrarian relations of production. More than 90 per cent of the country's population worked as subsistence peasants, either in independent peasant farming or in tenancy, dependent on a landlord.

By independent peasant farming, we mean a peasant household which operates a farm without having to make any recurrent payment of a portion of its produce or its labour services as rent or "tribute", as a pre-condition for the continued use of the farm land.[4] In the institution of landlordship and peasant tenancy, in contrast, the land cultivated by a village household is owned by someone else who is entitled to a share of farm output and often also labour services, in the form of contractual rent. It is characteristic of the institution of landlordship that landlords can lease out land that is large enough to enable them to enjoy a much higher standard of living than any one of their tenants without themselves engaging in farm work. In the Ethiopian agrarian scene of the 1960s, the relation of a landlord to his tenants was normally regulated by the *political power* he exercised over the latter, more often than not through an official government position. There was little intervention of a modern legal mechanism in the determination of levels or forms of rent or the conditions of commencement or termination of tenancy contracts. Contracts were mostly oral, and tenancy was very much merged with political and social servility. The form of rent was mostly in kind, often involved labour services, and ranged between a quarter and a half of the tenant's crop - cases of rent payments of up to three quarters are reported - depending on local tradition and whether the tenant was dependent on the landlord for the supply of oxen or seeds.

By 1970 close to 43 per cent of farmers in the south operated under this form of tenancy. According to official statistics, another 45 per cent of rural households in the same region worked as independent peasant farmers on land held as their private property.[5] In contrast, less than 10 per cent of farmers in the north (i.e. in northern Shoa, Gojjam, Gondar, Tigray, Eritrea and parts of Wello) fully rented their farm land. Tenants in the *rist* areas worked under conditions of tenancy that involved far less servility than those in the south. Here independent household farming was the dominant institution of peasant agriculture.

In Amharic speaking areas of the north, both independent farming households and landlords claimed land titles through the *rist* system of tenure that seemingly survived the dissolution of *gult*-lordship. In Tigrean speaking areas the same system coexisted with the more egalitarian system of "communal ownership" of farmland, *deisa* (or *shehena*) that excluded landlordship, periodized redistribution and guaranteed the equality of shares with respect to size of land as well as its equality. While socially recognized residence guaranteed titles to land in this system, titles in the *rist* system derived from socially recognized claims of descent from ancestors known to have had the same title to a share of land within the village in question. Land held by such rights could be farmed by the title holder himself or leased out as a source of rent income. The system excluded indigenous communities of artisans or minority religious or ethnic groups from the rights it defined. By 1970 those excluded could have constituted as much as 18 per cent of the rural population in the north.

Among those the system accommodated, everyone was guaranteed usufructuary titles to plots of land; the size of holdings increased with the members' status in the broader regional political framework and their wealth. Such correlation meant a situation whereby the poorest and least powerful 10 per cent of *ristegna* peasants had land that fell short of their subsistence requirement and tilling capacity. These had to work on the *rist* land of the most powerful minority as "partial tenants". It was a peculiarity of the *rist* system, at least as observed in the 1960s and 1970s, that *rist* titles to village land had to be redistributed as often as new claims were successfully made. A person's holdings of a particular plot had to be defended from time to time, and the successes of the defence depended on the current holder's wealth and power relative to the new claimant.

Urbanization as a New Dimension of Agrarian Overlordship

In the first instance, the evolution of *gult*-lordship into landlordship constituted a change in the property relations that defined overlordship in Ethiopian peasant agriculture. Secondly it relocated the same overlordship away from the village into newly emerging townships. It thereby created an urban environment of commerce and public finance close to the farmers. In the beginning landlordship and official capacity in the new state apparatus coincided, and gave rise to the towns. However, as the apparatus matured and its manpower requirement expanded, the rustic landlord-cum-civil servant was gradually replaced by better groomed generations of functionaries of increasingly humble origins. The new civil servants came from the more adventurous of village youth moving to the new towns in search of greater fortune and higher status than was available in the villages. It appears, therefore, that urbanization in Ethiopia started as a replacement of the institution of *gult*-lordship by a state bureaucracy, which created an opportunity to absorb "surplus manpower" from peasant agriculture. By the mid-1960s, this function was performed by a chain of some 200 towns of variable sizes spreading out along a system of unconnected highways radiating from the largest town of them all - Addis Ababa. Towns already accounted for almost a tenth of the country's population. The urban population was growing at an annual rate of about 7 per cent, mainly due to migration from the countryside.[6]

Initially, food came to the towns in the form of tribute and then rent in kind, which the new landlords marketed to the towns. Eventually, this was supplemented by direct crop marketing by farmers, first to meet tax obligations to the central government and, subsequently, also to acquire artisan products or imported substitutes. In the early 1970s, peasants in better endowed areas were marketing 10-25 per cent of their produce through three regional networks of grain and livestock marketing, terminating in Addis Ababa, Dire-Dawa and Asmara.[7] The sale of coffee on the international market converted a large part of the net output of peasant agriculture in the country into purchasing power over European consumer goods and urban facilities. This gave the finishing touch to the rural-urban duality. A newly emerging urban middle class life style, imitating cosmopolitanism, became characteristic of the urban elite but remained alien to villagers.

In all the three networks, village produce entered circulation with a peasant transporting his goods to the nearest rural market or town, often 30 km or more away from the village. The goods were mostly sold to purchasing agents of medium and large dealers, often to retailers and sometimes directly to consumers. Market towns could range in size from a few thousand to 50,000 inhabitants with at least five to ten, often 40 or more traders. Dealers numbered in the hundreds in the central markets of Addis Ababa, Dire Dawa, Dessie or Asmara. The majority of farmers had to dispose of most of what they could market during the harvesting season, partly because they had no proper storage facilities but mainly because they had to settle tax obligations. Individual sales were small. This gave the highly oligopolized grain and livestock dealers an absolute power to determine urban-rural terms of trade (Ministry of Agriculture 1973). These grain and livestock dealers, a small but powerful mercantile group, together with landlords and local officials, were the main channel through which resources were extracted from villages and pumped into the fast growing real estate and catering sectors in the towns.

The Ethiopian economy thus emerged as a clear-cut duality in which urban activity fed on peasant agriculture as an external source. This basic structure became less easy to distinguish with the rise of a small sector of industrial processing and relatively modern enclaves of merchandising and finance, in the wake of a limited flow of foreign aid and private capital in the 1950s and 1960s. By 1970, Ethiopian national income statistics were being interpreted to suggest that the towns produced no less than half of the country's GDP, with less than 10 per cent of the total work force. Such a reading would imply that the average urban employee, who was far more likely to be in the civil service, the army or the catering business than a factory hand, was ten times more productive than the average village cultivator. If this interpretation were correct, the barely 40 years of urbanization in Ethiopia would be one of the fastest instances of technical progress ever observed in economic history. Certainly, there is a contrast between the technical and managerial backwardness of Ethiopian peasant agriculture and the small islands of imported modern technology in the towns. Nevertheless, it is more likely that the decreasing share of the countryside in our GDP figures reflects the fast growing net outflow of resources from villages to the towns, and the growing dependency of the urban population on such outflow.

A New Urban-rural Relationship

By the mid-1960s, this outflow could not keep pace with growth in the urban population. Food and import prices started to rise more and more steeply in the towns. At the same time, the public sector - the main basis for urban growth - could absorb fewer and fewer of the younger generation of townspeople. It was becoming increasingly clear that the townspeople could not be sustained unless the villages were made to render more. Towns had to become more productive and economic both in internal structure and in their relation to the countryside. This need was reflected in public policy through the Imperial Government's Third Five-Year Development Plan of 1967. In the plan document, the government acknowledged the urgency of industrialising urban economic life through import substituting industrial ventures, and of boosting agricultural production through a more entrepreneurial outreach of the towns into the countryside. The government gave inducements to landlords, merchants and the better off in the civil service to adopt an entrepreneurial approach to farming, and it incorporated peasant farming into a more active fiscal and agricultural structure

A large proportion of the few manufacturing establishments dotting today's Addis Ababa were results of policy measures associated with this plan. However, such industrialization could not reach the level required to ease the pressure of urban unemployment, as the plan envisaged. A number of landlords and civil servants invested in "commercial farms" in the southern regions of the country.[8] This again did not occur on a scale which could significantly alter either the technology or the institutional profile of agricultural production in the country.

Even less impressive was the impact of the policy designed for the development of peasant agriculture. Development projects associated with the policy barely covered 100,000 farming households. In the southern areas where these projects concentrated, their intervention came up against the interests of the landlords. To the dismay of project personnel, greater productivity of tenancy farms simply resulted in landlords demanding increased rent from their tenants. In the better endowed localities of these areas, the projects also threatened the land security of tenants by attracting large-scale commercial farming ventures, run by urban entrepreneurs, into project areas. Thousands of peasants were evicted from their traditional farmland as a result. Although the percentage of households affected by evictions was rather small at the level of country-wide statistics, it was sufficient to signal the onset of a growing conflict between the development of peasant agriculture and large-scale urban enterprise in agriculture.

Still, by the end of the first decade of active government economic policy, little had changed in the economic structure of the countryside or its relations with the towns. The symptom of an urban economic crisis, sustained rises in unemployment and prices, had become even sharper. Famine ravaged many parts of the countryside, and the urban crisis sharpened so much that it eventually undermined the political supremacy of landlords in the towns, culminating in the overthrow of the monarchy.

The Ethiopian revolution can thus be understood *as an expression of the towns' decision to restructure its access to the countryside*. This decision was to be realized in the 1975-82 agrarian reforms. Behind these reforms was a radical reformation of economic and political power in the towns. With the overthrow of the monarchy all urban land and real estate enterprise, finance and medium-sized and large-scale manufacturing, merchandising and catering ventures were nationalized. This extended the hitherto mainly administrative domain of the public sector into the central management of urban economic life and resources, in pursuit of "the building of a socialist economy".

The reforms of 1975-82 established direct central government control over rural land administration, rural settlement patterns and the dynamics of the institutional structure of farming. This has opened the possibility of central government command over the mobility of resources both within the countryside and between villages and the towns. The last decade has seen a determined government drive to realize this possibility.

All indications suggest that the government is using its new fiscal, marketing and pricing policy instruments to tilt the balance increasingly in favour of the towns. Some observers consider the magnitude of net outflow from the villages so large that it makes internal investment in the countryside impossible (Cohen and Isaksson 1986, Pausewang 1988). In this way the government undermines its own declared strategy of using agricultural growth to generate resources for industrialization. The conflict between such practice and what might be perceived as the "populist" spirit of the 1975 land redistribution and of the government's declaration of "priority to agricultural development" leads to a pessimistic conclusion: that we are, after all, back in the pre-reform days in a fundamental sense, where, as in the old days, the elite of the towns "consider rural areas mainly as a reservoir of resources that can be tapped as the need arises" (Pausewang 1988).

One cannot help concurring with this observation. What one may disagree with is whether we are observing merely a gap between policy and outcome; and whether the 1975 redistribution of land represented even a temporary break in the traditional town-country relationship.

Concluding Remarks

At the core of urban economic life today is an anomalous public sector through which nearly half of the GDP passes. Over the past 40 years of its history, this sector has been feeding on the countryside to develop into a largely parasitic institution.

The sustaining of this kind of urban structure requires agrarian policies which get increasingly "extractive" rather than "entrepreneurial". Only to the extent that the government succeeds in establishing a basically productive mode of urban economic life can it afford to look for rational alternatives to current policies towards peasant farming. In this sense, the current "rural development problem" in Ethiopia is primarily an "urban development problem". But who is to say that Ethiopian towns are easier to reform than the countryside?

NOTES

1 Gult has obvious parallels to the European "fief" (or "Lehen"). Ethiopia has therefore been termed a "feudal" state; but particular features of the Ethiopian politico-economic system make many scholars dispute the term "Ethiopian feudalism" and the justification for this historical parallel.

2 The category of the estate of **gult** and the contextual definition of it are due to Hoben (1973).

3 This consisted mainly of unused arable land and the traditional grazing territory of semi nomadic pastoralists of the lowlands, the lands rights of which were apparently never recognized by the Imperial Government.

4 Editorial footnote:

Actually, this statement is misleading for **rist** farmers in the north. Also a peasant on **rist** land had to pay tribute to his gult-lord, who could evict defaulting peasants. But in contrast to tenants in the south, **rist** peasants held their land through their inherited and inalienable rights of descent, which entitled them to a share in the collectively held land. Neither legally nor **de facto**, they had a tenancy relationship with the **gult** owner. If for one reason or another they were forced to leave one village, they could always claim a share in another village where they had **rist** because of descent rights.

5 Editorial footnote:

Such figures, officially published in the sixties by Haile Selassie's government (Central Statistical Office and Ministry of Land Reform), are in fact grossly misrepresenting realities at that time. Figures are based on surveys in which people were asked whether they rented or owned their land. But peasants had no concept of ownership in a European sense. Asked whether a certain area was their land or whether somebody else owned it, a majority of peasants answered: it is mine, not knowing that in legal terms this was not the case any longer. Figures are therefore not even acceptable as guesses. Estimations vary considerably, both locally and in aggregation; but there is no doubt that by far the majority of peasants in the south had lost all legal rights to their land by the late 1960's - though many of them were not aware of this fact themselves. See also the following chapter in this volume.

6 Of this rate of growth, 4.5 per cent per annum was due to migration from the countryside. By 1970 this meant the migration of about 100,000 villagers per year (Taye and Beyene, 1982).

7 These were (1) the network of coffee markets of the towns of Keffa, Wellega, Sidamo and Hararghe that fed into Addis Ababa - Assab central and export markets; (2) the network of grain and livestock markets in the south that fed into the Addis Ababa and Dire-Dawa central

markets; (3) the northern system of grain and livestock markets that fed into the Asmara and Dessie terminal markets (Ministry of Agriculture, 1973).

8 Barely 5,000 "indigenous capitalist farmers" shared between them 200,000 ha of farm land, leaving peasant tenancy and independent peasant farming as the dominant institutions of the regions (Ottaway 1978).

3 "Meret Le Arrashu" Land Tenure and Access to Land: A Socio-historical Overview

Siegfried Pausewang

There is hardly any field in which so much confusion persists so obstinately as that of land tenure in Ethiopian tradition. Even the word itself is misleading: rather than tenure, it would be more correct to speak about access to land. Land holding practice changed over time, and tremendous variations can be observed not only in different regions, but even within the same village and family. Most confusing of all is the social dimension of conceptions about rights to land: a nobleman may have conceptions of his rights to the land which are completely different from those of "his" peasants. Moreover, urban viewpoints on rights over land are often completely different from the rural viewpoint.

Many misconceptions are still reproduced in public debate as well as in scientific literature and official documents. Misunderstandings are repeated time and time again. Many official statistics have been produced in such a confused and misguided fashion that the figures are not even guesses; they bear simply no relation to the reality of land holding. Nevertheless, they are quoted as scientific findings, and continue to mislead everybody.

It is therefore important for any examination of alternatives in agriculture to clarify some of these virulent misunderstandings. A realistic debate on options in Ethiopian agriculture is impossible without understanding that land rights are an integral part of rural culture and cannot be understood separately.

Some Basic Principles in Relation to Land Rights

The European concept of ownership is not applicable in Ethiopian tradition. To ask about ownership in Ethiopia is to invite misunderstanding. Ethiopia can only be understood within an African cultural tradition, in which land is a free gift to mankind, a resource which is necessary for everybody to live, which cannot be taken away from a person. Whoever has a right to life, has a right to land, just as he needs air to breathe, water, a community. Rules of distribution may have varied over time, in different areas, in different tribes, and within different categories of people. Land inheritance and transaction may have been practised. But rights always concerned the use of land, never land as a commodity, as property - until the development of a distinctive urban culture and mentality created a difference between rural and urban land. Ownership of land is an entirely urban concept in the African context, if it is not simply a European impostor.

In the Ethiopian cultural context, access to land was always interrelated with other rights. It was not a right in itself, but a function of membership in a kinship group, a community, a religious fellowship. This was manifest in the *rist* system by the fact that Moslems were excluded from holding land, but could nevertheless own urban land. The Felasha could not hold *rist* land, but could rent land or even clear and cultivate parts of the common land outside the defined area of the village's *rist* land. Amhara peasants referred not only to land when claiming to have *rist*. The term *rist* could equally refer to the right to residence in different places to which they could trace their descent, or simply the consciousness of security, founded on the proud feeling of being welcome in the communities of different villages, which included the right to membership in kinship, community and religious groups, as well as to the common use of land. It is essential to understand that land use rights are even today conceived as part and parcel of community rights and obligations, not as independent individual legal titles.

Land rights, conceived as an integral part of community membership, included a collective responsibility for a fair distribution of the agricultural land available. Fair distribution did not necessarily mean equality. Needs differed from family to family and from year to year. The available labour force varied through the family cycle. Moreover, the need for resources was also relative to community obligations and to merit, prestige and leadership functions in the community. A fair distribution had to reflect such different needs and capacities.

Those who used community land to produce food for their own livelihood also had also a responsibility to contribute to the community, and to the institutions guaranteeing its physical, organizational and spiritual integrity - that is, in Amhara culture, the village, the state and the Church.

Amharic language expresses this very concept: Amhara peasants are proud of being *gebar*, meaning a contributor. Until today, peasant associations are called gebarewoch mahber, not using the word *arrash* which, like "farmer" in English, refers to the work of the agricultural producer (as does the German *Bauer*). The word "peasant" like the French *paysan* and the Spanish *campesino*, refer to rural residence. The Norwegian word *bonde* or *husbond* refers to the settler, who lives on the farm and in that capacity is the head of its household (a term living on in the English word "husband"). Unlike all these professional terms, the Amharic word refers to a community obligation, contribution to the common well-being of all, as the criterion of an independent agricultural producer. At the same time, however, interesting changes in the content of the word *gebar* also indicate a historical dimension in the concept of access to land.

While different people with the same rights might be allocated land of different size, people with different community functions could be given different types of rights to land. One was allocated the right to till a certain parcel, another might be given the right to a share of the produce, in return for his service to the community as a Church or state functionary. A third person might have a right to administer the reallocation of land in a certain area. Hunting, fishing or passage or grazing rights were also allocated by the community. Yet another person might be proud of having a right to arbitrate in case of disputes on land. All of them might have the same reason to call the same area their land, claiming a right on it - but none of these rights could be considered ownership.

Cultural rules are one thing, social practice another. People with separate rights to land may also have differing conceptions of their rights. Also, theory and practice can differ considerably, especially as historical forms often evolve away from the original meaning of a rule. A system of common responsibility for distribution may have worked smoothly when there was enough land for everybody, but shortage and hence competition for land was bound to create problems for actual distribution. In practice, population pressure was not the only factor interfering with a concept of fair distribution according to everybody's needs and abilities. Influence in the community, prestige and power biased distribution. Growing extraction of resources was bound to increase pressure on land and competition for its allocation. It is therefore imperative to study land distribution not only at one point in history, but to envisage it as a system in flux, and to understand the original meaning of the rules in a system of collective responsibility but individual cultivation. It is even more important to study how this system was corrupted during the centralization of the Empire, which created channels for massive extraction of resources from agriculture into a central power structure with a new, distinctively urban national elite.

Lastly, if one wants to understand Ethiopian land distribution, an overriding principle is that every rule has exceptions. Whatever is said about land holding in Ethiopia fits some, maybe most areas, times and groups, but not all. As always in social laws, variety is the ultimate rule. But in Ethiopia, more than elsewhere, the many configurations make it difficult to see the rule.

Land Tenure in Ethiopian History

The *rist* system in the north of Ethiopia[1] demonstrates the difference between the inherent logic of a theoretically egalitarian and flexible system of regulating access to land, and a locally varying practice of intrigues, suspicion and conflict, as described for instance in Gojjam by Alan Hoben (1973). In theory - and in the consciousness retained by the Amhara until 1975 - the *rist* system gave every Amhara a claim on community membership in any village from which he could prove descent, and hence on a share of the common agricultural land. The community was collectively responsible for a fair distribution, and could re-allocate land at any time. How this was done varied considerably from place to place; but the principle of collective responsibility, vested in the elders, not in political leaders or the nobility, seems to have been retained almost everywhere. In theory, such a system should allow both local and social mobility: those who gained community responsibilities could claim access to more land; and anyone who felt discontent could claim his share in a village where more land was available, and escape from land fragmentation, troublesome neighbours or an over-demanding *gult*-lord.

Extraction of resources to finance overarching interests certainly existed. The Christian Church, physically organized around monasteries and parish churches, had access to resources for taking care of spiritual needs. The institution of *gult* financed the overarching common interests of political organization, defence, infrastructure etc. The *gult*-lords, a nobility of political and military leaders, had rights to collect a share of the produce of all agricultural land in a given area, in exchange for their administrative, political, cultural and judicial services. Each church and monastery had land from which it collected a share, in addition to some land for the priests who cultivated crops for their own upkeep. There was and still is a lot of confusion about the amount of church land in Imperial Ethiopia, because the fields which priests and monks cultivated, in return for their services, were never separated from church *gult* (rights on a share of ordinary peasants' produce in a certain area).

Peasant labour produced the resources needed to maintain such a system. Different rights related to land, its use, its distribution, and its produce guaranteed in theory a balance of powers: the local nobility depended both on the support of their peasants and on the state for their administrative authority of office. In the Church hierarchy, the local priests were peasants themselves; the Church leadership, with the *abuna* on top, could only be strong as long as they commanded the support of their peasant believers. And the Emperor could remove individual noblemen on any level of the hierarchy who dared to rebel against him, as long as the others gave him the power to enforce his decisions. Rebellions occurred where emperors exceeded the limits of their power. Noblemen could certainly evict peasants who defaulted or rebelled; but peasant rebellions had good chances of success if local noblemen misused their power or the authority of a king.

Much remained undefined and ambivalent in the distribution of resources, influence, and power. Practice was guided by the general rules, but determined by power relations which fluctuated with time and social processes. A strong central power could for some time tip the balance in favour of a national court. Peasant labour could be mobilized to build a rich and strong capital, as in Axum and later Gondar. In the Era of the Princes, fierce competition of provincial kings kept the Imperial court weak - at the expense of the majority of peasants who had to maintain the growing power of half a dozen provincial kingdoms. Centralization of the Empire, attempted in a grand design by Tewodros, established later by Menilek, and completed by Haile Selassie, was achieved through an unprecedented surge of resources to the new central administration and army.

The *gada* system of the Oromo was, in essence, the organization of a pastoralist cooperation, not only concerning land use, but social life in general. *Gada* was a social division into age groups with a distinct division of labour. Each age group had its specific social obligations, its religious duties, its work assignments, its distinct culture, language, rituals. Herding cattle, for long periods of time in distant grazing areas, was one age group's obligation, religious and political leadership, hunting and warriorship were vested in other groups. At regular intervals, all individuals were promoted to the next age groups, assuming new collective responsibilities.

When some Oromo tribes, during their expansion to the west, settled in sedentary agriculture, they developed a more permanent political organization built on social hierarchy. The Oromo kingdoms in the west also changed their distribution of access to land. While the literature asserts that the kings owned all land, it is likely that this merely expresses the translation of a complicated set of rights into an alien concept: the kings probably never had more than an ultimate privilege of arbitration about a fair distribution of arable land, and a right to extract tributes. In practice, their authority was invoked for distribution and redistribution. Their actual power, of course, decided to what extent they could expropriate individual peasants. But their interest was, in any case, not the land as such, but its produce.

There are probably at least a dozen other systems worth discussing. But in each case, after describing different rights related to the use of land, to its distribution, or to parts of its produce, one would have to explain that such rights had to complement each other. Those who had privileged access to parts of the produce saw themselves as much as "owners" as the peasants did. Their common interest was that the peasants could produce. Extractive "ownership" rights did not interfere with peasant producers "owning" their individual piece of land, irrespective of a communal responsibility for fair distribution. As long as individual cultivation was the only means to make land productive, a king or nobleman owning land only made sense together with peasant ownership: land without peasants was unproductive, was without value.

Expansion of the Empire to the South

Menilek's campaigns to the south were in principle a colonial[2] expansion, to create the material and demographic basis for a strong state, a standing army and a central administration. The conquered people had to pay the bill. It is often repeated that Menilek expropriated all land in the conquered south and distributed it to his followers. But this is a Eurocentric statement which does not define which rights he expropriated. It wrongly suggests a European concept of ownership.

Menilek remunerated his soldiers and administrators by giving them land rights in the conquered areas. Of course, these administrators and officers were not interested in land for cultivation, but in collecting contributions from productive peasants. Thus, Menilek expropriated all land in the south as far as rights of extraction are concerned, and redistributed these; but he expropriated very few peasants: they were the source of wealth in the south. Without their uninterrupted production, the "expropriated" land had no value. If anything, peasants were encouraged to continue to produce; no-one thought of evicting them from their land. To the contrary, a nobleman who was given land without peasants would offer attractive land rights to attract settlers, often from the north, to come and till the land. Peasants who rebelled would be punished, but the majority remained on their land and continued to cultivate the land of their fathers. They had to deliver larger contributions than before, to new masters, who were armed and had built their power on the gun. *Neftegna*, man with a gun, was their name until the land reform eliminated this new rural class. Heavy coercion was only used when peasants refused contributions, or when landlords wanted to increase these. Not even missionary activities were allowed to interfere in local affairs: the conquerors built churches in the south to cater for the settlers from the north, but seldom made more than sporadic efforts to Christianize the conquered peoples (Pankhurst 1966).

Centralization of the Empire led both the old *gult*-lords in the north and the new ones in the south to move into towns as civil servants, taking with them their privileges and the resources they collected in their villages. Those who returned as administrators and representatives of central authority came to the villages with less responsibility towards the peasants, but more power over them. Resources that were earlier consumed and redistributed in the village, were now sold in town, to finance an urban style of living, and to stimulate urban growth. Urbanization accelerated, the balance tipped once again at the expense of peasants, whose contributions were increased to meet growing urban expenses. The villages lost both the cultural, social and communal services of the nobleman and the resources he redistributed locally, while their contributions increased with taxes to the central administration.

In the north, peasants were able to defend their *rist* system, which preserved their right of collective control over redistribution of land. But pressure on land increased, as every peasant needed more land to cultivate enough for growing obligations on top of what he needed to feed his family. This made the system change character.

Power and positions had always been determinants of actual redistribution of land rights. But increased competition meant an outright fight of all against all, where intrigues, positions, alliances and patronage counted. What Hoben (1973) describes as *rist* in Gojam in the 1960s must be interpreted in the context of such sharpened competition, turning neighbours into rivals and making common ancestors a reason for suspicion. A situation where peasants spent more time in litigation than in ploughing clearly signals the corruption of a system of inheritance rights which peasants still defended with dedication and zeal.

From *Gult* to Freehold

In the south, landlords succeeded in convincing the Emperor to make their rights hereditary. While *riste-gult* (hereditary *gult* rights) was rare in the north, it became the rule in the south. Under Haile Selassie, growing economic relations with Europe introduced the European concept of one single and comprehensive ownership right into Ethiopian legal thinking.

Ownership in this sense appeared a precondition for investments in modern agriculture. Haile Selassie granted rights of freehold - an alien concept in Ethiopia - to owners of *riste-gult* and other recipients of Imperial land grants. Again, such changes were made at the expense of the peasants who were not even informed of the legal changes affecting their rights. For them there was no change: they continued ploughing their land and producing, for as long as the new land-owner had no interest in interrupting the flow of their contributions. Ownership rights expanded in the south, all unbeknown to the peasants.

After the Italian occupation, Haile Selassie instituted the payment of taxes in money, directly to the government, and legally recognized the tax payer, i.e. the contributor or *gebar*, as land-owner. All land for which no tax had been paid was declared the property of the state. Again peasants were not aware of the significance of legal changes. Their terms of contributions were not affected. But those who collected taxes had them registered in their own names, thus buying official recognition as *gebar*, land-owners, even where they had no such rights before. The legal expropriation of a majority of peasants proceeded, quite unobserved by most of those affected. It was only when urban investors became interested in commercial agriculture that the landlords intervened. Peasants often only realized the change when tractors started to plough up their crop.[3] When they went to court, to protest against what they considered illegal infringements on their inherited rights, they were told they were only tenants and had to move. Even when such events occurred on a regular basis, most peasants would attribute it to corrupt practices by courts and individual landlords, rather than understand the structural change that had occurred and the political system that had allowed and supported it.

This ambiguity of land rights was reflected in a change in the word *gebar*. In the north, peasants who had *rist* rights continued to be proud of contributing as *gebar*. In the south, in contrast, it was traditional to call the cultivator from conquered tribes a *gebar*; a peasant with no rights, subject to growing exploitation and the arbitrary power of the *neftegna*. More and more, the term was used to characterize the tillers as tenants, subjects, even slaves. In legal terms, at the same time, the word *gebar* meant the tax payer who, by virtue of having his name entered in the tax register of the state, was recognized as legal owner of the land. Those who were *gebar* in legal terms were precisely not the *gebar* in everyday language and in self-understanding.

This is why the students demonstrating against Haile Selassie's regime, in 1965 and later, sang *Meret le arrashu*, land to the tiller, as their slogan and battle song. They would certainly have had every reason to embrace the thoroughly democratic connotations in the word *gebar*, implying community obligation and shared responsibility. But this word was discredited in the south, where peasants characterized themselves as *irbo arrash*, *siso arrash*, and *ekul arrash*, indicating that they had to deliver one fourth, one third or one half respectively of their crop to their landlord, who paid the tax and considered himself the legal *gebar*. Using the word *gebar* could have been understood by many peasants as a support for those who were not tillers, but had usurped ownership rights on peasant land.

Similarly, the ambiguity of the concept of ownership created confusion in reports and statistics. At the end of the 1960s, the Ministry of Land Reform conducted a series of studies on land tenure in different provinces. The surveys conducted in the southern provinces are a classical example of imported scientific methodology producing nonsense. They calculate figures which have nothing to do with reality, - but which are nevertheless quoted even today to show that almost half the population of the south were tenants, the other half owning their land themselves. In fact, such results indicate that the interviewers should be given credit for asking not only the landlords, but also taking the trouble to go to the villages and asking at least some peasants. As the situation was at that time, asking people "Do you own this land" - translated to mean in Amharic something like "Is this your land" was meaningless. Peasants would insist it was their land, while the landlord would claim they were all tenants and the land was his. Had someone ever taken the trouble to calculate how much land was "owned" altogether, it would have amounted to about twice the province. The Central Statistical Office repeated the exercise in their sample surveys with no better results. Directed by foreign social scientists, with questionnaires designed by Indian experts, interviewers could only collect numerically exact answers to ambiguous or meaningless questions. But statistics, once they are printed, become the truth, and since it is no longer possible to repeat the exercise, it is hard to convince administrators that the only statistics they have got are useless.

The Land Reform

The land reform redistributed very little land. Most peasants just kept the land they ploughed. Only where a landlord himself cultivated much more than the average peasant was his land taken for distribution. In most villages, there was not enough land available for redistribution to the poor who had been granted rights to land. The newly formed peasant associations resolved the problem by ploughing up some areas of common grazing land.[4]

What made the difference was not the extent of ploughed land, but security on the land, the abolition of contributions to landlords, debts and work obligations. This explains the fact that the land reform was welcomed with great enthusiasm in the south, while in the northern *rist* areas, peasants were sceptical, and easy to organize for resistance against alleged attacks on Christianity, Amhara culture, and *rist* rights. Here peasants had preserved more security of land holding, at least in theory, through collective responsibility for distribution, and the *gult-lords* were considered patrons of the village and part of local culture. But once local resistance was broken and the land reform was effected, Amhara peasants too accepted its basic principles and understood its merits. The land reform freed them from the burdens of litigation, of having to defend their land against competitors. It gave them a limited but secure right to a share of the community's land and preserved the collective responsibility for distribution in the peasant associations.

Peasants were freed from contributions. This immediately enabled them to consume more. In 1976, it was easy to see that the peasants in the villages had more to eat - and also more to drink. But what was an advantage for the peasants was a disadvantage for the towns. For the government, growing food shortages in the urban centres became a nightmare. Conflicts between urban and rural population groups became virulent. At one point, in 1976, the government had to send soldiers to confiscate grain from communal stores built to give peasants better control over trade and price developments. New taxes had to be introduced, both because peasants had to be induced to sell grain, and, as the largest productive group in the country, they had to contribute to the costs of administration.

Since 1977, the situation in the villages has changed significantly. The government has not only re-introduced taxation, other contributions have come back, though not the landlord. Marketing and price policies have in effect caused a considerable deterioration in the terms of trade for peasant produce (see the articles by Eshetu and Taye in this volume).

I would thus suggest (in contrast to other articles in this volume - Dessalegn, Taye, Eshetu) that the land reform of 1975 did actually redistribute resources, giving peasants more to eat (and to invest), by allowing them to keep those parts of their produce which earlier had to be delivered to landlords. I would argue that in 1975 this was done quite deliberately, both by the political leadership which withdrew the first, less radical draft of summer 1974 and set up a new drafting committee, and by those young experts who drafted the land reform law of 1975. But the same leadership soon realized that redistribution to the advantage of peasants had been granted at the expense of the urban population. To satisfy the urban poor, and to finance growing state expenditures, they had to withdraw the distributed privileges again, step by step. At the same time, this process also withdrew most of the local autonomy and self-administration peasants had enjoyed from 1975 to 1977. This is the significance of the 1977-78 changes in peasant association leadership and in the assimilation of peasant associations as local organs of state administration.

Today, peasants resent not the land reform as such, but the forms of interference from above, the increasing taxes and contributions, the diminishing availability of land, and a general loss of autonomy and independence.

Conclusion

An observer remarked recently that without the land reform, Ethiopia might today face an Oromo resistance movement, compared to which the Eritrean and Tigrean fronts would look like Sunday schools. Indeed, Oromo peasants were the prime beneficiaries of the land reform. But the land reform would be more acceptable to most peasants anywhere in Ethiopia if its provisions and practice remained within the frame of certain traditional values of common relevance in peasant culture. Such a common cultural fundus limits options in rural policies. Land distribution, land rights and agricultural practice are an integral part of rural culture. Any intervention in rural production relations must take the cultural context into account, and give due consideration to how new laws, changes in contributions, or administrative innovations work within (or interfere with) the totality of cultural practice. Rural reforms will be accepted by the majority of peasants, it seems, as long as they guarantee that

1. land remains common property (not state property)
2. distribution of access to arable land remains in local hands
3. collective responsibility for distribution and social security is maintained
4. individual rights to a share in the community's land are preserved
5. individual control over the fruits of one's work (including permanent improvements on the land, trees, buildings etc.) is not restricted
6. there is some limitation of contributions, including taxes, to a level which allows the individual farmer a fair return for additional work

And above all, the land reform measures must be compatible with local cultural life. A reasonably detailed description of land distribution patterns in Ethiopia before 1975 is not possible in this context. Land tenure before and after the land reform is described in detail in: Cohen and Weintraub 1975, Pausewang 1983, Dessalegn Rahmato 1984, Alemneh Dejene 1987. There exists a number of descriptions of individual systems of land distribution, in the context of tribal cultures and their solution to the problems of individual access to land, and their rules to redistribute food and work to secure that every member of the community had access to at least the minimum needed. See Hoben 1973, Weissleder 1965 and others. Many of these texts are describing complex social relations at one particular point of time, and from a culturally centred view. For example, Hoben describes land tenure patterns from the viewpoint of the participant observer wondering why there is so much litigation about land in Gojam; the reports of the Central Statistical Office and the Ministry of Land Reform before 1974 tried to bring some order into the complicated differences of land-ownership relations in Haile Selassie's Empire. Other papers reflected urban interpretations of students who wanted to expose the exploitation of Ethiopian peasants. A critical reading, which keeps in mind the principles of Ethiopian land rights, can find a wealth of useful information in these publications, even if figures should not be accepted at face value, but scrutinized for what they really say.

NOTES

1 A reasonably detailed description of land distribution patterns in Ethiopia before 1975 is not possible in this context. Land tenure before and after the land reform is described in detail in: Cohen and Weintraub 1975, Pausewang 1983, Dessalegn Rahmato 1984, Alemneh Dejene 1987. There exists a number of descriptions of individual systems of land distribution, in the context of tribal cultures and their solution to the problems of individual access to land, and their rules to redistribute food and work to secure that every member of the community

had access to at least the minimum needed. See f.eks. Hoben 1973, Weissleder 1965 and others. Many of these texts are describing complex social relations at one particular point of time, and from a culturally centred view. For example, Hoben describes land tenure patterns from the viewpoint of the participant observer wondering why there is so much litigation about land in Gojam; the reports of the Central Statistical Office and the Ministry of Land Reform before 1974 tried to bring some order into the complicated differences of land-ownership relations in Haile Selassie's Empire. Other papers reflected urban interpretations of students who wanted to expose the exploitation of Ethiopian peasants. A critical reading, which keeps in mind the principles of Ethiopian land rights, can find a wealth of useful information in these publications, even if figures should not be accepted at face value, but scrutinized for what they really say. The following summary description of **rist, gult** and **gada** refers to: Pausewang 1983:17-85.

2 Comparable to the Roman Empire's colonies in Africa and northern Europe, or Prussian expansion to the East in 18th century, rather than European colonialism in Africa.

3 In parts of the south, especially along the roads offering easy access, peasants learned to understand the word **limat**, development, as synonymous with evictions, and tried to keep aloof of anything related to it (Pausewang 1983:75-83).

4 For more detail about the land reform and its consequences, see the contributions by Dessalegn Rahmato and Stefan Brüne in this volume.

4 The Evolution of Rural Development Policies
Dejene Aredo

The literature on past and present rural development policies in the country is scattered over different papers and reports. This study attempts to put the present policy in its historical perspective, as a basis for the study and better understanding of current issues in Ethiopian rural development. The first part focuses on the relationship between national economic planning and the agricultural sector, while the second deals with rural development projects. The third and concluding section attempts to summarize rural development policies in the country during the last 30 years.

National Economic Planning and the Agricultural Sector

In line with the development theories[1] and policies[2] of donors which accentuated only the instrumental role of agriculture to supply resources for industrial development, Ethiopia's agricultural sector was largely neglected in the late 1950s and early 1960s.

When issuing its first Five-Year Development Plan in 1957 the Imperial Ethiopian Government (IEG) felt "no need to bring about fundamental changes in present methods of (peasant) production" and stuck to the "kind of tools now used" (IEG 1957). At that time (1958 to 1968) there were only 100 to 120 agricultural extension agents scattered across the country (Tesfai 1975:2). Paradoxically, the very sector which was given little attention by the planners was expected to supply the industrial sector with "plentiful agricultural raw materials", notwithstanding the low productivity of labour in agriculture (IEG 1957, 1962).

The first two Five-Year Plans (1957-62 and 1962-67) heavily favoured large-scale commercial farms and export crops. Large-scale modern farming was considered to be the "right way to develop Ethiopian agriculture, especially since there was much virgin land to be settled". With regard to the production of cash crops for export, the "greatest attention was given to the cultivation of coffee". According to one estimate, the results of the first plan were such that cereal production increased by only 10 per cent, while coffee production increased by 20 per cent and hides and skins by 50 per cent (IEG 1962).

By the late 1960s the adverse effects of previous agricultural policies were being increasingly felt. Cereal production lagged behind the growth of urban and rural population.[3] As a result the country became, for the first time in its modern history, a net food importer[4] with imports amounting to 45,000 tons in 1959/60.

The "industry first" argument of the 1950s was being challenged theoretically as post-independent Africa's aspiration for a rapid industrialization process became increasingly frustrated (Johnston/ Meller 1961, Eicher/Witt 1964, Myrdal 1966), and the major donors made a significant shift in their aid policies in favour of rural development *vis-à-vis* urbanization and construction of infrastructure.

In an attempt to realize this change of policy, donors subjected the Ethiopian government to strong pressure. Foreign assistance agencies, particularly the World Bank (IBRD) and American organizations, advised Ethiopia to give high priority to the agricultural sector and recommended the package approach concentrating on the more promising regions. This idea was also supported by FAO (Nekby 1971:9). It strongly influenced the third Five-Year Development Plan (1968-1973), which "was to a great extent the work of international experts" (Stahl 1973:9).

The plan exhibited a marked departure from the previous ones. It recognized the importance of the agricultural sector, and charted out a relatively clear and well-articulated agricultural development strategy. The plan argued that "modernization of peasant subsistence agriculture in all areas of the country simultaneously is hardly feasible", but "no time should be lost in making a start in strategically selected areas in which good results can soon be seen". Accordingly, package projects were established in high potential geographical areas in order to bring about a "long, slow, experimental and gradual diffusion process of the transformation of peasant agriculture" (IEG 1968).

The primary objectives of the aid-financed package projects were to raise the real incomes of smallholders, eliciting their participation - and that of local government officials - in rural development efforts, to generate additional employment opportunities and to narrow the prevailing income disparities in the rural areas (Tesfai 1975:41). Another aim was the expansion of large-scale commercial farms, to realize relatively quick increases in the marketable surplus needed by a growing urban population and the export sector.

However, during the 1960s capital expenditure in agriculture averaged only about 6 per cent of total investment, and of this the smallholders received only some 13 per cent (Cohen 1987:61; Tesfai 1975:3).

It was envisaged that still more attention should be given to the agricultural sector in the fourth Five-Year plan (1974/1978). Pressure from donor nations and international agencies increased (see Pearson 1969, MacNamara 1973, Chenery et al 1974, Martin 1970, Codippily 1985:3, Cohen and Weindtraub 1975:1-10). The agricultural development strategy in the draft fourth plan, as provided by the World Bank, was to concentrate scarce resources on areas of high potential, in line with the on-going package programmes. Cereals and pulses were identified as priority crops.

However, the fate of the fourth plan was sealed by the onset of the 1974 revolution which opened new opportunities for the agricultural sector. The historic land reform proclamation of 1975 removed what had been considered as major constraints to rural development. It established peasant organizations at local and national levels as a means of mobilizing the energies of the rural toilers.[5]

However, during the four years following the February Revolution, virtually no new agricultural policies or rural development projects[6] were introduced to exploit the opportunities created by the 1975 land reform. This period could have been the most opportune time for accelerating agricultural growth, had the government not been preoccupied with the political and military struggle which followed the revolution. In fact, this period (1974-78) was characterized by stagnation and in some cases decline in the production of goods and services in almost all sectors of the economy.

The question of economic reconstruction and rehabilitation came to the forefront in 1978, when, as a result of the government's victories over its internal and external opponents, political power was consolidated and a period of relative peace and stability began.

Following the establishment of the Central Planning Supreme Council (NRDC & CPSC) in 1978, six annual development campaigns were successively launched in an attempt to revive the economy. In 1979 guide-lines concerning the nationwide promotion of agricultural producer cooperatives were passed. Rural administration was increasingly centralized, and two more ministries (Coffee and Tea Development in 1980 and State Farms in 1982) were created. The marketing sector was brought under central control by expanding the operation of the Agricultural Marketing Corporation (AMC) and the Coffee Marketing Corporation (CMC).

Between 1978/79 and 1980/81 the economy regained momentum and experienced a noticeable rate of growth of GDP. This was mainly due to good weather conditions and the utilization of excess capacity in manufacturing industries. Since then per capita agricultural output has steadily declined. In 1984 the annual campaigns, six in number, were replaced by the Ten-Year Perspective Plan(TYPP).

The plan, over-ambitious as it is, calls for a 4.3 per cent annual growth rate in agriculture (growth rate of GDP:6.5 per cent), a structural transformation of the sector (the sector's share in GDP was envisaged to fall to 39 per cent), and for the allocation of 22.5 per cent of total investments to agriculture. However, the plan made no attempt to deal with such related issues as pricing and population policy.

The TYPP expected to achieve the plan targets by accelerating the social transformation of the rural areas.[7] According to the plan, smallholder farming "cannot be a viable undertaking" and "the organization of farmers into producer cooperatives is expected to facilitate the gradual introduction of larger-scale farming and mechanized agriculture. In order to induce farmers to join producer cooperatives, preferential treatment will be given to members of cooperatives with regard to access to various types of productivity-raising inputs and the marketing of their produce" (PMAC 1984:52).

However, the great drought and famine of 1984, coupled with other problems, did not allow the plan to proceed as expected. The drought "gravely affected the activities of all other sectors of the economy" and brought about "a further fall of 6.7 per cent of GDP in real terms in 1984/85". Therefore, the target of the two-year plan (1984/85-1988/86) remained unfulfilled" (ONCCP[8] 1987). The share of domestic savings in GDP dropped from 4.8 per cent in 1980/81 to 1.8 per cent in 1984/85, and consumption exceeded total domestic production. In the same year, investment was wholly financed by external loans and assistance (ONCCP 1987:5).

Thus, it became imperative to modify the provisions of the TYPP in the Three-Year Plan (1986/87-1988/89). The original objective of "realising self-sufficiency in food supply and the holding of three months stock of food reserves (and attainment of a minimum 2000 calorie intake) at the end of the plan period" was replaced by a less ambitious and more concrete objective: to "increase food production in order to alleviate food deficits; emphasis will be given to the major staple food crops such as teff, barley, wheat, maize and sorghum" (ONCCP 1987).

Another major modification made in the TYPP in response to the ever-increasing food deficit was the strategy of concentrating modern farm inputs and extension work in the grain surplus regions of the country:

> Administrative regions will be selected according to their potentials for surplus production. This new strategy is selected for a more efficient allocation of resources. In the light of this strategy, administrative regions have been categorized into 31 surplus-producing *awrajas* (sub-districts), 14 potentially surplus-producing *awrajas* and others. The allocation of resources and distribution of inputs ... will be determined on the basis of this strategy during the period of the Three-Year Plan(ONCCP 1987:47).

The evolution of major rural development projects in the country has been summarized in Fig. 1. In 1968 the third Five-Year Plan had provided for promotion of large-scale commercial farms[9] and two types of integrated rural development projects, *comprehensive* and *minimum package* projects. The first three comprehensive package projects were the Chilalo Agricultural Development Unit (CADU), the Wolamo Agricultural Development Unit (WADU) and the Ada District Development Project (ADDP) which were launched in 1967, 1970 and 1972, respectively.

As package projects they aimed at integration of agronomic research, dissemination of research results, provision of modern farm inputs, marketing and credit facilities as well as the promotion of cooperative societies. A major feature of the projects was that all of them were largely aid-financed. The Swedish International Development Agency (SIDA) was supposed to cover 67 per cent of total operating costs of CADU, the Ethiopian government contributing the rest. Of the total cost of 44,371,400 birr during the period 8 September 1967 to 7 July 1975, SIDA contributed 28,995,600 birr and the Ethiopian government 15,375,000 birr. SIDA actively participated in the design of the project which was under its tight control and provided high level manpower (Sileshi 1982:161). Among others, as late as in 1972, the heads of

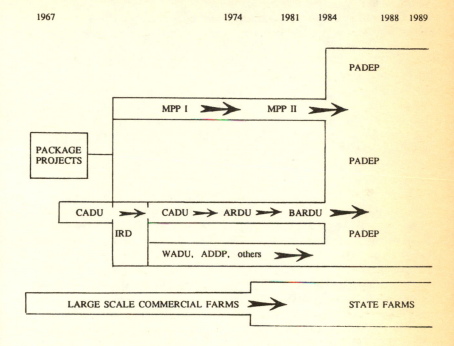

Fig. 1:
**Rural Development Projects
and Large-scale Mechanized Farms
(1967 - 1989)**

Notes:

MPP:	Minimum Package Projects
IRD:	Integrated Rural Development
CADU:	Chilalo Agricultural Development Unit
ARDU:	Arsi Rural Development Unit
BARDU:	Bale - Arsi Rural Development Unit
WADU:	Wollaita Agricultural Development Unit
ADDP:	Ada District Development Unit
PADEP:	Peasant Agricultural Development Extension Programme

the Marketing Division and of the Extension and Training Department were expatriates (Holmberg 1972:89-90).

Following the 1974 revolution CADU, the most important comprehensive package project, evolved into Arsi Rural Development Unit (ARDU) and then into the Arsi-Bale Rural Development Unit (BARDU). Finally, when PADEP was established in 1984, CADU-ARDU completed its gradual transition from a semi-autonomous unit to a fully integrated regional office of the Ministry of Agriculture (MoA), and became part of the South-Eastern zone (Arsi and Bale) of the new programme[10] (see Fig.1). The other comprehensive package projects were either terminated or were incorporated into the minimum package projects which will be reviewed below.

In the late 1960s the comprehensive package projects were found too costly to be duplicated in other parts of the country. It was decided to launch a scheme which was thought to be less costly per farmer. Thus, in 1971, minimum package projects (MPP), involving only those minimum services considered critical for rural development (mainly fertilizers and credit) were established along all-weather roads.[11]

It was planned that the MPP should cover all parts of the country by the end of the 1970s. Ten project areas were to be set up each year, and the programme was to make use of existing organizations, rather than chosing a more costly option of creating new ones. The minimum package projects (MPP) continued well through the post-revolution period, but their implementation and further expansion were constrained, among other things, by the reluctance of major donors to release funds on schedule. This was reportedly due to their dissatisfaction with some of the government's policies, for example the question of compensation for the nationalized industries.[12]

The World Bank renewed its commitment to the MPP after a hiatus of two years, and the programme entered into its second phase (MPP II 1981-84) with 60 per cent of its total financial expenditure coming from external loans and grants (Codippily 1985). Influenced by the political philosophy of the socialist-oriented government, the MPP II was over-ambitious in both its objectives and geographical range. It was expected to co-ordinate the various government activities (e.g. the efforts to create cooperatives), to disseminate modern farm inputs (chemical fertilizers in particular) and to develop rural infrastructure. It covered 13 administrative regions, 80 *awrajas* and 440 *woredas*.

Beginning June 1984, MPP II was expected to be replaced by PADEP, a programme which was seen as a happy medium, as its proposed costs lay midway between those of comprehensive and minimum package projects. PADEP was supposed to differ from previous rural development projects. It attempted to develop appropriate technologies at the zonal level, to strengthen coordination between research and extension activities. It was to prepare annual plans for the different zones, incorporate livestock development in its programmes, and to provide extension services at local level, taking service cooperatives (about 1,250 households) as a unit of extension work. Moreover, PADEP sought to promote smallholder production and resource conservation by forming stronger institutions. It concentrated extension resources and finance for small-farm fertilizer requirements in high-potential areas.

PADEP divided the country into eight zones, which were formed on the basis of similarities in natural resources, climatic conditions, cropping patterns, and proximity. Nevertheless important socio-economic criteria were left out in determining the various PADEP zones, as existing administrative boundaries were taken for granted.[13]

The feasibility studies for PADEP were undertaken by the major donor agencies and by high level experts from the Ministry of Agriculture. PADEP was expected to be financed largely by major donors who had delineated their respective spheres of influence right from the beginning of the feasibility study: the World Bank (the Central and the South-Western Zone), SIDA (the South-Eastern Zone), IFAD (Eastern Zone), and African Development Bank (South-Eastern Zone).

However, the launching of PADEP was delayed and its implementation was hampered by unduly prolonged negotiations. Within the framework of the World Bank's recent policy of structural adjustment lending, a policy dialogue dragged on for considerable time. It was only in 1989 that PADEP could finally be officially started.

Concluding Remarks

This study has attempted to shed some light on the patterns of evolution of Ethiopian rural development policies during the last 30 years. It has outlined attempts of donors to influence rural development policies in Ethiopia, in the past by suggesting strategies for national economic planning, and at present through a "policy dialogue". The interesting question here is therefore whether it is actually possible to formulate alternative policies and implement them without taking into account the role of foreign finance and aid. Of course, one may ignore donors and have one's own way, as shown by the villagization and resettlement policies. But one should also ask how far such programmes have succeeded in achieving their declared objectives.

Past and present policies have been characterized by various types of biases: spatial bias (concentration of modern farm input and extension activities in limited geographical areas), scale and technological bias (preferential treatment of large farms), gender bias (women have been neglected in the design and implementation of rural development projects), and approach bias (the bottom-up approach in planning has been largely neglected). The question at hand is therefore whether these biases are unavoidable or whether different options are available given the circumstances.

NOTES

1 Theories on the role of agriculture in economic development in the 1950s were based on dual economy models which were first propounded by Arthur Lewis and later elaborated by others (Lewis 1954, Ranis and Fei 1961, 1964; Jorgenson 1961). In these theories, the agricultural sector was considered as an instrument for the growth of the other sectors, as a "black box from which people, and food to feed them, and perhaps capital could be released" (Little 1982:105). Moreover, "it is fairly obvious from reading their works that the leading development economists of the 1950s know little about tropical agriculture or rural life" (Little 1982:106).

2 Donors' policy of this period was biased in favour of urbanization vis-à-vis rural development. The World Bank for example, by far the largest single source of development assistance to Ethiopia in recent years, allocated 85 per cent of its total loans to modern roads during the 1950-59 period, and nothing to the agricultural sector (World Bank 1985). Similarly, Sweden allocated no funds to the agricultural sector up to the second half of the 1960s. Prior to this period, Swedish aid totally went to largely urban-based education and health facilities (Sileshi 1982:147-167).

3 The introduction of medical technology into the rural areas (e.g. the largely successful malaria and smallpox eradication programmes in the 1950s and 1960s) led to a sharp decline in mortality (Robinson and Yamazaki 1986:327-338).

4 Some five or six years earlier the country used to export food (IEG, 2nd Five-Year Plan:45).

5 Peasant associations, and later rural service cooperatives, have succeeded in demonstrating the enormous potential that peasants have in self-management. The active role they played in redistributing and administering rural land, with limited interference from above during the initial period of the revolution, demonstrates this potential.

6 Of course, certain policy declarations were made during this period, though neither concrete nor effective measures were taken. The Programme of National Democratic Revolution (1976) stated: "...since the building of a strong and an independent national economy is possible only through the balanced development of the industrial and agricultural sectors of the national economy, it is necessary to have a centralized national plan based on socialist principles. Such a plan must take agriculture as a foundation of the country's economy and proceed towards establishing light industry that serves the immediate needs of the broad masses".

7 However it is not clear whether socialization was considered as a means or as an end in itself.

8 In 1984 the Central Planning Supreme Council was renamed the "Office of National Committee for Central Planning" (ONCCP).

9 During the pre-1974 period, fiscal policies (e.g. duty-free imports of tractors and fuel) were employed in order to attract, in particular, foreign private capital and managerial know-how into the mechanized, large-scale farming sector which was deemed to be the "most propulsive" mechanism for boosting the marketable surplus. By 1975 these farms accounted for less than 3 per cent of the total cultivated area. An excellent assessment of the performance of large-scale commercial farms during the pre-1975 period is given in Dessalegn Rahmato (1985). Following the land reform proclamation 1975, most of the large-scale commercial farms

were converted into state farms; the rest were transferred either to agricultural settlements or to producer cooperatives.

10 The process, causes and implications of the gradual area expansion of CADU are well-documented and extensively discussed in Cohen (1987).

11 The establishment of the MPP also coincided with a shift in donor policies. SIDA shifted from project aid to the country-frame approach (Seleshi 1982:161), and the World Bank began to increasingly cherish the idea of using chemical fertilizers as an open sesame to the problems of rural development.

12 During this period the country must have lost millions of dollars in foregone foreign aid. This loss, coupled with the then prevailing chaos and economic disruption, might have made a significant contribution to the on-going structural food deficit.

13 The eight PADEP zones were: North-Western Zone (Gondar and Gojam), South-Western Zone (Wollega, Keffa and Illubabor), Southern Zone (Gamo Gofa and Sidamo), South-Eastern Zone (Arsi and Bale), Eastern Zone (Hararghe), Central Zone (Shoa), North-Eastern Zone (Wollo and Assab), and Northern Zone (Eritrea and Tigray).

5 Gender Relations in Mobilizing Human Resources

Hanna Kebede

Ethiopian women have played a traditional role of mother and housewife in both rural and urban areas. However, their work has never been limited to the household and the family. Women's productivity is predominant in the processing and marketing of food and in related cottage industries. In urban areas, women are employed for domestic work, child rearing, food processing and in service industries. In rural areas, women engage in a wide variety of economic activities, including the construction of housing, land cultivation and harvesting, food storage and marketing. However, women's work in the agricultural sector has often been erroneously documented as marginal, and they have been considered more as consumers than as producers.

While farming is traditionally considered a male activity, women participate in every aspect of farm production. Ploughing is about the only activity women do not usually undertake, but they will take on even this task when there is no male assistance available. From soil preparation to sowing, weeding, harvesting and winnowing, as well as storage and marketing, women are involved every step of the way in manual farm labour.

Women have secondary status within the family and in society, which is why they get little credit for their productivity. Their status also limits their access to the economic resources which could enable them to promote their independence. Hence, women continue to be regarded as an appendage to the family, as helpers to the male head of household, as consumers but not as producers.

It is important to understand how conditions for women have changed, if at all. In what ways has the country mobilized the labour of women to optimize human resources in the overall economic development of the nation ? Does the changing society offer women credit for the productive work they do, and access to resources for improving their work situation, their self consciousness, and their productivity ? This analysis will focus on four areas: Marriage, education and the family; Economic activity, productivity and labour compensation for women; Property ownership, income generating and purchasing power for women; and decision making within the household, along with participation in economic and political life.

Important changes have taken place with the introduction of the socialist ideology which advocates equal rights for all, irrespective of sex, religion, racial or social origin. Women, along with other minorities, were among the underclass for whom the 1974 revolution heralded "equal rights". Rural women (including, to a limited extent, nomadic women) have begun to assert themselves within the household and in their communities. Urban women particularly have forged ahead to compete in the employment market.

One of the factors which influenced women to demand employment, education and access to land and economic resources was the Development Through Cooperation Campaign launched in December 1974. At that time, students were mobilized to educate the people in rural and urban communities. Girls were deployed alongside boys to participate in the development effort. This equal treatment of the sexes was an enlightening experience in itself. Furthermore, the students' contributions in challenging traditional values, beliefs and customs which undermined women's positions within the household and in the communities were highly significant in raising consciousness among both males and females.

Ethiopian women seem to have fared somewhat better since the 1974 socio-economic and political transformation. They have expanded their horizon both with educational advancement and increased economic activity. Before we consider the many changes which have either increased or decreased women's participation in the mainstream of social, economic and political life, it is important to understand the social setting within which women operate.

Marriage, Education and the Family

Radical measures have been taken towards implementing ideological reforms, but the institution which organizes labour between the sexes, the family, continues to be central in role assignment and status definition for the sexes. Redefining women's roles and increasing their participation are challenges to the patriarchal system, as are women's struggles for self determination.

The family is a major training and employment institution for women. It is within this framework that girls are prepared for their future, and women find their vocation as housewifes and mothers. Girls marry at a younger age than boys, limiting their opportunities for education or gainful employment outside the household. Traditionally, non-marital alternatives have had adverse social consequences for women; prostitution was the primary means of livelihood for women who did not marry.

This is not to say that women were not formerly employed except as prostitutes. Domestic work and services within the food and beverage industries were always open to women for minimal wages and sometimes for as little as room and board only. This was probably because women's nurturing roles involved food preparation and serving people, which translated to serving in bars and restaurants, working as domestic help in cooking and child rearing, clothing care and household maintenance.

Table 1 reveals that 53 per cent of girls get married before they are 20 years old, while only 5 per cent of boys are married at this age. Ironically, at age sixty only 25 per cent of women are married, in contrast to 90 per cent of men at this age. As the women grow older, they are less likely to remain married, since the men often contract second and third marriages, choosing younger wives. This explains the high rate of divorcees (11 per cent) among women above the age of sixty, while only 3.4 per cent of the men live as divorcees at the same age. This appears curious given that divorce is so highly discouraged for women in both Christian and Moslem families.

Twelve per cent of women are widowed by the age of fifteen, and 8.4 per cent are divorced. The average age for marriage is 17.7 years for girls and

Table 1.
Marital Status by Age Group and Sex (in percentages)

Years	Age	Currently Married		Never Married		Widowed		Divorced	
		M	F	M	F	M	F	M	F
1982	0-14	69	71	26	8	2	12	3	8.4
	15-19	5	53	94	39	0.08	0.45	0.8	7.4
	20-24	43	84	53	5	0.51	1.0	3.4	9.3
	25-44	89	86	6	0.9	1.2	5.4	3.6	8.0
	45-59	95	60	0.5	0.7	1.9	2.4	2.6	9.3
	60+	90	25	0.5	1.4	6.1	6.2	3.4	11

Source: UN 1986:88

25.5 years for men (UN 1986:111). These figures appear distorted, probably by data from urban centres where women pursue education and wage labour which enables them to marry at an older age than traditions and customs permitted previously. Rural average marriage age is probably closer to 13.5 years for girls and 21.5 years for men. The ideal age gap between a man and his wife was traditionally considered to be ten years. A man was expected to establish himself financially, with a farm, housing and other requirements, before he could start a family. He should also be sufficiently mature to handle the responsibilities of a head of a household and patron of a family. Such traditional values may be gradually eroding, but for most women, the family remains the major source of employment.

Primary school enrolment for the female population increased from 1,081,885 girls in 1974/75 to 2,811,910 girls in 1985/86. In secondary school, 16,774 girls attended grades 9-12 in 1974/75, while the figures jumped to 113,686 in 1985/86. Enrolment at institutions of higher learning shows an increase from 72 females in 1974/75 to 1,998 in 1985/86. Female enrolment at college alone had increased from 7.8 per cent in 1970 to 11 per cent in 1983 (CSO 1987a:105, tab.61.1). By 1983, 37.5 per cent of all children enrolled at primary level were girls, a significant increase from the 31.4 per cent in 1970. From 1970 to 1983, the enrolment ratio of girls was almost tripled, from 7 to 19 per cent, while boys doubled their ratio from 15 to 33 per cent (UN 1986:386). These figures are strong indicators of a shift in the allocation of productive resources, as women seek to find gainful employment outside of the family institution. Still, in absolute terms, enrolment of boys increased more than enrolment of girls.

The family continues to function as a viable socio-economic unit. It is still the main employer of women, particularly in the rural sector. Women's nurturing duties are still emphasized regardless of the change in ideology. Whether monogamy or polygamy is practised, the family household determines the position of women within their respective ethnic and cultural communities. Women continue to participate in farming work, and continue to be regarded as mere consumers and reproducers, in contrast to their male partners whom society regards and compensates as producers.

This perception continues to tie down women's productive energies, demobilizing the nation's human resources even in terms of the planning and programming of national development. Traditional values have not evolved along with the changing living conditions of women. They continue to affect the way women can contribute to society and to shape how the planners set the trend for future generations.

Economic Activity, Productivity, and Labour Compensation for Women.

Since 90 per cent of the Ethiopian population inhabit the countryside, our focus is on rural women. Women in urban centres are a small minority by comparison. Urban changes, such as the rise in the literacy rate, an increase in school enrolment, and growing competition in the employment market, have not directly affected the lives of rural women.

Table 2 shows that the "economically active" population of both sexes has been increasing in absolute terms over the last two decades. These figures do not reflect the downward trend in productivity both in agriculture and manufacturing industries. Furthermore, 59.7 per cent of females aged 15 and above were "economically active" in 1970, but figures went down to 54.3 per cent in 1980. Similarly, economically active males for ages 15 years and above were 84.5 per cent in 1970 but declined to 77.2 per cent in 1980.[1]

Table 2.
Economically Active Rural and Urban Population by Age and Sex (in 000)

Area	Sex	Age	1975	1987
Rural	Female	10-24	1,827	2,456
		25-49	2,243	3,016
		50+	660	888
	Male	10-24	3,458	4,476
		25-49	3,572	4,833
		50+	1,796	2,407
Urban	Female	10-24	194	267
		25-49	182	286
		50+	35	56
	Male	10-24	186	220
		25-49	433	596
		50+	76	114

Source: CSO 1987a:30, tab. 7.5

Despite the differences in the numbers of "economically active" men and women presented by these figures, women are increasingly productive, be it on the family farm or the producers' cooperative, in agriculture, cottage production, marketing and other related economic activities. The difference between males and females is of course due to a highly inadequate definition of "economically active" persons as people in paid employment or in agricultural production, while housework is considered consumption and reproduction, and the work of a woman helping in the fields is treated as part of her husband's activity rather than as her own.

The decline in productive employment may be attributed to a combination of economic policy, geo-physical and political factors. The annual rate of change for the economically active showed a 1.7 per cent growth for females and 2.1 per cent for males between 1970-1985 (UN 1986:198-9), which is considerably below population growth. The projections for 1985-2000 show an annual growth rate of 1.6 per cent for economically active women and 2.5 per cent for men. Economically "non-active" populations are shown as on the rise by 2.8 per cent in 1970-85 and 3.4 per cent in 1985-2000 for women and by 2.7 per cent and 3.3 per cent respectively for men (UN 1986:229). It is interesting to look at why the non-active population grows. Is this a function of a baby boom, resulting in a growing under-age population ? Does it represent an increase in dysfunctional adults due to war, poor health and dislocation from drought and famine ? Or does it reflect the shift from unskilled labour to white collar work by an expanding educated population ? Could it simply be a sign of rising unemployment ? To what degree have women been pushed aside, left with no choice but to work as a housewife, a job which is not considered as "economic activity"?

The overall decline in productivity and productive employment may be attributed to population shifts caused by war, drought, famine, and may also be due to lower incentives for production, along with the price fixing and quota systems of AMC. But while overall employment declined both in agricultural and in manufacturing industries, actual working hours for women have increased, since they are increasingly involved in activities organized by peasant associations and producer cooperatives which demand their time. However, this does not necessarily result in increased production, as most of their time may be spent on political meetings and administrative functions. If leisure time is considered as an indicator of improved living conditions, it is noteworthy that the family responsibilities of rural women remain the same while their out-of-household production activities have increased.

The average day for a rural woman involves food processing, water and fuel collection, assisting on the family farm, marketing, cottage production, and labour exchange for community services in *debbo, ijjige, wonfel,* or *dado*. Women receive no remuneration for their labour, no monetary or material gains and no benefit in leisure time and improved living conditions.

Women have had to take on an increased work load within the community and in the household in the rural sector, but the compensations are clearly lacking. Assisting the male head of household to fulfil his time allotments on producer cooperatives and meeting their own obligations to the women's associations, on top of regular duties in food processing, storage, marketing, child rearing, and family care, takes women twelve to sixteen hours a day.

Women are expected to derive their gratification from nurturing the family while providing their services as mothers and wives. Even rural women in polygamous marriages, widows and women whose husbands have migrated for wage labour do not get monetary remuneration for their work, except for a small cash income from cottage products they market themselves. All they can hope for is to feed themselves and to keep a roof over their heads. It is the men who preside over all production matters and resource allocations. Women who take employment on state farms are paid the minimum wage. Equal terms of employment do not apply to work that is classified as an exclusively male function.

The point is not that women should place themselves above the needs of their family, or that their needs and wants are similar to those of urban women with higher income. Rural women spend their time in productive activities which directly benefit their families and society in economic terms. There should be some measurable means of remunerating their productive services and of providing incentives for them to produce efficiently and use their energies meaningfully

Property Ownership, Income Generation and Purchasing Power

In the past, women were not owners of the means of production, except if they inherited land from their families. With the Rural Land Proclamation of March 1975, land was nationalized, transferring its control and redistribution to peasant associations. In practice, women do not have access to land unless they are widowed or registered as independent heads of household within the peasant association. Under the previous system the majority of women were landless tenants anyway; and even if in theory female inheritance was possible, the social structures in both Moslem and Christian families were such that properties were almost always transferred to the male heir in the family.

The Rural Land Proclamation has given women legal access to organize themselves in peasant associations as heads of household, if they have an independent residence, even within the framework of polygamous family structures. Although women are also legally authorized to organize themselves in producer cooperatives, land (the most significant means of production) is still in the hands of peasant associations. It appears that women's cooperatives are still limited to horticulture, poultry and similar activities of moderate scale and limited income. The situation may be different in peasant associations and cooperatives where membership consists of large numbers of women heads of households. Again statistics are lacking; it may be only in resettlement sites that such cases occur.

Undoubtedly, some new trends emerged during the pre-1974 modernization process which encouraged urban girls to attend formal education and to participate as a work force for wages. However, fields of employment were limited for women, because manufacturing and retail industries and similar economic sectors were not adequately developed. White collar work was limited to a small minority of women, with only certain professions such as teaching, nursing and secretarial service open to them.

In the last decade and a half, urban women have branched out into employment areas which do not require formal education, to earn their subsistence. Jobs in the construction industry and in factories, as well as in sales and marketing services are now filled by women. Blue collar employment of women has started to expand, probably as a direct result of changing attitudes among women themselves.

Education is now more of a priority for urban women, marriage is being postponed, and alternative employment is a possibility for women; women are no longer limited to domestic work and nurturing services. Unfortunately, both agricultural and non-agricultural production have declined since the mid seventies. Manufacturing and retail industries have not been expanding to absorb the growing labour force. The great majority of women are still employed in marginal areas and are not adequately compensated for their labour.

With the rise in literacy of the overall adult population, some urban women are benefiting from non-formal education and can compete for blue collar jobs which require few skills. Formerly male-designated jobs such as masonry, carpentry, construction and similar forms of manual labour are now being increasingly handled by women.

In contrast, most rural women have no independent budget, but are part of their husband's household. As far as they have control over money, they derive their income from what little grain or cash crop the male head of household allocates for their discretionary use. Mostly, this portion is for the woman to purchase household goods necessary to sustain the family. A woman may be allowed to use some cash for her own personal use if she deems it necessary. However, conditions are such that there is scarcely enough to get the household through the season until the coming harvest. So women rarely spend on themselves or their children without the approval of the patron, and even then only for special occasions such as holidays. As of today, most women consider their productive work and income as a means of caring for the entire family, and not as a way of protecting themselves in the marital relationship.

Decision Making in the Household; Women's Political and Economic Participation[2]

The land reform legislation did not redefine the relationship of men and women within the family. Both in monogamous and polygamous households, women continue to exist under the jurisdiction of their husbands.

There are forces operating to diffuse the cohesiveness of the family as the tightly knit unit it used to be when the patriarch had full control and when women had no say about how the family economy should be organized. The results of resettlement, war, migration due to famine and drought certainly caused many families to break up. Unfortunately, we do not have statistics which reveal how many households on resettlement sites and within village dwellings are headed by women. It would also be intriguing to know how resources are allocated to women in peasant associations and producer cooperatives. It would be enlightening to study the dynamic changes in decision making and participation which take place between the sexes in these families due to such changes.

In the cultural context of rural society, female-headed households are a minority which have little influence and less effect on the "normal" family household. Women's decision making in family finance and economic activities is limited to income generated from cottage production (crafts, food processing, etc.) and possibly to small income generating agricultural and related activities (horticulture, poultry, bee keeping, etc).

Normally, women do not determine what crop to plant, or whether a cow should be sold or not. Women do not participate in decisions to take out a loan for the farm or to meet the household's economic needs. These and similar major economic decisions are male responsibilities. Of course, even in traditional times, exceptions existed, where women have been able to make decisions or to influence the male's decisions on economic and production related matters. The rule still remains that within the family the male makes all the decisions and the female follows his direction.

However, raising the consciousness of the women has also helped to influence the way men think. Some men begin to understand that women have the intelligence and the wherewithal to make decisions on major issues of economic and political life in the community and in the family. Variations in ethnic and geographical norms notwithstanding, farmers may nowadays give their wives some control over cash crops like coffee, oil seeds, grain and bee keeping.

Women have more control over their social rights in the household, for instance regarding physical abuse, as a result of the creation of people's tribunals in which women have voting power. However, their working hours have not lessened, and their financial benefits have not improved.

Literacy programmes, political committees, people's judicial groups, and development programmes are among the forces which have helped to enlighten women to their rights by raising their consciousness and self-esteem. As a result of their increased economic participation, women are taking more responsibility in the household for family expenditures. However, women do not have a great deal of influence over production activities, although they assist the head of household in carrying out both the household's economic activities and mandatory services in the community.

In the eighties there was in principle acceptance of the idea of women being organized and even forming their own producer cooperatives. However, except for appreciation of the economic gains which heads of households consider a necessary and welcome addition to the family income, women's position in the community or in the household does not show drastic changes. Individual attitudes continue to limit the ways women can participate in community affairs and in their families' economic life.

The issue remains one of power dynamics which cuts deep into the way men perceive their status within the family and in the community. Since involving women in all economic activities is helpful to the male as well, men are in favour of women's increased participation and equal opportunities for earning income. On the other hand, men were conditioned for centuries to consider themselves superior to women because they made all major decisions while women followed. Such attitudes may gradually change as women assert themselves more and as they prove to be indispensable in raising family income.

Women depend on the approval of the male head of household in order to participate in community organizations which are focused on women as a group. Approval is mostly dependent on whether the woman's participation in these organized entities brings financial gains. In most cases, men consider these gains very small and a diversion from women's family responsibilities. Generally, women's participation in organized efforts which help to raise their political and social consciousness are not well seen by the male members of the communities, particularly in the rural areas.

During the late 1970s, there were instances where peasant associations clashed with women's associations over issues which touched on the economic and political rights of women. In some communities, peasant associations refused to act as collateral in processing loans for women's associations as producer entities. Where groups of independent women gained strength, those women were ostracized in the community. The male head of a household would not allow his wife to be active in these groups, or succeeded in making her feel she was not fulfilling her duties as a wife and mother by joining these groups and actively pursuing the interest of her sex group. Sometimes, there was stiff competition between male and female organizations. Men used traditional structures and customs to coerce the women's organizations. Membership dropped and women abandoned their projects.

In 1985/86, women members in producer cooperatives totalled 12,790, while male members totalled 190,372. These are female heads of household in cooperatives run by a male majority. On the other hand, membership of women's associations reached 2,218,496 in 1981/82 and doubled to 4,917,347 in 1985/86 (CSO 1987a:39, tab. 8.5).[3]

The discrepancy in female membership between producer cooperatives and women associations is glaring. It is apparent that despite legislative encouragement for women to organize as producer entities, women producers are still in the shadow of peasant associations and male-dominated cooperatives. Financial opportunities and material resources are not as readily available to women as they are to the male members of society. The purchasing power of women is very limited. Even organized in cooperatives, their opportunities to generate income and to make sizeable financial gains are very often undermined.

Figures on political participation are not available other than on membership in associations and various political and judiciary committees. Actual participation by women requires close scrutiny to confirm whether women are asserting themselves in society, and whether this has implications for their relationships within the household. Since political and economic status go hand in hand, increased political involvement through women's associations and internal committees in peasant associations have helped to raise their consciousness. However, political participation is definitely marginal not just for women but for the peasantry in general. There are semblances of increased participation, but certainly none significant enough to secure women's access to economic resources either as an organized cooperative or as members of independent households.

Conclusion

Evidently, women's productivity is essential for family and the community well-being, whether the benefits accrue proportionately to women or not. The perception that women are merely reproducers within the family, processing and marketing what the male member produces is erroneous and requires a redefinition. Production, consumption and "reproduction" are common activities of both sexes within the family and in the community. This may be more accepted as women are now organized and take part in community decisions even if at times their decisions may be coerced. Providing incentives is a sure way to increase productivity both for rural women and men. If it is considered important to optimize the efficient use of human resources in the productive sectors of the nation's economy, there is a need to rationalize labour in rural production including household work.

Furthermore, incentives are important for women not only to allow them to earn an income, but to ensure recognition of their capabilities in society. Women must know that their activities and decisions make a difference in building their communities. The incentive for men should be the increasing income and improving conditions in family life of those who allow women to take a bigger part in economic and political life. This would help them to understand that women's increased participation and equal opportunities need not compete with their social status nor undermine their position in the family.

Planning and implementation of human resources management for national development, i.e., policies on education, finance, employment and institution building, have to address the position of women, considering their changing roles and status. Women are half of the population. One of the ways to mobilize human resources for the country is to provide opportunities for them to be gainfully employed and to increase their purchasing power. Mobilizing women's labour may require capital and material resources, diversified production and increased productivity. But first of all it requires rationalizing labour in the household sphere, where women spend most of their time, to free them for more productive work.

NOTES

1 These figures should be taken with caution since the parameters used to determine economic activity are not clear. Generally, the tradition of registering women as "housewives" and considering work in the home not as economic activity discriminates against women in spite of their considerable contribution to the household's total work load and income. In addition, it is not clear whether the given figures determine women's actual productivity in working hours or just the number of women and men statistically considered as "economically active".

2 Data gathered from a sample of farm families in selected villages from 1975 through 1978 are the basis of the author's contentions. Sources: Attitudinal Case Studies in Robe, Gobessa and Lemu, ARSI Publication No. 2. Rural Reconstruction: Women and Rural Development, UNDP/FAO Eth. 73/003 Study. Both the above studies were based on primary data collected by the author.

3 Unfortunately, separate figures for producer cooperatives which have exclusively female membership are not available.

6 Options for Rural Development in Ethiopia: The International Context

Fantu Cheru

Although Ethiopia has received more publicity than any other African country in recent years as a result of the widespread famine in 1984/85, it is not the only country experiencing a sharp economic deterioration reported across the continent. In discussing the Ethiopian case in the context of the larger debate on Africa's future, this chapter examines external factors that are likely to influence the efforts of *any* Ethiopian government to restructure the agricultural sector and the economy as a whole.

Like the rest of Africa, Ethiopia is being warned by some that excessive state intervention hampers economic development and that only the adoption of free-market policies is likely to provide a lasting solution to the country's agricultural decline. Such advice, in the spirit of a new orthodoxy, appears promising on the surface, but is basically a reincarnation of the widely contested *Accelerated Development for Sub-Saharan Africa: An Agenda for Action*[1] issued by the World Bank in 1980.

While the UN Economic Commission for Africa (ECA) holds that a decade of free market economic reform imposed by the World Bank and International Monetary Fund has failed to reverse Africa's economic decline (UNECA 1989), the World Bank tries to provide evidence that its reform programmes are working. In a recent study the Bank compared countries that have implemented its "structural adjustment" programmes with those that have not. It concluded that those governments that paid fair market prices to farmers, devalued inflated currencies and trimmed bloated bureaucracies, enjoyed higher growth rates. This view, which is shared by many donor institutions,[2] has been challenged by the ECA, which called the study inaccurate and even charged that the bank manipulated statistics to prove its reforms are working when in fact they are not (UNECA 1989). Those claims amount to a direct challenge to the Bank and western donors who increasingly insist on "structural adjustment" as a precondition for economic aid.

At the abstract level, it is hard to disagree with many of the reform proposals advocated by western donor agencies. But in practice, implementation of these reforms in the absence of an enabling international economic environment is likely to foster dependence, and not self-reliance. The current debate focuses on efficiency and productivity, and often overlooks the exploitation and the conflict that governs economic relations between North and South. Simply instituting free-market solutions in African societies is not by itself translating into increased agricultural production at local level. Also, more production does not necessarily mean more money for peasants, if the income they earn from the sale of exports fails to cover the cost of what they buy.

For reasons outlined below, free-market pricing in agriculture needs to be complemented by a major package of governmental programmes to assist peasants - hence the need for an active government (Schatz, 1987:134). In fact, many of the successfully developing countries, such as South Korea, have relied on government activism. Even when "good government" is in place, "good" policies are implemented, and production targets are met, the reality of the world system can have a profound impact on foreign exchange earnings and the benefit accrued to individual peasants.

The Private vs. Public Debate

In September 1985, a team of Soviet advisers working at the Ethiopian National Committee for Central Planning submitted a five-year economic perspective. The so-called Sokolov report (GOSPLAN 1985) called for a redirection of government policy and resources toward peasant agriculture. It urged the government to supply peasants with tools, seeds, fertilizers and other inputs and to clarify, through legislation, the rights and duties of individual farmers concerning the use of land and water. The provision of credit and increased access by farmers to consumer goods and the establishment of flexible pricing for farm products are also emphasized.

Some commentators have wrongly interpreted the findings of the Sokolov report as Soviet endorsement of the development strategies of the World Bank (Henze 1988). While no one disputes the need for such fundamental policy reform in Ethiopian agriculture as the report suggested, the Soviets did not in any form declare that socialist development was incompatible with Ethiopian reality. The report recommends giving more support to service cooperatives, rather than producer cooperatives, since the former enjoy greater acceptance among peasants. Its emphasis on peasant farming does not amount to a retreat from cooperative policy and a state farm approach. Instead, the report underlines the need to improve the profitability of state farms, and to establish, on a limited basis, large private and public commercial farms which would be allowed to employ labour.

While the need for policy reform in the area of marketing, pricing and other forms of liberalization is important no matter who said it, it looks as if the purported neo-liberal tone of the Sokolov report has been over-exaggerated by the proponents of *laissez-faire* economics in Ethiopia. In some respect, the Soviet document is even too orthodox in its approach, as it fails to urge the government to democratize the decision making process at local level and to give adequate autonomy to local organizations. Recent events in China are instructive of the dichotomy between narrowly defined free-market solutions and the drive to genuine democracy.

From a different perspective, criticizing the agricultural policies of African governments, the World Bank has presented itself as the champion of peasant rights. As reasons for the poor performance of agriculture in Africa, it pointed to mismanagement of marketing boards, government subsidies of urban food consumers, taxation on agricultural exports, and the lack of sufficient price incentives for agricultural producers. On its part, the Bank advocates changing incentive structures by hiking producer prices, developing more open and competitive marketing agreements, curtailing parastatal involvement, and involving farmers in decisions that affect them.

Indeed, some of the policies advocated by the World Bank and the IMF are desirable. No one would quarrel, for example, with the idea of paying farmers more, or the abolition of badly managed marketing boards. However, the beneficial effects of some of the other policies advocated by the multilateral financial institutions, such as cuts in social spending, import restrictions and drastic curtailment of public sector involvement, are less obvious. While realignments of monetary and fiscal policies are important, they alone do not remove any of the fundamental constraints upon agricultural development in Africa. The structures of production, consumption, technology, external dependence and distribution of power serve as an important impediment to long-term, equitable development. These fundamental political issues require first and foremost a political answer. Thus, in Ethiopia and Africa in general, great emphasis must be placed on efforts to make the public sector responsive to the needs of peasants who can not succeed without government support in the area of infrastructure, training, input, and markets.

Finally, while peasant participation in production, marketing and other key decision making processes is critical, how such improvement will be facilitated and which peasant groups should be assisted is not clearly outlined by the Bank. Given past experience in Ethiopia and elsewhere in Africa, there is a danger of supporting "Kulaks" who produce for export, rather than subsistence farmers. What the Bank and its supporters propose is essentially the revival of export oriented growth strategies in order to correct what they view as African mistakes (World Bank 1981).

The Bank's anti-public sector stance is not practical given the political realities of sub-Saharan Africa. While inefficiency and corruption are widely known to exist among some parastatals, as is the resistance by bureaucratic elites to any moves aimed at empowering peasants, the Bank is wrong when it advises African governments to dismantle parastatals arbitrarily and to hand over their activities to private institutions. It is unlikely that the private sector in its present form will take on long-term, highly expensive public sector projects such as the construction and management of rail transport, irrigation projects, electric generation and harbours (Colclough 1983:24-29). The private sector in Africa is not well developed because of deficiencies in education, skills, and training experience.

At the same time, there is a large sector of the domestic economy that could benefit from private sector competition. Wholesale and retail trade, real estate, insurance and domestic transportation could often be handled more efficiently by the private sector. The move by some African governments in this direction has been shown to benefit domestic entrepreneurs. Beyond that, there is no realistic alternative to government involvement, unless foreign private enterprises are called upon to take over a significant chunk of African economies.

Therefore, the real issue is not the degree to which the state intervenes in economic matters, but how and on whose behalf it intervenes. Indeed, when one looks at the allocation of public resources and institutions in Africa, there is enormous bias toward the export sector, largely dominated by the ruling class and their foreign counterparts (Beckman, 1982:37-51, Langdon 1985). Using their control of the structures of the state, African elites have conferred upon themselves monopoly power over a vast area of economic activity, while peasants and small producers are left to fend for themselves. But while criticizing African governments for mismanagement, the Bank tacitly ignores its own role in supporting the elites through the promotion of development strategies which created widening inequalities.

In short, there is no easy free-market solution. Problems like the improvement of environmental and human conditions cannot be solved solely under a private enterprise market system with price as the allocation. There must be some room for intervention by society to establish standards. Those standards become the basis by which the social cost is internalized in the cost of production. The market system is then free to work again.

Export-oriented Growth: A Way Out?

The World Bank and other western donors also advise African countries to export their way out of their debt predicament by actively participating in international trade. Consequently, emphasis is given to primary export, despite the rhetoric of donors on peasant farming and the need to strengthen Africa's food security. The prescriptions offered are based on the assumptions that world trade will grow, commodity prices will stabilize and that protectionist barriers will not be erected by the western powers. However, reality has been quite different. Increased protectionism, burdensome debt-servicing requirements, declining development assistance and deteriorating terms of trade are hampering successful implementation of the most carefully crafted economic recovery programmes in Africa.

The dismal performance of African economies throughout the 1970s and early 1980s can partly be explained by the fact that the continent relies heavily on the export of a few primary commodities and minerals for the generation of foreign exchange. In 1983, for example, coffee provided 82 per cent of Burundi's total export earnings and 62 per cent of Ethiopia's. Petroleum accounted for all the export earnings of Libya, 95 per cent of Nigeria's and about 92 per cent of Algeria's. Copper brought 90 per cent of Zambia's total export earnings and 38 per cent of Zaire's (UN,1988). Altogether, these primary commodity exports constitute some 94 (!) per cent of merchandize trade, with prices being dependent on world market forces entirely outside the control of African countries (UNECA 1987:37).

In addition, the demand for most of these items in the developed countries has stagnated or has been persistently declining despite rapid expansion of exports by African countries. Moreover, many such products are facing mounting competition from the Common Agricultural Policy of the EEC, as well as substitutes such as synthetics for cotton, aluminium for copper, corn syrup for sugar (GATT 1985:17; UN 1984:29). A sharp fall in international prices, and a fluctuation in external demands have severe consequences for Africa's foreign exchange earnings, import capacity, level of employment and, indeed, development process at large.

In addition to export dependence, Ethiopia and other African countries rely even more on imported inputs, machinery and capital goods to maintain the momentum of economic growth. Since the Arab oil embargo of 1973, however, import demands have exceeded the capacity of many of these countries to generate sufficient foreign exchange from the sale of exports. A deterioration in the terms of trade resulting from declining commodity prices and increased cost of imports has led to a chronic trade and balance of payments deficit, requiring additional external borrowing. The decline in the volume of imports has exacerbated the transport bottle-neck which in turn creates disincentives in food production, marketing and distribution.

Ethiopia's terms of trade declined by 4.7 per cent per year from 1970 to 1984 (World Bank, 1986:5). The value of merchandize imports has been running at more than double the value of merchandize exports since 1981. The current deficit increased to the equivalent of 8.6 per cent of GDP in 1983/84 and to 8.8 per cent of GDP in 1984/85. The wide disparities between the import and export volume growth rate on the one hand and the import and export price indices on the other, led the economy to a state of widening external trade deficits (World Bank, 1987a). While terms of trade improved temporarily in 1986 as a result of increased earnings from coffee and a drop in the price of petroleum, price projections for Ethiopia's exports by the World Bank for the early to mid-1990s are expected to be lower than those attained in the mid-1980s (World Bank 1987b:41). Ethiopia either has to expand export volumes or increase its cost competitiveness in order to increase its foreign exchange earnings. This is highly unlikely given the massive production and export subsidies being undertaken by the EEC. Export markets will remain oversupplied and export prices are likely to remain low in the foreseeable future.

African countries tried to offset lower world prices by increasing their share of production for the world market. However, this simply drove prices further down, as dozens of African and other developing countries flooded the world market with their coffee and cocoa as part of IMF or World Bank "structural adjustment" programmes to generate foreign exchange to service their external debt obligations. Under present conditions, it is impossible for Ethiopia and other African countries to export their way out of debt. To the extent that the western powers have prevented Africans from earning a reasonable income on international markets, they themselves must take some responsibility for Africa's inability to pay its creditors (Fantu Cheru 1989). The international economic order established after WW II still reflects the old patterns of dominance and dependence. It rewards the developed countries disproportionately and creates unmet human and financial needs in the underdeveloped countries. Because their export-oriented economies are dependent on trade with the developed countries, most African countries are vulnerable to decisions made in the North. When the US economy sneezes, the Third World catches pneumonia.

The demands of the Third World for partial restructuring of the world

Share of Leading Exports for Selected African Countries (per cent)

Coffee		Cocoa		Cotton	
Ethiopia	62	Sao Tome	75	Burkina Faso	48
Burundi	62	Eq.Guinea	48	Mali	39
Madagascar	33	Côte d'Ivoire	26	Chad	69
CAR	33	Ghana	47	Sudan	25
Kenya	26	Cameroon	14	Tanzania	13
Tanzania	32	Sierra Leone	15	Benin	10
Côte d'Ivoire	22				

Petroleum		Copper		Diamonds	
Angola	89	Zambia	90	Botswana	78
Cameroon	43	Zaire	38	Lesotho	41
Nigeria	95				
Congo	86				
Gabon	69				

Source: Compiled from UN, Financing Africa's Recovery

economy have gone unanswered by the developed countries. Starting with the first session of UNCTAD held in Geneva in 1964, through the 7th session, which ended in July 1987, African countries have actively sought negotiations with the industrialized countries to establish a mutually beneficial international economic relationship. Instead of fair trade practices, however, protectionism has become the order of the day. Negative transfers from the South to the North are also growing at an alarming pace (UNECA 1986).

Despite these facts, the Western countries continue to put all the blame squarely on the doorsteps of developing countries. Consequently, they have strongly supported IMF retrenchment measures in face of depressed commodity markets and growing protectionism. Under present conditions, it is impossible for these countries to export their way out of debt and still be able to meet basic human needs and preserve their natural resource base. As African governments adopt austerity measures, cuts in social services are often accompanied by the dismantling of state environmental controls and programmes to control soil erosion, and by over-intensive cropping, resource depletion and desertification. These cuts occur when the programmes are needed the most.

One key issue of great interest for Africa has been commodity trade and the need to ensure remunerative prices for producing countries, and for an effective system of compensatory financing in the event of falling world commodity prices. The establishment of the Integrated Programme for Commodities (IPC) and the Common Fund are among the major decisions taken by UNCTAD in this field. However, the momentum seems to have stopped despite the fact that the economies of commodity-dependent countries such as Ethiopia continued to be under considerable strain (UN 1985). Now, there is great doubt whether UNCTAD can serve as an effective forum to resolve the global trade anarchy.

With regard to international commodity agreements (ICAs), only one agreement with pricing provisions, covering rubber, has been signed since 1976. Measures on processing of primary products and the need for compensatory facilities have yet to materialize. Past experience on the renegotiation of existing ICAs like those for coffee points to a difficult road ahead and could prove to be arduous (UNECA 1986:6).

The Common Fund, which was to become the financial core of the system of ICAs, has not yet become operational because of lack of support by major industrialized market economies (Avramovic 1986:31). It is unlikely that we will see any breakthrough on trade and finance in the near future.

Structural Adjustment: A New Orthodoxy?

In the wake of the 1984 disastrous drought and economic collapse, the need for policy reform in Africa has become a centre of national and international attention. The Organization of African Unity adopted Africa's Priority Program for Economic Recovery, 1986-1990 (APPER) (OAU 1985), emphasizing the need to pursue self-reliant strategies. The member states publicly acknowledged their own mistakes, and agreed to implement a variety of policy reforms consistent with the overall development philosophy of the Berg Report.

At its Special Session on Africa held in May 1986, the UN General Assembly adopted its Programme of Action for African Economic Recovery and Development, 1986-1990 (UNPAAERD) (UN 1987a). The UN programme recognized the importance of international measures to implement reforms, while at the same time stressing the ultimate responsibility of African governments. Both the OAU and UN Programme of Action gave priority to agriculture and related sectors, with emphasis on remunerative producer-pricing policies and incentives schemes for agricultural producers. Policy reforms were called for in a wide range of areas, including public enterprises, domestic savings, and fiscal administration. At the same time, Western nations promised a two-pronged approach: increased and better coordinated aid, and more equitable terms of trade through commodity price stabilization and debt relief.[3]

The African nations have largely held up their end of the bargain. Since 1986, more than 30 African countries have concluded arrangements with the IMF and other creditors and implemented policy reforms established within the framework of APPER and UNPAAERD (UN 1987b:8-11). According to a recent survey by the Economic Commission for Africa, over four-fifths of countries surveyed have adopted price incentives, and two-thirds have taken action to improve internal distribution channels. Nearly two-thirds of report-

INDEX OF PURCHASING POWER OF EXPORTS

1970 = 100

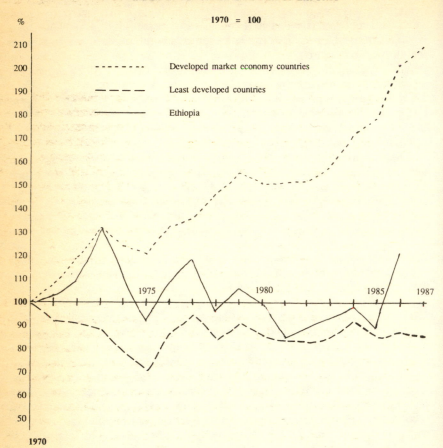

Source: figures from UNCTAD Handbook of International Trade and
Development Statistics, 1987   (Supplement, p. 45 and 534)

ing countries have achieved the target of 25 per cent of total investment allocation to agriculture. About two-thirds of the countries surveyed have also reduced subsidies (UN 1987b).

Despite great sacrifices made by African countries in implementing the above harsh measures, the response of the international community has so far been disappointing in light of the resource needs of African countries. A progress report issued by the United Nations on its Programme for African Economic Recovery warns that the continent is regressing toward disaster and cites the following statistics:

- Commodity prices dropped across the board to their lowest levels in 30 years. This cut Africa's export earnings from $65 billion in 1985 to $46 billion in 1986. During the same period, costs of imports of manufactured goods rose by 20 per cent (UN 1988:11-12). The deterioration in terms of trade is expected to grow.

- Despite the fact that the majority of African countries developed new investment codes to attract foreign capital, there has been virtually no significant private sector investment in Africa since 1985. In 1981, foreign investment reached $1.5 billion in sub-Saharan Africa, but since 1984, it has been only about $400 million annually. Bank lending has plummeted from $3.5 billion in 1980 to $1.5 billion in 1986, and export credits have almost ceased in 1987 (UN 1988:13). The IMF alone took out $1 billion more in 1986 than it put into Africa (UN 1987b:28-30).

- With regards to trade, discriminatory tariffs still exist, and market access for African products remains limited. Neither commodity price-stabilization agreements nor assistance in diversifying agricultural export bases have been forthcoming. While industrial countries have offered temporary debt relief measures, such as rescheduling loans, they have failed to make significant efforts that might lead to a lasting solution to the crisis.

The events of the past seven years have shown clearly the pitfalls and dimensions of the sacrifices which African countries have to confront on the way to recovery. Structural adjustment and policy reforms are virtually impossible to attain in an environment of uncertain commodity situation. As a result, all governments in Africa are facing potential turmoil because of the harsh austerity measures imposed to repay the debt. Over the past five years, cuts in food subsidies and social programmes required under the IMF stabilization programmes have sparked demonstrations in Tanzania, Ghana, and Zambia, and food riots in Morocco, Egypt, Tunisia, Algeria, Sudan and Zambia (Fantu Cheru 1989).

There is no doubt that the international trade and economic environment over the past decade has adversely affected African countries. The present order rewards in the first place the developed world and creates unmet human and financial needs in the poor countries. Thus, without fundamental redistribution of power within and between societies, the prospects of achieving sustainable development at multilateral level are exceedingly dim.

This does not mean that there are no shortcomings at the domestic level. It is not possible to eradicate poverty and preserve the natural resource base without transferring some real power to the marginalized groups. If farmers are given titles to land and other incentives, they will devote the energy and the resources needed to produce food and conserve their land. Governments could reward environmentally sound land use practices, such as terracing and building check dams, with price subsidies for agricultural implements and supplies. After all, development is not what the experts claim it to be, but what the people see as their immediate need.

NOTES

1 Often called, after one of its main authors, the Berg Report.

2 Particularly the US Agency for International Development (AID).

3 The cost of these measures has been estimated at $128 billion, of which $45 billion was expected to come from external sources (UN 1987a).

7 Soviet-Ethiopian Cooperation in Agriculture

Grigori Polyakov

Unlike other African countries, Ethiopia chose the road of socialist orientation during the second half of the 1970s. Moscow soon became the major
benefactor of the new regime, providing both economic and military assistance. At that time, the dismal performance of Soviet assisted projects in
other African countries was no secret any more. Several projects in Mali,
Ghana, Guinea, Tanzania had been transferred to private hands while
others still operated, wasting extensive government subsidies. Because of
this experience, the Soviet Union was not in a hurry to establish large-scale
projects in the Ethiopian agricultural sector after the revolution (*Sovremienaia Etiopia* 1988:215).

It should be kept in mind that Soviet cooperation started before the time
of perestroika. The Soviet Union was - and still is - a country where some
Soviet scientists speak of the marginalization of most of the population
(Starikov 1989); where the construction of a state based on law has just
started; where by international standards some 80 per cent of the population
is categorized as poor. At the same time, this society, which in terms of the
level of consumption per person is ranked somewhere between 50th and 60th
in the world, spends 5.6 times more than the USA, 3.2 times more than Great
Britain and 2.6 times more than West Germany[1] on assistance to other
countries (*Argumenti i Fakti* 1989),[2] exporting as aid goods which are not
available to the consumer at home. Such a paradox is explained by some as
part of a system to keep the majority of the people poor and submissive, while
offering privileged jobs abroad to the few.

Agricultural Cooperation in the 1970s

The Ethiopians themselves were in no hurry to adopt large-scale agricultural projects. Unlike the countries mentioned above, Ethiopian officials
were not prepared to sign contracts before feasibility studies had been
conducted and the profitability of projects was assured. Secondly, key officials within the Ethiopian bureaucracy tried to slow down the economic
cooperation with the USSR and other socialist countries. They considered
Soviet projects, given the experience of other countries, as too expensive,
needing subsidies, and not profitable. Plans to establish two state farms and
milk processing plants in Bahr Dar were abandoned when it was discovered
that the land provided by the Ethiopians was considered to be useless for
agriculture. In 1979, projects for construction of two meat canning plants
in Melga Wondo and Dire Dawa were abandoned for the same reasons.

The lessons from many project failures are simple. Soviet policy makers failed to understand Ethiopia's needs, and to design projects which were sustainable and mutually beneficial to both sides. Projects were easily approved by the Soviet bureaucracy without consideration of financial requirements, because they were considered politically important. A good example is the oil refinery near Nazareth. Nobody had any hope of finding oil around this resort town. To provide the refinery with oil, it was decided to connect it with the port of Assab by a pipeline and to pump Soviet oil from sea level to 1,000 m in altitude across a distance of more than 800 km.

At the first stage of Soviet-Ethiopian cooperation, agriculture stayed in the shadow. This main sector of the Ethiopian economy, with five million peasant holdings, was considered by Soviet experts as uncontrollable and opposed to socialism. Experts equipped with a Stalinist CPSU short history course were sent out to restructure Ethiopian society. Since 90 per cent of the agricultural production was in "private" hands, they recommended that Soviet aid should support state farms and cooperatives, on which they hoped to build the foundations of true socialism. What they failed to understand was the fact that the revolution, which they were sent to support and consolidate, actually broke out for the sake of the peasants, who after all comprise some 90 per cent of the population.

In 1979, Ethiopian experts elaborated a very original programme for agricultural cooperation, nicknamed the "Green Book" among Soviet experts. This plan of cooperation took the historical and cultural traditions in Ethiopia as well as the needs of the peasantry and the economic possibilities of the government into account. But while translating the "Green Book" from Amharic into English and then into Russian, its main ideas were lost, and its basic philosophy was never understood by Soviet experts.[3] They chose instead only one aspect from the proposal: producer cooperatives, which are similar to the Russian *kolkhozy*. Emphasis shifted to mechanization and state control of the economy. Priority was given to the construction of a tractor factory to service state farms, while peasants were left to fend for themselves with outmoded technology. Having the support of the Workers Party of Ethiopia which needed prestige projects, Soviet experts simply by-passed the Ministry of Agriculture which was calling for a peasant oriented strategy.

New Signals in Soviet-Ethiopian Cooperation

Just at the time of the famine emergency in the mid-1980s, Soviet economic cooperation started to change. Emphasis was to be given to the peasant sector. Unfortunately, this recognition came too late and was too indecisively applied to help Ethiopian peasants who were already on the way to feeding centres or being moved to settlement camps further south.

With the advent of perestroika in the mid-1980s, Soviet experts openly acknowledged the pitfalls of a Stalinist approach to agricultural development in the USSR. This meant a re-assessment also of Soviet-Ethiopian relations. Review reports about Soviet projects in Ethiopia exposed questionable results. The catastrophic famine of 1984–85 demonstrated the failure of a state farm approach despite millions of roubles spent on making this strategy work. There was also concern among Soviet experts that the food crisis might destabilize the existing regime which was friendly to the USSR. By the time of the 1986 drought, the Ethiopian food problem had become the Kremlin's political headache.

At the same time it became clear to Soviet experts that Ethiopia would not be able to pay her debts unless the agricultural sector was restructured and became viable. Since efforts to find oil in the Ogaden and gold extraction in Adola had shown no promise, it was recognized that agriculture remained the only source of surplus extraction from which repayment could be made. This new self-serving approach is reflected in the Long-term Programme of Economical and Technical Cooperation and Trade between the Soviet Union and the People's Democratic Republic of Ethiopia for 1984 to 1993.

The urgency to move the focus of Soviet-Ethiopian cooperation to agriculture was also understood by the Ethiopian leadership. Several projects under the category of agriculture appeared on the list of cooperation projects before the 10th anniversary of the revolution.

Present Cooperation and Current Problems

In the Long-term Programme for 1984 - 93, it was agreed to render assistance on a compensational basis. But most of the projects planned or implemented so far did not emerge from the new thinking; rather they are an extension of agreements signed before 1985.

Two main agricultural projects of cooperation are the Alvaro and Awash irrigation projects. Technical studies for the construction of dams and irrigation channels for 10,000 ha of land have been completed. Irrigation work for the first 1,000 ha of land is underway. In 1984, a feasibility study for the construction of a dam in Tendaho was submitted to the Ethiopian government. When completed the Awash project will irrigate some 60,000 ha of land, of which an area of 35,000 ha will provide 237 tons of long-fibre cotton, part of which can be exported to the USSR on a concessional basis. From the same land, Ethiopia is expected to get 350, 000 tons of maize and 200,000 tons of vegetables for local consumption (Polyakov 1988).

The second major effort involves the tractor assembly line in Nazareth which has produced more than 1,500 tractors. According to the original contract, the USSR was expected to supply about 1,000 disassembled tractors yearly. In recent years, however, the Ethiopians have complained that Soviet made tractors are unreliable and maintenance costs are excessive. To remedy the problem, the Soviets built six maintenance centres. A plan to construct a second tractor assembly and three exemplary state farms was dropped after a feasibility study found them not profitable.

The Minister of Agriculture wanted the Soviets to build machine and tractor stations (MTS) to serve the rural cooperatives and individual farmers instead. But the Soviet embassy preferred to neglect his ideas about "small private farms" and turned the demand for MTS into a request for repair shops. Plans were made for a huge tractor repair factory, which proved unfeasible because Ethiopia had neither sufficient numbers of tractors to be repaired, nor the capacity to transport broken equipment over long distances for repair. Small decentralized repair shops were never seriously considered. Five million peasants who were in need of machine and tractor services received nothing.

Many agro-industrial projects in developing countries put in operation with Soviet assistance survive only through heavy government subsidies, if at all. There are may ways of making up for losses in the state sector. Regardless of whether losses are covered through artificially high consumer prices, direct subsidies, or debt cancellation, the main source for such support is higher taxes levied on the peasants. Thus, Soviet aid which commits the state to pay heavy subsidies, hits those who receive it: peasants who use spades and hoes are made to pay for loss-making tractor plants. Compensation projects in particular, which are supposed to pay back their debts through their own produce alone, are unlikely to be able to do so. If such projects do not meet international standards and are too costly and inefficient, they just add new debts to the old ones.

Of course there are also some Soviet projects which have been very important to the Ethiopian economy. These include oil reservoirs constructed in the port of Assab and in Bahar Dar, Agaro, Shashemane; refrigerators with a capacity of 100 tons in Addis Ababa; two grain elevators in Aseb and Addis Ababa; and grain stores all over the country (Polyakov 1982:224).

In addition to these projects, Soviet-Ethiopian cooperation is expected to finance cattle farms in the provinces of Bale, Arsi and Hararghe; introduce production of oil crops in an area of 700 ha, and construct a small oil processing factory; and start a tobacco growing and processing project in Gojjam province and a cattle raising farm on an area of 23,000 ha, with veterinary services, MTS and meat and skin processing plants.

Even in this period Soviet assistance did not foster the "strong points" in Ethiopian agriculture and the economy. More often than not, it created enclaves of modern technology detached from the surrounding rural economy. Consequently their economic performance was inadequate, undermining the foundations of cooperation.

The bureaucrats organizing such projects did not worry about profits. For them, the most important criteria of success were schedules met and amounts of resources spent on time. This departmentalized approach created a vicious circle: instead of purchasing African produce from the compensational projects built with Soviet assistance, the Foreign Trade department purchased goods of African origin in London, paying in hard currency. The State Committee reached plan targets, and all the bureaucrats were satisfied because they had spent the money according to the plan (Polyakov 1989).

The hunger in Ethiopia in 1985 demonstrated the failure of such policies. We should take part of the blame for this tragedy. If our advisers had demonstrated more intelligence, initiative, courage and honesty, the famine could have been averted or at least could have been met with more efficient preparedness. Instead, the Soviet embassy reported to Moscow "plan fulfilled" but did not react to the famine before the Ethiopian Government announced the campaign to fight hunger.

Under the Soviet-Ethiopian Inter-Governmental Commission for Economic and Technical Cooperation and Trade, a Coordinating Committee was created in 1988, with the main objective of organizing joint ventures with Ethiopia in agriculture and agro-industry. But no such enterprises have been started up to now. Not long ago the only Soviet-Ethiopian joint venture organized before 1974 and working in trade stopped its operation due to inefficiency. Despite all the theories and all the hopes this form of cooperation gave rise to, Soviet and Ethiopian officials have so far found no practical way to organize joint ventures.

Glasnost, Perestroika, and Ethiopian Agriculture

When Mikhail Gorbatchov came to power, it was mostly his personality, courage and initiative that started the process known as "perestroika". At that time, Soviet-Ethiopian economic relations were at a difficult stage. The drought in 1984/85 took more than one million Ethiopian peasant lives and demonstrated the shortcomings of the agricultural policy of the Ethiopian leadership which followed a Stalinist model. The failure of this model was evident already on the 10th anniversary of the revolution. It was time for the USSR to change course.

If we understand perestroika as the process of making the bureaucracy responsible to the newly elected parliament, and glasnost as giving the people and their representatives proper information in all fields, we have to admit that these processes have only just started. Mikhail Gorbatchov cannot spell out the consequences of this new thinking to each specific region and country. Rethinking earlier conceptions of Soviet cooperation with foreign countries was left in the hands of bureaucrats. They were often in a position to use perestroika as a means to support their own position.[4] For a long period, the personal career of Soviet bureaucrats depended on their ability to obey their superiors. So it is not surprising that they still wait for directives from above instead of thinking by themselves and finding new solutions in the spirit of perestroika. There is a tendency to continue old projects and plans but present them as new success stories.

To start with, Soviet agricultural policies went through three stages. For a long period of time it was believed that only large-scale industry and highly concentrated agricultural production could lead the USSR to a higher level of economic growth. This doctrine was also applied in cooperation with developing countries. But practice proved that neither a free market nor state control could make this approach work, and the necessity to combine large-scale, medium and even small enterprises was recognized. Since perestroika, it has also been recognized that small peasants must have control over their means of production as well as access to government services.

The new thinking at home was extended to Soviet development assistance, and top priority was given to the task of making Ethiopia self-reliant in food production. A special report from the USSR State Planning Commission (GOSPLAN) Advisory Group in the Ethiopian Commission for Central Planning, delivered in September 1985, stressed that priority.[5] The report recommends state support for the individual farmer; increased production and provision of simple consumer goods for the peasants; balanced pricing policies which stimulate peasants to grow the food items which are in demand; reorientation of state farms from food production to production of export goods and raw materials; contract relations between the state and producer cooperatives as well as individual peasants, based on reciprocal commitments; development of cottage industries processing agricultural raw materials. It was also recommended that peasants be allowed to hire labour under certain conditions, and that prices be adjusted in a flexible system allowing peasants some income on top of covering production costs. More realistic quotas for the AMC, and a legal right to sell on the free market whatever exceeds the quota, were suggested, among other measures, to stimulate peasant initiatives to increase output.

Such recommendations were not a result of careful scientific investigation, but rather a transfer of our own new agricultural policy to Ethiopia. To be more precise, we are pushing a development strategy on others which we have ourselves still to try out. The old principle of "follow me" has changed very little. What is presented to the world as perestroika is, in this respect, essentially Stalinism with a new face.

The new Soviet enthusiasm for the virtues of privatization appears basically like a restatement of recommendations made by ILO, FAO, the World Bank and other international bodies. Soviet ministries are ill-equipped to undertake policy based research, and to discard old principles in favour of more pragmatic decisions. The same happens in our advice to Ethiopia: while advising the government to change policies from administrative control to market methods, we still have not understood, or at least not officially recognized, that it would be absurd to gather 53 per cent of the total peasant population in producer cooperatives by 1993. The architects of the GOSPLAN report still believe that much of government assistance should go to cooperatives and state farms, with the unsubstantiated hope that they should become more profitable. While in theory Soviet assistance claims to build on "new thinking", our advisers in practice implement the programmes adopted before 1985.

A new form of cooperation which puts the peasant in the centre of planning and assistance is nowhere in sight. Real perestroika in foreign aid should lead us to investigate priorities and needs of peasants, and orient assistance towards their interests and demands.

Toward a New Soviet-Ethiopian Economic Cooperation

There are big problems ahead for Soviet-Ethiopian cooperation. However, if at the present stage this cooperation faces hard times, this reveals more a lack of constructive ideas about how to put Gorbatchov's "new thinking" into practice, rather than the absence of objective conditions for the future development of our cooperation.

First of all, cooperation should not be a matter of charity. Soviet assisted projects should be advantageous to both sides. Assistance is not a matter of more credit - but making better use of the already existing loans.

Even with perestroika, it appears unlikely that a peasant policy can replace the present preoccupation with large-scale cooperation projects, as long as such a reorientation of agricultural policy towards the small producer has not been applied practically within the Soviet Union. In the near future, as long as positive experience with such policies has not yet changed bureaucratic attitudes in the USSR, it seems unlikely that such proposals will gain influence in Soviet-Ethiopian cooperation.

There is ample proof that it is high time to stop gigantomania. Several African countries are by now wondering how to get rid of monumental but unproductive projects like the Ajaokuta dam in West Africa. Experience shows that it was wrong to shy away from small-scale projects. Indeed, some micro dams built in five or six months proved more efficient than a major irrigation project for which pre-contract preparations alone took four to five years. A small plant making farm implements is more useful than a tractor assembly plant, in a country having no oil of its own. Costs for building about a hundred small repair shops for craftsmen would not exceed those of setting up one machine and tractor station. Unless we bear this in mind, we can hardly expect economic ties with Ethiopia to intensify.

Cooperation should, moreover, be giving more direct support to peasants, and plans should start from an investigation of what they need. For example, there is a tremendous need for consumer goods in the rural areas. Since those goods are not available in Ethiopia, peasants have no other recourse than to smuggle their own produce out of the country to get from outside what they need. In this way, scarce agricultural raw materials which are needed for processing in Ethiopia and for export are smuggled out, while cheap goods made in Hong Kong are imported unofficially. The quality of these goods may be far from satisfactory, but their prices suit the poor in Ethiopia.

Ethiopia has considerable potential for export. Yet some 225,000 head of cattle, 750,000 goats and sheep, 10 to 15,000 tons of coffee and other commodities are smuggled out of the country every year, while the tanning and meat packing industries run on only 60 to 70 per cent of their capacities due to shortage of raw materials. Soviet advisers want to set up fattening facilities comparable to American ranches, though such projects in other African countries, built with Soviet aid, have failed miserably (Polyakov 1987). Why not rely on peasants to raise the bull calves instead? Better price incentives could induce peasants to sell enough cattle to fully utilize capacities in existing processing plants. This would eliminate the need to control smuggling, and encourage state trade.

To induce peasants to sell their produce, it is also necessary to supply consumer goods. If peasants cannot buy what they need in the rural areas, they have little incentive to sell there, or even produce for the market. But Soviet organizations show little interest in adjusting the possibilities we have today to Ethiopia's potential.

The Soviet Union is one of the world's biggest producers of consumer goods. Unsold consumer goods worth billions of roubles pile up every year in the storehouses of our trade ministry. For a long time to come, we could supply sufficient quantities of goods like textiles, footwear, knitwear, pants and other items to Ethiopia without neglecting our own demand.

We could use such goods to finance internal expenditures in Ethiopia. This would be better than supplying Ethiopia with oil products, iron, steel reinforcements, cement, glass and other materials we need ourselves. A Soviet-Ethiopian trading company, organized as a joint venture, could supply the peasants with consumer goods for cash or by contract in exchange for their produce.

There is nothing dishonourable about such a deal. As long as these goods are not considered unfit for use, large sections of the rural population would finally get access to goods, and derive practical benefit from Soviet assistance. Both politically and economically this can only stimulate a form of cooperation which is beneficial to both parties.

Humanizing aid and getting it to the people who need it most is a strategy long used by Western countries in Ethiopia and elsewhere. We, however, build oil refineries and dams which never work. The majority of the Ethiopian people can barely meet their basic needs, let alone use electricity. If "incentive goods" which everybody could afford were to appear on the empty shelves of the cooperative shops, peasants would no longer want to sell coffee, livestock, skins and oilseed on the black market or smuggle them across the borders. They would be in a position to exchange these products for goods they need without running the risk of being penalized for smuggling.

Joint ventures could facilitate trade by signing contracts with peasant cooperatives and individual farmers, offering them consumer goods in exchange for rural produce. In five to seven years time, having accumulated some capital and experience, they could also engage in production by setting up small enterprises to supply peasants with craft products. Improved implements and spare parts for simple farm equipment can be produced in rural craft shops. Specialists estimate that replacing the iron tip of the wooden plough by one made of alloyed steel could increase productivity of peasant labour by 10 to 15 per cent. At country-wide level, such a change could mean a far higher increase of agricultural output than two or three new, up-to-date state farms could provide.

Joint ventures in trade, later expanding into small-scale local production, could also create conditions for more active use of traditional forms of cooperation, and at the same time benefit an expansion of economic ties between the Soviet Union and Ethiopia. They would, by processing agricultural raw materials, create linkages, supply incentive goods, and provide additional buying power in the rural areas.

In conclusion, Soviet foreign aid must undergo considerable revision to fit the "new thinking" of perestroika. First of all we must stop projects with high costs which will bring no economic return either to us or to the Ethiopian people. Such projects should be replaced by others which serve the peasantry directly. Our policy makers should be aware of the social, economic and ecological consequences of projects to be funded. Aid should serve the people's urgent needs, but not dead ideas. Especially, aid should take care to respect the rights of minorities, peoples who have not been reached yet by European civilization. They, too, have a right to exist, their culture has a right to survive, and aid should avoid doing anything that may have repercussions on them against their will.

We must respect the right of the Ethiopian peasants to exist within their culture and their social and economic adaptation without being pressed into alien social structures, such as producer cooperatives. Agriculture can only be developed out of its own conditions. These conditions include a historically based peasant culture building on individual production but community cooperation and mutual help. Cooperation should therefore not be enforced as a matter of ideology, but supported where it helps the local people, and is initiated by them. Involving the peasants themselves in projects, from planning to practical implementation, is important, because they know best what works and what will not. Soviet experts must learn to listen to peasants instead of waiting for directives from Moscow. An openness for discussion of policies and of their consequences is necessary, if the new thinking of perestroika is to have practical effects in Soviet assistance to Ethiopia.

NOTES

1 Measured in the percentage of Soviet assistance in Gross National Product.

2 The quoted figures probably stem from a rather unconventional calculation. OECD figures document Soviet foreign aid (in expenditure per GDP) as considerably lower than American aid. Western statistical estimations do not include military aid, and use different definitions in other aspects of cooperation. As a result, Western and Soviet sources differ considerably on the volume of Soviet aid. Moreover we suspect that the author may refer to an article in which the way aid flows from particular sources are calculated suggests a greater concern with polemics than with statistical accuracy (Editorial footnote).

3 For example, the Amharic term for "service cooperative" implies mutual help and service to peasants in improving production and living conditions. The Russian translation implies trade, i.e. cooperatives engaged in buying and selling. More examples are given in an article by Paoukov and Polyakov (1986).

4 Economic cooperation with foreign countries is still not a subject for glasnost. At the first Congress of the Supreme Soviet, our foreign policy makers received a pat on the back, but all serious discussion was avoided. Only deputy Nikolai Schmeliov criticized aid policies. He just said that his country had spent, according to the estimates of American experts, 6 to 8 billion dollars every year on the assistance to some Latin American states. It is quite remarkable that

neither Schmeliov nor anybody else mentioned Africa and specially Ethiopia where our expenditure may even exceed that in Latin America (Yanov 1989).

5 The report was published in English translation by Paul B. Henze (1989).

8 Agriculture and Surplus Extraction: The Ethiopian Experience

Eshetu Chole

The Problem

There are divergent views and experiences on how to generate capital formation, particularly on the relative roles of the state and the private sector, on the instruments and institutions required for surplus mobilization, and on the contribution of various sectors to this process. But there is no dispute on the point that growth requires capital accumulation.

This chapter examines the importance of Ethiopian agriculture as a source of surplus for investment. As in most underdeveloped countries, the agricultural sector in Ethiopia looms large in the structure of output and the structure of employment. Although agriculture's share in the GDP has tended to decline over the last quarter century, this share is still over 40 per cent. Its contribution to employment is even more pronounced, being variously estimated at between 80 per cent and 90 per cent. It might be added parenthetically that this discrepancy between agriculture's contribution to output and employment vividly portrays the low level of labour productivity that prevails in this sector.

More germane to our present task is the role of agriculture as a source of surplus. Since the notion of surplus is a slippery one, it would be useful to indicate in what sense(s) it is used in this chapter. Nurkse (361-2) distinguishes between a marketable surplus and an investible surplus, the former referring to the portion of agricultural output sold, while the latter represents "an act of saving in the farm sector". The marketable surplus stands for what the farmer brings to the market, but this does not necessarily suggest that it represents an excess over his "subsistence" requirements, for the simple reason that the notion of surplus is a fairly elastic one. The significance of the marketable surplus is that, because it represents the agricultural sector's demand for non-agricultural goods, it determines employment in the non-agricultural sectors.

But a marketable surplus may not necessarily materialize into an investible surplus; it could easily be consumed. On the other hand, an investible surplus may be generated even in the absence of a marketable surplus, as when "surplus" labour is transferred from agriculture to capital construction projects.

In this chapter the word surplus is used in both of the above senses. Further, following Baran, one could distinguish between the size of the surplus and the mode of its utilization. But our concern here is only with the first part of the problem.

At a conceptual level, one line of argument has it that, given the dominant role of agriculture in backward economies, it is incumbent upon this sector to contribute its due share to surplus mobilization. More extreme versions of this argument assert that the agricultural sector should be squeezed to finance industrialization. This point of view is buttressed by reference to the historical experiences of Japan and the Soviet Union, experiences which are vastly different from each other. In the former country, immediately after the Meiji Restoration of 1868, stiff taxes were imposed on agriculture to wring out a substantial surplus, which was instrumental in financing the country's industrialization and in the building up of her military might. In the Soviet Union, the task was accomplished through the collectivization drive of the 1930s which managed to boost to a considerable extent the country's marketable agricultural surplus, without which the country's industrialization (at least at the pace at which it proceeded and in the magnitude it assumed) would have been inconceivable. This forced march is often referred to as the Stalin strategy.

There is, however, a school of thought that counsels against such a strategy. It argues that the agricultural sector should be viewed not merely as a repository of surplus to develop industry but as a sector that should be developed in its own right. To emphasize industry to the neglect of agriculture, it is argued, would lead to stagnation in agriculture and - consequently - to stagnation in the economy as a whole, owing to the sector's pivotal role in the economy. While the imperative need to generate surplus from agriculture is not denied, the argument is that a surplus must be produced before it can be extracted. In other words, at early stages of development, priority should be given to policies that promote agricultural development. The experience of countries such as Brazil and Argentina is cited to show that even with natural resources conducive to agricultural development, it is possible to lose this advantage if the policy framework is inappropriate (Nicholls 1964).

In principle, there is a variety of instruments available for extracting surplus from the agricultural sector, the most obvious one being tax policy. Although it is the one that comes most readily to mind, tax policy may not always be the most important instrument. Price and marketing policies may also serve the same purpose. In this connection, a deliberate policy of turning the terms of trade against agriculture may be pursued. Surplus may also be generated by utilizing unpaid or underpaid labour. Another possibility is the soliciting of contributions in cash, whether or not these are dubbed "voluntary" being immaterial. At the extreme, there is also the alternative of compulsory requisitioning of the peasant's produce by the state. It is against this background that we now turn to the Ethiopian experience.

Surplus Extraction through Agricultural Taxation

The taxes that fall directly on the agricultural sector are (a) the land use fee, (b) the tax on agricultural incomes, and (c) taxes on exports of agricultural products. There are also special taxes that are levied from time to time

Table 1
Actual Budgetary Revenue
(in million birr)

Revenue Source	1982/83	1983/84	1984/85	1985/86	1986/87
Taxes on Coffee Exports					
Export Duty	14.0	14.3	10.1	9.1	12.2
Surtax	174.0	225.6	148.7	236.7	118.1
Cess	4.6	4.4	3.8	3.4	3.5
Total	192.6	244.3	162.6	249.2	133.8
Transaction Tax on Exports*	10.3	11.ᴧ	9.0	11.3	12.4
Export Duties on Hides and Skins	0.8	ᴜ.9	1.0	0.8	0.3
Land Use Fee	51.3	48.1	41.4	48.8	46.0
Agricultural Income Tax	52.6	48.6	41.9	51.7	49.9
TOTAL AGRIC. TAXES	297.6	353.3	255.9	361.8	242.4
TOTAL TAX REVENUE	1814.0	1731.5	1677.5	1 876.1	2108.5
ORDINARY REVENUE	2143.4	2268.7	2254.5	2717.8	2746.3
Agric. Taxes as % of Total Tax Rev.	17.0	20.4	15.3	19.3	11.5
Agric. Taxes as % of Ordinary Rev.	14.4	15.6	11.4	13.3	8.8
Share of Coffee as % of Agric. Tax Rev.	62.6	69.1	63.5	68.9	55.2

* This figure is slightly exaggerated because it includes transaction taxes on non-agricultural exports. But, given the dominant role of agriculture in the structure of exports, the distortion is not significant.

Source: Ministry of Finance

(e.g. taxes earmarked for drought relief and war efforts), and to the extent that these also fall on the rural population, they should be considered as surplus contributed by the agricultural sector.

The land use fee is paid by peasants for the use of the land given to them. The annual rate is 10 birr for those who are not members of cooperatives and 5 birr for those who belong to cooperatives. It is a flat sum paid irrespective of location or soil fertility. State farms are also required to pay 2 birr per hectare on their holdings.

The tax on income from agricultural activities applies to individual farmers and cooperatives. Annual incomes not exceeding 600 birr are subject to a fixed tax of 10 birr, incomes above that being taxed on a progressive basis.

Of the taxes on exports of agricultural products, the one that applies to all products is the 2 per cent transaction tax on exports. However, the most important taxes in this category are those that fall on coffee. In addition to the 2 per cent transaction tax, coffee exports are subject to payments of export duties, a surtax and cess. While the export duties apply to hides and skins as well, the surtax and cess are imposed on coffee exports only. The surtax is designed to capture greater revenue for the state in times of rising coffee prices. The cess, which was originally introduced to provide revenue for the now defunct National Coffee Board, is currently part of general revenue.

The above are effectively the only taxes of consequence levied on the agricultural sector. Strictly speaking, however, we may note two more categories of taxes. The first relates to the tax obligations of state enterprises. The law stipulates that "any government or privately owned judicial person or association that carries out business actively excluding cooperative society" is required to pay 50 per cent of its taxable income as income tax (*Negarit Gazeta*, 38th Year, No.3). But it is difficult to determine the contribution made by state agricultural enterprises under this heading, because the data available do not show this information separately. The second category concerns the "residual surplus" which state enterprises are required to surrender to the treasury in addition to the 50 per cent income tax. However, since most state farms are losing concerns, there is no surplus to speak of. On the contrary, they are themselves appropriators of surplus produced elsewhere in the economy.

What, then, is the contribution of the agricultural taxes to surplus generation? To answer this question, we will look at the data for the period 1982/83 - 1986/87, which are summarized in Table 1. Contrary to a widely held impression, the figures show that the agricultural sector is not an important source of tax revenue, especially considering its contribution to output and employment. For the three years indicated, the agricultural sector contributed, on the average, 16.7 per cent of total tax revenue and 12.7 per cent of total ordinary revenue, figures which are quite low compared to the sector's share in GDP, which is more than 40 per cent.

Another striking fact that emerges from the table is the dominant role of coffee in the structure of agricultural taxation. For the period indicated, this crop accounted for about 64 per cent of the tax revenue generated from the agricultural sector. By far the most important item here is the surcharge on coffee exports.

In contrast, the role of the agricultural income tax is modest. It is noteworthy that in all the five years the contribution of this tax is almost exactly equal to that of the land use fee. This suggests that peasants pay the minimum 10 birr obligation as income tax, which makes the progressive rate structure for annual incomes above 600 birr entirely fictitious. Therefore, the image of an Ethiopian peasantry over-burdened by taxes does not square well with the facts. But, one should hasten to add, there are other modalities for surplus extraction at work. It is to these that we now turn.

Surplus Extraction through Grain Marketing and Pricing

A frequently encountered problem in the pricing of agricultural products is the conflict between two objectives. On the one hand, the agricultural sector is expected to generate a surplus for investment as well as a steady supply of food to the urban population and raw materials for industry. This requires a policy of keeping agricultural prices low. On the other hand, rural incomes should be rising so that an effective market for manufactured goods can be guaranteed. And this requires that agricultural prices be incentive prices, i.e., adequate enough to stimulate producers. In the conflict between these important objectives lies the dilemma of policy making. And the choice becomes especially difficult in circumstances of low productivity.

This dilemma is encountered in the Ethiopian setting as well. While one objective of government marketing policy is "to provide farmers with incentives to produce and market more output", another is "to ensure adequate food supplies at reasonable prices for urban consumers and for food deficit areas" (World Bank 1987:41). But expert opinion is unanimous that the balance tips heavily in favour of the latter objective. If this is indeed the case, then the government's grain marketing and pricing policies serve as instruments of surplus extraction. It is this point that we wish to explore here.

The government's grain marketing and pricing policies are well-known and they can be briefly summarized as follows:

a) All farmers are required to sell to the state marketing enterprise, the Agricultural Marketing Corporation (AMC) a certain quantity of grain at a price fixed by the government.

b) Any surplus over this quantity may be sold on the free market.

c) Licensed private merchants must sell 50 per cent of their grain purchases to the AMC at state-determined prices (which are 4-5 birr per quintal above the official farm-gate purchase prices). As of January 1988 the remaining 50 per cent may be sold anywhere. Prior to this date, this was not true for all regions. Private exporters are required to sell only 25 per cent of their purchases to the AMC. Private merchants may buy grain only from farmers.

d) The AMC sells to urban dwellers' associations (*kebeles*), state enterprises and the armed forces, among others. It may be noted here that about two-thirds of the AMC's purchases are from the peasant sector and merchants while the remaining one-third is from state farms (Study on Grain Price Determination).

What is the magnitude of the surplus generated through the government's marketing and pricing policies? This is a fairly difficult question to answer in precise terms, and so we will be content to suggest general orders of magnitude.

One way of looking at the surplus is by considering if the quota deliveries are too high. A second form in which the surplus appears is as the difference between the official farm-gate price paid to the peasant and the price paid by the final consumer. A third way of looking at the surplus is by considering differences, if any, in the terms of trade of agricultural products *vis à vis* those of non-agricultural goods.

Quota Deliveries

Let us take the magnitude of peasant quota deliveries first. To establish‘ whether these are too high or not would require an accurate determination of the peasant's output, the consumption needs of his family, the seeds he has to put aside for the next harvest, and the surplus that he requires to finance his purchases of non-agricultural goods. In the absence of readily available information on such matters, this is not an easy task. Moreover, it is misleading to make broad generalizations, because the setting of quotas, at least with respect to individual farmers, varies from locality to locality. Although some tentative observations can be made on the basis of information obtained from the AMC, the data are unfortunately aggregated and averaged for selected *awrajas* and not disaggregated by crop type, which makes them inadequate for our purposes.

Quotas allocated per farmer per year range from a low of 0.02 quintals in Sidama (not a grain-producing area) to a high of 7 quintals in Chilalo (a major grain-producing area and one that comes closest to having experienced a "green revolution"). Quotas actually fulfilled vary from a low of 0.03 quintals in Gofa and Wolaita *awrajas* (again not grain-growing areas) to a high of 3.13 quintals in Chilalo. Like all averages, these figures hide a lot of diversity, which makes them unreliable for firm generalizations.

What can be stated with confidence is that there is no uniformity in the procedures for setting quotas and that there is arbitrariness in enforcing them. We do know, for example, that in at least certain areas farmers are under serious strain to meet their quota obligations (Study on Grain Price Determination:46); in fact, cases are known of peasants buying grain on the free market to deliver the required quantity to the AMC. As much is admitted by an official document: "It is known that, since the allocation of quotas is not based on uniform procedures and reliable information, it has created misgivings among farmers. Not only is the system of quota allocation haphazard and inequitable as between different localities, it has also been causing problems of implementation in some *weredas* because the quota happened to be in excess of what the peasant could bring to the market after deducting his requirements for seeds and for his own consumption" (Study on Grain Price Determination:45-6, author's translation).

We do not know how widespread this practice is, but in the areas where it applies it means too high quotas and therefore represents a hidden form of taxation.

Agricultural Prices

Secondly, are the prices paid to the peasant by the AMC too low? There is no doubt that, relative to free-market prices, the prices received by the farmer are too low. As far as the peasant is concerned, to the extent that the price he receives from the AMC falls short of the free-market price, the difference is surplus extracted from him. A general picture can be gained by comparing AMC buying prices with wholesale prices on the Addis Ababa free-market. The relevant information appears in Table 2. As is evident from the table, AMC farm-gate prices are in all cases less than 50 per cent of the Addis Ababa open-market price. Even if not all of this would have gone to the peasant in the absence of compulsory quota deliveries, there is no doubt that a sizable fraction would have accrued to him. The sizable differences between AMC selling prices and free-market prices are proof of this.

Table 2
Wholesale prices of Grain
Addis Ababa Grain Market*
(birr per quintal
13.3.89 - 18.3.89)

Grain Type	AMC Farm-gate Price	AMC Selling Price	Free Market Average Price
Teff			
white	48.00	69.55	124.83
mixed	41.00	61.90	112.00
red	37.00	57.55	93.67
Wheat			
white	36.00	57.55	110.67
mixed	32.00	53.15	74.00
black	31.00	52.10	67.83
Barley			
white	30.00	49.90	115.00
mixed	28.00	47.70	63.50
Maize	22.00	44.45	52.00
Chick peas	30.00	49.90	135.67
Lentils	45.00	66.30	186.50

*called "ehel berenda" in Amharic

Source: AMC

It may be objected that, in view of considerable segmentation in the market for grain, looking at Addis Ababa market prices will give a misleading picture. For this reason, we have attempted to look at price differentials in various markets. For this exercise we have taken the prices of red teff for illustrative purposes, and the relevant information appears in Table 3. An examination of this table reveals that free-market prices for red teff are higher than AMC selling prices by about 60 per cent on the average.

How much of a surplus is extracted through these price differentials? Without pretending to answer this question fully, we will perform a small exercise to suggest orders of magnitude. In Assela, for example, the AMC farm-gate price for wheat (the average for all three grades) is 33 birr. This compares with a free-market retail price of 50.83 birr for July-December 1988. Given an average quota delivery of 3.13 quintals per farmer in Chilalo *awraja*, this represents an average differential of 55.81 birr per farmer. True, not all of this represents a surplus, but it ought to be recognized that many farmers in the *awraja* deliver larger quantities. Similar exercises reveal differentials per farmer of 33.14 birr for teff in Debre Markos and 16.05 birr for maize in Ambo. Thus, after all the qualifications have been made, there is no doubt that pricing and marketing policies represent an important means of surplus transfer from agriculture.

Table 3
Comparative Prices of Red Teff
birr per quintal

Town	AMC Selling Price* (1984/85-1985/86)	Open Market Price Average for 1987/88
Addis Ababa	56.05	88.00
Ambo	54.49	71.00
Asmara	87.88	176.00
Assela	50.66	75.00
Bahir Dahr	51.71	76.00
Dire Dawa	64.65	136.00
Debre Berhan	54.42	95.00
Debre Markos	50.39	79.00
Gonder	50.46	74.00
Metu	52.48	58.00
Nazareth	54.82	97.00
Nekemte	53.28	57.00
Shashemene	49.56	75.00

* excluding 2 per cent turnover tax. Note that the AMC wholesale purchase price for 1984/85 - 1985/86 was 39 birr.

Source: AMC

Terms of Trade

Finally, there is surplus extraction through a deterioration of the agricultural terms of trade *vis à vis* those of manufactured consumer goods and industrial inputs purchased by farmers. Unfortunately, the only price index we have is the Addis Ababa retail price index, but it is adequate for obtaining a general picture.

AMC's farm-gate purchase prices had for the most part shown no increase between 1980/81 and 1987/88, and the price increases which became effective in January 1988 involved increases of only 2-3 birr per quintal for most grains. This contrasts with a steadily rising consumer price index, which means an equally steady decline in the peasant's purchasing power. Therefore, surplus is extracted from the farmer in this manner too. For example, real 1985/86 price expressed as a percentage of real 1979/80 price was 68 per cent for mixed teff, 91 per cent for mixed wheat, 58 per cent for maize and 85 per cent for sorghum (World Bank 1987:46).

It may be argued that, since prices of some industrial products are also controlled, the deterioration in the agricultural terms of trade may not be as suggested above. But one should not exaggerate the significance of this point, for the simple reason that, in 1987/88, for example, of the total sales of the Ethiopian Domestic Distribution Corporation, only 14 per cent went to peasant associations, compared to 34.9 per cent for private traders (ONCCP:35).

We conclude, therefore, that due to (a) high delivery quotas (at least in certain cases), (b) low farm-gate prices relative to those on the free-market, and (c) a deterioration in the agricultural terms of trade, the government's grain marketing and pricing policies are highly instrumental in extracting surplus from the peasant sector. It might be added in passing that the prices the AMC pays to state farms are higher than those paid to peasants.

Surplus Extraction through Foreign Exchange Generation

From the viewpoint of the farmer it matters very little whether his products are marketed within the country or internationally. But as far as surplus extraction is concerned, it is necessary to consider the export sector separately for at least two reasons. First, our discussion has so far concentrated on cereals but has said nothing about important exportables such as coffee. Secondly, foreign exchange being a crucial factor in the Ethiopian economy, explicit consideration of the role of agriculture in this regard is mandatory. However, since the general picture is a well-known one, we can afford to be brief.

The most obvious fact in this connection is that, over the last fifteen years or so, agricultural products have, on the average, accounted for close to 90 per cent of the country's total export earnings. Worthy of special mention is coffee, whose relative role has been increasing in recent years, so much so that its share in total export value has risen to over 60 per cent lately. It is estimated that coffee exports may be about 50 per cent of total production, about 95 per cent of which originates in the peasant sector (World Bank 1987:25). Some calculations show that the price received by the producer for unwashed coffee is about 40 per cent of the international FOB price (World Bank 1987a:145-6). Of the remaining 60 per cent, 44 per cent is taken by taxes and duties (which we have already considered), which leaves 16 per cent for interior costs, finance and insurance, and cleaning and other costs. Although the 40 per cent received by the farmer is not too low by international standards, it still suggests a high degree of surplus extraction.

Important as the share of agriculture in foreign exchange generation is, however, the following qualifications need to be made. First, major Ethiopian exports (notably oilseeds and pulses, fruits and vegetables) have been declining in volume in recent years. Second, owing partly to rising import volumes and prices, the country's trade balance has been deteriorating. Third, there is a sizable leakage of potential foreign exchange through contraband trade that has reached alarming proportions. Fourth, the share of food and inputs for use in agriculture in total imports has been rising, which means the agricultural sector is not only a generator but also a user of foreign exchange. On balance, of course, its generation of foreign exchange far outweighs its utilization. All told, therefore, whatever foreign exchange the country earns is largely accounted for by the agricultural sector.

Other Forms of Surplus Extraction

Although reliable data are not available, it is well-known that farmers are from time to time required to make cash contributions for a variety of reasons, including the construction of meeting halls, roads, etc. and the financing of festive occasions, among others. They are also required to participate in various construction projects, but the magnitude of this contribution is difficult to quantify. However, one can get a general impression by referring to the Ten-Year Perspective Plan. It is significant that of the total investment of 7.2 billion birr allocated to agriculture, 1.9 billion birr (or 26.4 per cent) is expected to come from individual peasants and agricultural cooperatives. Perhaps even more significant is that more than 68 per cent of this contribution is expected to take the form of peasant participation in such activities as the conservation and development of soil, water and forest resources. This topic represents a fertile and fruitful area for future research.

Postscript in Lieu of a Conclusion

What, one may ask, does the agricultural sector receive in return for the surplus that it contributes to the rest of the economy? An answer would require an examination of the structure of current expenditure, the sectoral allocation of the capital budget, and the sectoral distribution of loans from the banking system.

In 1984/85, for example, actual total current expenditure was 2,636 million birr, of which agriculture's share was 453 million birr, or about 17 per cent. We are also told that the actual total investment between 1984/85 and 1988 was 7.4 billion birr, of which the share of agriculture was 1.7 billion birr, or about 23 per cent (Central Report of the General Secretary of the Workers Party of Ethiopia). Although this figure is the highest for any sector, there is widespread expert opinion that agriculture deserves more. Of the bank loans extended for economic activities between 1984/85 and 1987/88 (3.1 billion birr), 1.2 billion birr , or about 39 per cent, was extended to the agricultural sector.

The issue, however, is not only one of sectoral allocation but also one of the allocation of financial resources within agriculture itself. The evidence is incontrovertible that state farms, which for the most part are losers, receive the bulk of financial allocations. Between 1980/81 and 1984/85, for example, state farms absorbed 43 per cent of all the financial resources allocated to agriculture, although their share of agricultural output was less than 5 per cent.

In concluding, an important qualification is in order to forestall a possible misunderstanding. Far be it from us to paint Ethiopian agriculture in rosy colours or to cast it in a heroic light. In fact, if there is a villain of the piece in the Ethiopian economy, that role belongs to the agricultural sector. It has failed to meet the most basic objective of feeding the population. Beyond this, the stagnation and decline that have characterized this sector for a long time now have taken their inevitable toll on the performance of the economy as a whole. The underlying causes of this deep malaise go far beyond the scope of this short chapter, but no diagnosis of Ethiopia's economic ills will be complete if it ignores the problem of surplus extraction which we have attempted to sketch here.

9 Cooperatives, State Farms and Smallholder Production
Dessalegn Rahmato

The Policy Framework for Transition

Since the overthrow of the absolute monarchy in 1974 Ethiopia's peasant society has been significantly restructured. The first and perhaps most central measure was the land reform of 1975 which provided the economic and institutional framework for all the major rural policy changes carried out by the government to date. There are three major aspects of the land reform which have had a significant impact on the structure of post-revolution rural Ethiopia:

- the abolition of landlordism, and the distribution of land to peasant households;
- the abolition of tenancy and other forms of social dependency on propertied classes (but not dependency itself):
- the establishment of rural mass organizations, particularly peasant associations.

The reform was thorough and all-embracing, and here lies its strength, but it was also radical in the extreme, and here lies its weakness.[1]

Land, the reform legislation says, is the "collective property" of the Ethiopian people, and private ownership is prohibited. This in effect means that the state is the real owner of property, and peasant cultivators have only usufruct rights over the land they are allotted by their peasant association. Here is a form of ownership in which the state acts as the real landlord with the right, in the last instance, of allocating or disposing of land.[2]

A major problem of the reform is that it gives rise to a process of diminution of peasant plots. A rural household has access to land only in its community, whose land and other natural resources are fixed. Young peasants who become eligible for land can only acquire it if land is alienated from peasants in the community who are considered to possess "large" plots.[3] This progressive levelling down of individual possessions has created deep uncertainty among the peasantry, and will continue to have a discouraging effect on peasant production.

While the reform legislation prohibits tenancy, the leasing/renting of land, and the hiring of labour, all three are widely practised in many parts of the countryside with the tacit approval of rural mass organizations. Renting land, the most widespread of the three, takes a variety of forms, but the chief objective is basically the same in all cases: for the peasant who rents land from another it is a means of supplementing his income, while for the peasant who leases his plot it is a survival strategy. In the latter case, the land would not otherwise have been worked either because the family concerned is physically unable to do farm work, or more commonly it does not possess work oxen and other necessities (Dessalegn 1987). These, and other similar "illegal" practices are clear indications that while land reform has satisfied some of the basic needs of the peasantry, it has not tackled the root causes of peasant poverty and rural underdevelopment. Insufficiency of holdings, land fragmentation, insufficiency of plough oxen and livestock, land degradation, and the very limited use of green revolution technology have been in the past and continue to be at present among the main causes of agricultural stagnation in the private peasant sector. [4]

Although the process of transition to socialism in rural Ethiopia is not discussed in depth from a theoretical perspective in the major public policy documents, its general outlines can be deduced (WPE 1984:21-32). The government talks of completing what it calls the National Democratic Revolution (NDR), while laying the foundations for socialism. It is not clear exactly what the NDR really involves, nor how this is to be seen in the context of a developing national economy. In rural areas the programme calls for expansion of cooperative and state-owned enterprises. It is assumed that agricultural growth will only accelerate if there is a move from smallholder to large-scale production, and from private to social or state ownership. There is a passing reference to the need to develop the "productive forces", but no clear analysis is made as to how this is incorporated in the transition and what precise role it will play in the process.

The Ten-Year Plan (1984-94) attempts to put a time scale on the process of change. By the end of the plan period (initially 1994) the transition in its formal sense will have been completed in the main, and the socialist sector of rural production will have become the dominant sector, as is shown in Table 1.

Table 1
Socialist Agriculture in the Ten-Year Plan

Farming Sectors	1984-5		1994	
	Area	Prod.	Area	Prod.
Peasant	95.4	94.8	39.6	36.6
Cooperatives	1.4	1.4	52.2	51.9
State Farms	2.8	3.6	6.4	10.0
Settlement sites	0.4	0.2	1.8	1.5

Source: ONCCP September 1984 (d):191

There is reason to believe that the pace of cooperativization has slowed down since the plan was prepared. At present rates, far fewer peasants will find themselves in cooperatives than was envisaged by the plan. As the table shows, planners have placed high hopes on the cooperative endeavour which they see as the engine of rural modernization.

On the other hand, there are now some misgivings about state farms among policy makers, and the rate of expansion of state agriculture may be slowed down to some extent in the years to come.

The underlying tenets of the socialist transition revealed in policy documents are neither new nor conceptually or programmatically adapted to Ethiopian conditions. There are two aspects worthy of note, and these are that the transition is seen in terms primarily of *property ownership* on the one hand, and in terms of *scale of operation* of enterprises on the other. In other words, it is the *formal* aspects of production rather than the real stimuli to improvements in production that are given prominence.

Policy guide-lines for what are called producer cooperatives were issued in June 1979, and the process of implementation was begun soon after. It is curious to note that among the major objectives mentioned, the struggle against capitalism is given an important place. Cooperatives (and here we shall be concerned mainly with producer cooperatives, and not with what are called service cooperatives)[5] were to bring an end to capitalist exploitation, and to prevent the re-emergence of capitalism in agriculture. This is surprising as rural capitalism was never a threat to begin with, not even under Emperor Haile Selassie, and was quietly laid to rest by the land reform itself in 1975. Besides laying the foundation for socialist production in the rural areas, producer cooperatives are meant to introduce modern technology and to pave the way for the transition to large-scale agriculture.

Cooperatives were to be organized on a three-tier basis, each lower tier succeeded by a higher one after a certain period of time. At the lowest level are primary cooperatives (called *malba*) in which there is common ownership of land combined with individual ownership of livestock and agricultural implements. These were to develop into secondary cooperatives (called *welba*) where all agricultural resources are commonly owned. At the highest level are *weland* which are formed of two or more *welba* and which involve complete collectivization.[6] *Weland* resemble, at least on paper, the Russian *kolkhozy* (collective farms) of the 1930s. Peasants involved in the primary and secondary level cooperatives are allowed to keep individual garden plots measuring half or a quarter of a hectare for their own use.

Theoretically, a producer cooperative may be formed by as few as three persons living in the same peasant association, but a minimum of 30 members is needed for the organization to be formally registered and recognized, a process which can take one to two years or more. As of 1986, the last year for which there is reliable information, less than 10 per cent of the producer cooperatives organized in the country, i.e. 225 out of a total 2,323, had received their registration. Registration is necessary to obtain credit from banks, to enter contractual agreements with state enterprises, etc. The slow pace of registration probably suggests that the men behind the cooperativization drive - political and extension agents - are finding it difficult to set up full-fledged cooperative enterprises. Cooperators are free to villagize if they so wish, and a number of cooperatives have built villages for their members.

State agriculture was formally launched in May 1977 with the establishment of the State Farms Development Authority, which later became the Ministry of State Farms Development (MSFD). Among the major objectives of state agriculture were to alleviate the country's food problems, to produce raw materials for domestic industry, to expand output for export purposes, and to create employment opportunities. State farms also seem to be a reliable source of food for government procurement agencies, and were to play a strong role in the expansion of agro-industries. We shall see that state agriculture is still no nearer to its goals than it was when it was organized about a decade ago.

Peasants, Cooperatives, State Farms: A Comparative Analysis

Examining the strengths and weaknesses of each of the three sectors we shall begin with peasant agriculture. In the Ethiopian context, the inherent weakness of peasant agriculture flows from the interplay of the following factors: 1) Smallholder agriculture is oriented mainly towards auto-consumption, and this, more than the market, largely determines land-use and cropping plans. 2) The standard of technology is poor or of limited potential. Improved technology is, for most peasants, either too costly to acquire, too complicated to operate, or too dependent on external economies. 3) Most peasants are plagued by inadequate holdings; their plots are too often fragmented, and soil and water erosion are frequent hazards.

Historically, attempts to overcome the first and second problems have often involved the establishment of multi-purpose marketing or service cooperatives, while the solution to the third constraint has been thought to lie in land consolidation and collectivization.

On the plus side, peasant production benefits from high personal motivation, flexibility in cropping strategies (particularly in response to unanticipated environmental changes), and high levels of farming skills and agricultural knowledge, all of which is frequently lost when collectivist policies are imposed on peasant agriculture.

Peasant cultivators have not often been given the credit they deserve for their traditional farming skills and environmental knowledge. While not all peasants are equally capable, the level of know-how of the more accomplished ones is quite impressive (Dessalegn 1987, Adams 1986). Hardy peasants in the highlands of Gamo Gofa, south Ethiopia, for example, have for decades exploited the full potentials of their ecology thanks mainly to intensive, bi-modal cultivation which relies on a package of sophisticated irrigation and drainage techniques, skilful terracing to minimize erosion, and a complex cropping and crop rotation system. Konso peasants in the same region employ twenty-four distinct varieties of millet, and are reputed to have developed one of the most sophisticated soil and water preservation techniques in the area (Jackson 1969, Hallpike 1970). In both the southern and northern highlands, extensive knowledge of plants enables peasants to make use of a wide variety of "wild" plants for construction, medicine, food preservation and decorative purposes; some of these plants are also used as emergency food in times of serious food shortages (Dessalegn 1987).

In brief, peasants have developed sufficient capabilities to make full use of the resources of their environment. This ability and know-how are threatened by collectivization and may eventually be lost if individual peasant initiative is smothered by collective discipline.[7]

The management of a large-scale enterprise is more complicated than that of small enterprises. Ethiopian peasants are not familiar with the advantages of large-scale farming, nor do they have the ability to manage such enterprises. Most extension agents are themselves untrained in this field. Some cooperatives in the cereal growing regions of the country operate farms measuring 500 ha, others as much as 800 to 1,000. Before the land reform, peasants who had access to large holdings worked some of it and leased the rest to others or left it fallow. Rare was the peasant who was able on his own to manage more than 5 or 6 ha of land.

Compared with family based peasant production, producer cooperatives are fragile institutions. Their rate of success in developing countries - measured by the ability to be self-supporting - has been very disappointing. One of the most critical elements in all forms of cooperative labour, a factor which is often ignored in the debate on the subject, is the "ideological" motivation of the members themselves. A group strongly motivated by a set of ideals and a high sense of purpose is more likely to succeed in its endeavours than another which lacks this motivation. The success of the "communistic" enterprises of monastic orders in the past, and of the Israeli collective agricultural schemes in our own time must in large measure be attributed to the drive inspired in the members by transcendental values and goals. State sponsored cooperatives in Third World countries often lack this inspirational element, and a majority of them will remain dependent on government subsidy and other forms of support.

In Ethiopia cooperatives are entitled to privileges not offered to private peasant cultivators, or even to state farms. Cooperators pay less tax per head than individual peasants. Modern inputs like fertilizer, pesticides, etc. are offered at subsidized prices, and bank interest rates are comparatively lower. Cooperatives are also given priority in extension work.[8]

Not infrequently, rural extension agents alienate farmland and common pasture belonging to peasants and peasant associations, and allocate it to cooperatives, whenever the latter complain of shortage of land and request more. This practice, though not universal, is fairly widespread and has aroused resentment among individual peasants. During our field work in 1980 in Wollaita sub-province (southern Ethiopia), we were informed by a district administrator that some 200 peasants in one peasant association had angrily beaten up a couple of extension agents, because these had allowed a cooperative which had just been set up (and which involved about 35 households) to enclose for its sole use a grazing area commonly open to all members of the peasant association. Moreover, producer cooperatives have access to additional labour during the peak seasons from peasant association and rural youth association members. Individual peasants living close to a cooperative are often obliged to work one to two days per season on the cooperative's fields, without pay. Similarly, members of the youth association (an arm of the peasant association) provide labour during land preparation and weeding. This partly explains the disparity in constraints between individual and cooperative enterprises shown in Table 2.

It may be of interest to note that the marketed surplus of cooperatives and individual farms is about equal: on the average both sell about 20 per cent of their harvest, and the rest is consumed at home (68 per cent) or reserved as next season's seed (12 per cent).

Despite many limitations of rural cooperatives, there are, we believe, certain areas in which they can play an important role. Certain forms of specialized agriculture, for example vegetable, fruit and spice growing as well as dairy and meat production, may produce better results if organized in cooperatives and operated on a scale calculated to maximize efficiency and to encourage intensive endeavours. As a general rule, small-scale cooperatives - with 10 to 15 members, for example - are much more manageable and efficient than large-scale ones. The advantages of specialized agriculture are that production is geared to the market, enterprises are not highly capital intensive, and specialization allows intensive operation.

Secondly, cooperatives are much better placed to serve as conduits for the transfer of improved technology than peasant or state enterprises. The leap from traditional ox-drawn ploughs to tractors and advanced technology is often a hazardous undertaking. The diffusion of intermediate technology among peasants has proved difficult owing to a wide variety of factors including cost and serviceability. In many ways cooperatives are closer to the small cultivator, and new technology which is also appropriate for peasant needs could be developed in cooperatives and diffused to the surrounding peasantry.[9]

Table 2
Comparison of Constraints for Peasants and for Producer Cooperatives

Constraints	Severity	
	Peasants	PC
Land Scarcity	More	Less.
Lack of Work Oxen	Less	More
Soil Fertility Problems	Equally severe for both	
Frost, Natural Hazards	Equally severe for both	
Pest Damage	More	Less
Drainage Problems	Less	More
Shortage of Dry Season Cattle Feed	More	Less
Peak Season Labour Shortage	More	Less

Source: Based on IAR Farm System Surveys 1987

The story of state agriculture is one of mismanagement, of wasted resources and financial loss on a large scale. Since 1977, when the government formally gave its blessing to state farms, the enterprise has incurred a total accumulated loss of 613 million birr. In the period 1980/1985, annual recorded losses have averaged nearly 80 million birr. In the same period, state farms absorbed on the average 64 per cent of the annual state capital expenditure allocated to agriculture. State farms, it should be noted, operate less than 4 per cent of the cultivated area of the country and contribute about 1 per cent to the nation's food requirements[10] (MSFD 1986: 385).[11] In the words of an in-house document prepared recently, state agriculture has been a "financial disaster" since its inception.

In the first decade of their formation, state farms, encouraged by generous government grants and liberal bank credit, carried out large expansion schemes in many parts of the country. At the beginning, their land holdings measured a mere 55,000 ha, but five years later their holdings had grown four fold, and the regions they were operating in had increased considerably. The feverish expansion of this period turned out later to have been poorly planned, and in some cases environmentally damaging. At present the cultivated area under state control measures over 210,000 ha of which more than 86 per cent is rain-fed agricultural land which in a number of instances was taken from peasant associations. At the height of state farm expansion, some peasants were evicted from their land to make way for mechanization, particularly in Arsi, Bale, and Gojjam.

One of the chief aims of state farms was to help alleviate the country's food problems, and to be a reliable source of food grain for state purchasing agencies. How far has this goal been achieved?

The total contribution of state farms to the nation's food requirements stood at 2 per cent in the agricultural year 1981/82, but fours years later, in 1985/86, this figure had declined to just about 1 per cent (MSFD 1986:389). The Agricultural Marketing Corporation (AMC) is the chief customer of state farms for all food crops except barley which is sold to breweries. In 1980, state farms supplied 70 per cent of AMC's total purchases, and the peasant sector only 30 per cent. However, their contribution has been declining since then. In 1985/86, comparable figures were 41 per cent and 59 per cent respectively. An exception was 1984/85, which was a famine year and peasant agriculture was badly hit by drought.

State farms' contribution to the country's exports and its share of foreign currency earnings has been declining for the last six to seven years. In this period, the farms' annual export, which consisted mainly of live animals, horticultural produce and oil crops, averaged 6 per cent of total exports. The enterprises use up large amounts of foreign exchange because their operations are highly capital intensive, and all their chemical inputs (fertilizers, pesticides, etc.) are purchased from outside with hard currency. It is estimated that state farms can only cover about 40 per cent of their foreign exchange requirements from exports of their own products (MSFD 1986: 393). Thus, far from earning the national economy hard currency, as the planners had hoped, state agriculture continues to be a big drain on the country's export earnings.

The record of state farms in the area of employment creation is equally disappointing. At present MSFD has a permanent work force of 35,000, and employs some 50,000 labourers on a seasonal basis (MSFD 1986: 394). In comparison, private mechanized agriculture annually provided seasonal employment for over 300,000 labourers on the eve of the revolution (Dessalegn 1986: 81). On a number of regional farms, particularly those in the Awash Valley, the agency's seasonal labour needs are met through a system of peasant mobilization which in reality is hardly different from commandeered labour. The future trend of state farms is such that very few jobs will be created in the years ahead.

Some have argued that state farms could play an important role in modernizing agriculture; the sector could serve as a carrier of new technology and new ideas which could then be transmitted to the peasantry. This argument has few supports at present. State agriculture, like its predecessor commercial agriculture, operates as an isolated enclave within peasant production, offering very little assistance to the surrounding peasantry. On the other hand, it has over the years greatly abused the technology it employs, and its equipment handling and stock management methods as well as its cropping and land use practices are now so poor that nothing short of a major restructuring will save the enterprise from sinking deeper into the morass.

This, however, is not the same thing as saying that there is no future for mechanized agriculture in the country. Modern agriculture will have to find for itself a niche where it can operate profitably. This will certainly mean engaging in specialized agriculture geared mainly to the foreign market. A restructured, slimmed down large-scale farming sector, administered as an autonomous agency with decision making at enterprise level, may fruitfully engage in growing certain kinds of industrial crops, and in running plantations for rare plants which have a high demand in the world market.

In the long run large-scale agriculture can benefit greatly not just from product specialization, but also by building up a viable and mutually beneficial partnership with smallholder agriculture. Certain forms of partnership, notably contract farming, are proving successful in a number of Third World countries (Glover 1984).[12]

Whither Socialist Transition ?

The dilemma of socialist transition theory, particularly as it relates to rural production, is that the underlying arguments which were formulated in the second half of the 19th century have remained unchanged for nearly one hundred years. Briefly, the arguments are the following: there will be greater gains in social accumulation once private property is abolished. Workers will benefit more in a socialized economy, and hence labour productivity will grow much faster. Socialist production (which is erroneously understood to mean state-managed enterprises and planning) is inherently more efficient than private production. The progress towards large-scale agriculture is inevitable, since among other things large-scale production is more efficient and more rational. Smallholder agriculture on the other hand is destined to disappear because it is and will remain uncompetitive.[13]

These same arguments were uncritically accepted by the Bolsheviks in the Russian revolution and eventually became the cornerstone of Soviet agricultural policy under Stalin's leadership. Lenin's New Economic Policy of the early 1920s, which envisioned the co-existence of smallholder, capitalist and socialist production during an extended period of transition, was rudely shoved aside in favour of accelerated collectivization and expanded state-management of agriculture (Lewin 1968, Davies 1980). Soviet agriculture has not yet fully recovered from the ravages of the Stalinist collectivization of the 1930s.

The arguments in favour of socialization of agriculture may have appeared convincing in the context of European economic development in the 19th century, where new technology was for the first time employed on a large scale to revolutionize all sectors of society. Accumulation was taking place at a high rate, and an active and autonomous labour movement made the prospects for socialist revolution look promising. Third World socialist states, on the other hand, face today deep-rooted and in many ways unique problems in the light of which the classic arguments of socialist agriculture need to be reconsidered.

To begin with, these countries are all dependent on foreign earnings for their own development, and hence dependent on the world economic community, which does not make special allowances for ideology or doctrine (however appealing they may be) but apportions benefits or penalties on the basis of performance. Secondly, due to the extreme poverty and backwardness of these societies, the major objective of economic effort is the satisfaction of basic needs, and very little accumulation takes place. Moreover, many of the countries concerned continue to suffer from war and insurgency, famine, and economic dislocation. Thirdly, the politico-cultural climate is such that large collective or state-controlled units invariably give rise to a huge and stifling bureaucracy which in turn leads to great wastage of resources and poor economic performance. And finally, there are deep-rooted economic and social factors which strongly discourage the diffusion of new and advanced technology in these countries.

In view of these factors, the goal of "socialist transition" should be to build an appropriate environment for a competitive and complementary rural economy based on private, cooperative, state[14] and joint forms of operation. The different sectors should compete with one another on an equal footing, and at the same time complement each other through the exchange of goods, services and support. The advantages of each sector will be lost - and society will be the poorer for it - if preference is given to collectivist tendencies merely on grounds of doctrine. The competitive element is important in a transitional economy, as competition provides the needed stimulus for efficiency and increased effort. One can thus envisage a mixed and multi-sectoral economy not just in the "period of transition" but in "mature socialism" as well.

NOTES

* This chapter was written before the Central Committee's March 1990 announcement of a new mixed economy policy. So far (October 1990), the government has not expressly renounced the long-term aim of a transition to a socialist agriculture, and the peasants' insecurity as to future policies is to be felt everywhere in rural Ethiopia today. A discussion of options and alternatives seems more timely than ever. This chapter sets out to clarify the issues central to such a debate (Editorial footnote).

1 For a full account see Dessalegn 1984.

2 On occasions, government agencies in the rural areas have actually alienated land belonging to peasants or peasant associations for a variety of purposes, including cooperatives and state farms.

3 The maximum plot size a rural household is allowed to hold according to the land reform laws is 10 ha. However, in practice average plots are minuscule, in some regions ranging from 0.25 to 0.5 ha.

4 See also Stefan Brüne in this volume.

5 Service cooperatives are a grouping of four or more peasant associations and their main task is to provide marketing and credit services to peasants.

6 The origin of the words **malba, welba**, and **weland** which were coined when the policy guide-lines were prepared remains a mystery to this day. One is not sure whether the words are taken from local languages, whether they are acronyms, or new coinages.

7 At present there is a good deal of consensus among specialists in both West and East that smallholder agriculture is productive and can play an important role in rural development. In the West, a debate on the question "small vs. large" has been going for many years, but the current view is decidedly in favour of small-scale operations. Indeed, some studies have shown that there is an inverse correlation between farm size and output, i.e. as farm size increases, output per unit of land decreases (Cornia 1985). There is lately a growing criticism of plantation agriculture for showing less competitiveness, and for being an agent of stagnation and under-development (Kemp 1987).

That private peasant production has considerable potential is now recognized by Soviet specialists as well. A document prepared by a team of Soviet advisers attached to the Ethiopian government's central planning agency (GOSPLAN 1985:23-34) criticizes the wastefulness and inefficiency of state agriculture and recommends instead privately-run mechanized farms. The major effort of government, they stress, should be directed towards stimulating production in the private peasant sector. It is anyway interesting that Soviet-bloc planning and agricultural experts do not often recommend collectivization of agriculture to Third World socialist countries (see, e.g., Progress Publishers 1986).

8 In several parts of the country extension agents were instructed by their superiors to give top priority to cooperatives and to pay only minimal attention to private farmers. In 1985 during the early phase of the post-famine recovery in Wollo province there was a great shortage of farm oxen, and the government bought and distributed oxen to cooperatives only, even though private peasant cultivators were worse off than producer cooperatives.

9 Cooperatives could also serve as a testing ground for new ideas designed by concerned agencies, before these ideas are offered to the small cultivator. Cooperatives have advantages over state farms or experimental stations in this regard. New systems can be demonstrated in real conditions with the active participation of cooperators who are not too different from ordinary peasants.

So far marketing cooperatives (or service cooperatives as they are known here) have been well received by many peasants, and positively evaluated by most students of rural Ethiopia. They provide an important service to their members, and it is worthwhile to encourage them to grow and prosper. The present collectivization policy of the government, however, envisages these enterprises eventually to be absorbed by advanced level producer cooperatives.

10 Here and in the following, state-run coffee and tea plantations are not included in the discussion of "state agriculture".

11 The five volume work, **Towards a Strategy of State Farms**, prepared by a team of specialists from MSFD, Institute of Agricultural Research, and Addis Ababa University, is the most comprehensive study of state agriculture done to date. See also MSFD January 1982, September 1982; State Farms Development Authority 1978; Central Planning Supreme Council 1984; and ILO 1982. For mechanized agriculture before the revolution, See Dessalegn 1986.

12 Contract farming was not uncommon in Ethiopia before the revolution, and the Awash Valley was the region where the practice was most successful (Dessalegn 1986). This was a practice in which the big commercial agro-industrial projects (HVA, Tendaho, etc.) agreed to purchase crops from smallholders (or "outgrowers" as they were called then) who worked land leased either from the projects themselves or from large landowners in the area. While no hard evidence is available to substantiate it, the companies concerned were satisfied with the arrangement and were willing to depend on a large number of outgrowers in the area rather than on their own plantations for a good part of their crop requirements.

13 The views of Marx, Engels and Lenin are different in several respects, but all assume the co-existence of small and large-scale agriculture for a considerable period of time. Marx in particular favoured active assistance to peasant agriculture by the "proletarian state". For a summary of their arguments see Dessalegn 1985.

14 So long as societies in the Third World fail to evolve a vigorous and enterprising class capable of involvement in large scale economic ventures, the state sector will continue to be an economic force. Large-scale agricultural projects which involve water diversion schemes, complex construction works, etc. cannot be handled by private investors.

10 The Marketing and Pricing of Agricultural Products in Ethiopia

Befekadu Degefe and Tesfaye Tafesse

Introduction

The marketing and pricing of agricultural products is of central concern to policy makers throughout the world (Hallet 1981, Wadekin 1982, Lele 1976). Broadly speaking, marketing policies fall into two categories: the protective type and the extractive type. The marketing and pricing policy found in most Western industrialized market economies has as its objective to limit inequalities in income distribution between farm and non-farm incomes and to maintain a viable and dependable agriculture, both for economic and non-economic reasons. In these countries, agriculture is nurtured by a number of instruments including supporting prices at a level above world prices, barriers to competing imports, purchase and storage of surpluses and subsidization of exports. The pro-agriculture policies have had the effect of increasing production, mainly due to technological progress, despite attempts to limit over-production through special incentives.

A second policy approach is dominant in the socialist and developing countries. The basic policy objective is to use agriculture to support the development of the non-agricultural sector. The authorities play an interventionist role in the extraction and exporting of agricultural produce. They impose a policy of depressing the prices of agricultural outputs. Essentially this amounts to an anti-peasant policy.

Marketing and Pricing Policies

In Ethiopia, before the revolution, agricultural marketing and pricing policies were governed by the operation of the market (Befekadu, 1978). The government did not intervene directly in the marketing and pricing of agricultural products. In marketing, its role was limited to one of quality control. Its involvement in price and pricing was even more feeble than its attempts at establishing marketing standards and procedures. If ever there was an active marketing and pricing policy, it was a bias towards increasing producer prices, not so much because of sympathy for the producing peasant, but to placate the landed gentry who were the power base of the regime (Thodey 1969, Pausewang 1983).

In post-revolution Ethiopia, agricultural marketing and pricing policies have followed the experience of the socialist countries. To appreciate the logic behind this policy change, it is necessary to go back to the early days of the

1974 revolution and review the factors that contributed to the overthrow of the Imperial regime.

The revolution, in its early days, was an entirely urban phenomenon. Rural Ethiopia was not a major party to the civil disorder that eventually led to the revolution. Among the issues that galvanized the urban population was the increase in the price of basic necessities, particularly food and transportation. It was within this environment that the Dergue came into the picture. The first major decision it took was the rolling back of prices. The lessons learned from this experience seem to have left a lasting imprint on the minds of the policy makers.

While appeasing urban residents by rolling back prices for agricultural goods, the Dergue quickly nationalized land and abolished the landlord-tenant relationship. This was interpreted as a gift of the urban based revolution to the peasantry for which they should be grateful and respond in kind. Under such conditions, it was felt that to allow peasants to sell their output at market determined prices would create a rural/urban rift, by transferring income from urban to rural groups, and might therefore pose a threat to the revolution.

The second reason for controlling prices of agricultural products has to do with the lessons learned from the experience of socialist countries. In all the major socialist countries, industrialization was made possible through the extraction of resources from agriculture. The new government, keen to promote rapid industrialization, was thus particularly receptive to the argument in favour of fixing prices.

Domestic Market and Export Policies

While the main thrust of official policy is known, there are noticeable differences in the administration of marketing and pricing policies between export crops and goods intended for domestic consumption.

Marketing and Pricing of Export Commodities

Ethiopia earns more than 90 per cent of its export based foreign exchange from agricultural products. The main exports include coffee, pulses and oilseeds, fruit, vegetables, live animals, hides and skins (National Bank of Ethiopia 1985/86).

The export business is carried out both by state and private enterprise, and export goods are produced by private and public enterprises. The private sector is the junior partner, and is mostly confined to those goods in which the government has no or limited involvement, obtained from private producers. The share of the state amounts to no less than 90 per cent of merchandise export earnings. State marketing corporations obtain their supplies from private producers, the Agricultural Marketing Corporation (AMC), state farms, and settler farms. The latter two are required to sell all their produce to the respective export corporations and/or the AMC. Some of the export corporations enjoy a monopolistic or quasi-monopolistic marketing position while others face strong domestic competition.

Hides and Skins

The marketing and pricing of hides and skins has undergone a rapid change over a short period of time. Until 1984, the hides and skins market operated in a condition of intense competition between private exporters and parastatals such as the Leather and Shoe Corporation (LSC) and the Hides and Skins Marketing Corporation (HSMC). Since prices were influenced by the international market, the LSC was unable to compete effectively with private exporters.

In 1984 the government sought to alleviate this problem by assigning the responsibility of exporting raw hides and skins to HSMC, and revoked the export licences of private traders. However, the government's attempt to shore up these parastatals failed, and the HSMC was dissolved in 1989. The export of raw hides and skins was banned as a rule, and the LSC was given the monopoly of purchasing domestic hides and skins, processing them and supplying both the domestic and external markets.

Along with this institutional rearrangement, the domestic pricing and marketing mechanisms were also revised. Prices began to be institutionally determined by a committee composed of members from the ministries of agriculture, industry and foreign trade on the basis of international prices.

Oilseeds and Pulses

There are three independent participants in the marketing and pricing of oilseeds and pulses; private traders, and the two governmental enterprises, the Agricultural Marketing Corporation (AMC) and the Ethiopian Oilseeds and Pulses Export Corporation (EOPEC). While the position of the first two is unambiguous, that of EOPEC is more contentious.

Table 1
The pricing of Oilseeds (birr per quintal), 1987

	Purchase Price	AMC's Selling Price	EOPEC's cost to Assab	Export Price F.O.B.
Sesame	80	115	175.84	109.00
Niger seed	50	68	122.27	145.00
Rapeseed	46	64	117.03	61.00
Linseed	46	64	115.82	37.00

Source: EOPEC

The AMC was granted the right to purchase oilseeds and pulses from producers (private, producer cooperatives, service cooperatives, and state farms) and from private merchants for sale in the domestic economy. EOPEC, on the other hand, was established by the government for the sole purpose of exporting oilseeds and pulses. Its exports were acquired directly from producers and the AMC.

A problem soon arose between EOPEC and AMC. EOPEC's purchasing arm did not reach as many producers in the major producing areas as the AMC. EOPEC lacked the purchasing infrastructure to penetrate the market, and the legal power to force merchants to hand over part of their purchase to it. Furthermore, EOPEC did not have the financial capacity to compete against the two stronger actors: private traders and the AMC. On top of these structural inadequacies, EOPEC has to compete in the international market and this has only added to its unviable financial situation. The government has been forced to subsidize the operation of EOPEC. Clearly then the creation of a marketing institute such as EOPEC is uneconomical (Ministry of Foreign Trade 1987).

Coffee

Coffee is the most important export crop, accounting for more than 60 per cent of the foreign exchange earnings of the country. Due to its critical role, the government has taken an intense interest in the marketing and pricing of coffee. The existing marketing and pricing of coffee has retained an auction nomenclature but this has no functional bearing.[2] Both private and public exporters engage in the business of exporting coffee. However, private trade accounts for less than 10 per cent of the total export and exists only to the extent that the Coffee Marketing Corporation (CMC) allows it to operate. The latter is responsible for 91 per cent of total exports and for all domestically consumed coffee in the non-coffee producing regions.

Public exporters operate on the basis of centrally assigned quotas; private exporters are not allowed to compete with them until this quota requirement is met. More than 98 per cent of the coffee comes from private farms operating under an elaborate marketing arrangement. At its base are the producing farmers and the assemblers, people licensed to purchase coffee from the small producers and sell their purchases within 24 hours to collectors. They are required to dispose of their purchases by sales to CMC, which operates 56 purchasing posts spread through the main coffee producing regions.

Coffee is priced FOB Assab and cost adjustments are then made in Addis Ababa. In turn the Addis Ababa price becomes the benchmark for producer prices. The benefit which accrues to the coffee producers depends on the international price, which is reasonably stable due to the role of the International Coffee Organization (ICO). Nevertheless, the producers' share has declined since the revolution due to the very high tax imposed on coffee. In addition, producers pay additional tax in the form of income tax and land use fees.

Marketing of Agricultural Products Intended for Domestic Consumption.

A large number of agricultural products are traded to satisfy domestic needs, rather than exported. Private producers account on average for 95 per cent of products for domestic consumption. The balance comes from state farms (3-4 per cent), producer cooperatives and resettlements (1-2 per cent). The marketing arrangements correspond to those of export products. Some products are traded entirely by the private sector (e.g.

meat), in others both private and public enterprises are involved (e.g. cereals, pulses, oilseeds), and yet others are under a public sector monopoly (e.g. coffee). The Agricultural Marketing Corporation dominates where it operates.

Domestically consumed coffee is distributed in the non-coffee producing regions by the Domestic Coffee Marketing Enterprise (DCME), a subsidiary of the CMC. Coffee below standard export quality is purchased by the DCME which in turn sells it to retailing enterprises such as the Urban Dwellers Association shops and supermarkets at prices fixed by the state. Strict control on the flow of coffee from the producing to the consuming regions and inadequate quantity released through DCME have pushed open market prices to as high as twice the official price (National Bank of Ethiopia 1985/86b).

For products which the private sector dominates, there exists a free market.

Table 2
Share of Coffee Producers in the Value of Coffee Export

Year	Producer Price (birr/ton)	FOBExport value (birr/ton)	Producers' Share %
1960-65	1193	1934	62
1966-70	1360	2077	66
1971-74	1486	2393	62
1975-76	2107	3260	56
1976-77	3567	11001	32
1977-78	5931	17445	34
1978-79	4871	15222	32
1980-81	4335	13136	33
1981-82	4681	13375	35

SOURCE: 1961-77, Teshome Mulat, Ethiopian Journal of Development Research, Vol. 3, No.1 (April 1979); 1978-82 calculated from data obtained from CMC.

Attempts at price stability are made through the urban dwellers association price control policy. But since they do not extend to producer prices, these efforts are of little consequence. Dairy products are distributed by the Dairy Development Agency (DDA) which purchases milk from private producers through its extensive purchasing network and distributes it to public enterprises and private retailers. Fruit and vegetables from state farms are distributed, mainly wholesale, by ETFRUIT.

The development of marketing and pricing policies over the last decade can be divided into three phases:

Phase 1: 1974-79
During this phase, the government attempted to stabilize prices through legislative price control. Beginning in mid- 1974, the government came up

with a series of fixed prices, which were changed very often since their effect proved to be detrimental both to the producers and consumers. Between 1974 and 1979 seven revisions were made, but all of them proved unsatisfactory (Alemayehu Lirenso 1987, Committee of Experts 1987). The major cause for the instability of fixed prices was that they were never established at a level attractive to producers and traders. As a result, supply fell way below demand.

Phase 2: 1979-87

In 1979, the government abandoned its price control approach and sought to stabilize prices indirectly by supplying urban consumers at the official price. The free marketing system under which the AMC had competed with private traders was changed to a quota system. State farms were directed to pass their output to AMC. Private producers were to sell at government established ceiling prices to AMC until they fulfilled their quota and thereafter were free to sell to private traders, who were in turn required to sell part of their purchase to AMC as a condition for receiving permits to transport cereals, pulses and oilseeds from one region to another.

In 1983, revisions were made with respect to quota assignments. Private merchants were now restricted to 50 per cent of total purchases. Quotas for producers were changed from a flat quota assignment (for example 100 quintals of teff per peasant association) to one that ostensibly took production into account. An annual purchase plan was established at the centre and given to AMC as its annual purchase quota.

Quota assignments to the different regions were based on past records of production and sales. A Grain Purchase Task Force (GPTF) in each region assigned the quota at each level of administrative hierarchy. To ensure compliance by each peasant, punitive measures were built into the quota administration. Peasants who failed to fulfil their quota were not allowed to use the service cooperative shops to buy non-agricultural commodities. As a final sanction, they could be deprived of the right to use land. There is anecdotal evidence that in some cases at least, peasants who failed to fulfil their quota obligations from their own produce were forced to purchase the shortfall from other producers or on the market.

Phase 3: 1987 to the Present

In 1987, the government set up a committee of experts to look into the pricing and marketing arrangements which had yielded unsatisfactory results. In addition to their inadequate performance on the domestic market, existing operational arrangements faced strong external pressure mainly from the multilateral institutions such as the IMF, the World Bank, the African Development Bank and the International Fund for Agricultural Development. The committee of experts found that the quota system imposed undue burdens and hardship on the peasantry, since purchase decisions made at higher hierarchical levels often failed to take local conditions into account.

Officially established prices were found to be unremunerative. Often they fell below the cost of production or very close to it. This led at best to a stagnation of output. The committee then made the following recommendations:

(a) Private traders should be permitted to purchase in the surplus regions and export to deficiency areas.

(b) A uniform 50 per cent of quota should apply to all traders.

(c) More rational quota allocations should take local production conditions into consideration.

(d) AMC should aim at a drastic reduction of its overhead costs by taking administrative and organizational measures.

(e) With respect to prices, the committee proposed three alternatives, based on production costs, the difference stemming from labour costs calculated at 2.29, 1.92, and 1.50 birr respectively per working day.

In December, the government increased the price of all crops under review by 2 to 3 birr per quintal. The new official prices were on average based on the second and third cost alternatives.

The Peasant Viewpoint

The current marketing and pricing policy has grown unpopular and unproductive. Our study in two service cooperatives in Northern Shoa (Fasil Amba and Armania in Mafud Woreda) confirms this conclusion.

Pricing and Marketing
The residents we talked to told us that they are obliged to dispose of their produce in the immediate post-harvest period to fulfil various obligations to the state, such as income tax and land use fees, special contributions (as for famine victims or the war), and many informal and unaccounted contributions requested by the peasant associations, service cooperatives and *awraja* offices. Only after all these obligations have been met can the residents consider the purchase of necessities, seed reserves and the surplus they can keep for their own consumption.

Quota Delivery
Over and above these contributions, peasants are obliged to deliver a specified amount of grain as their quota to the Agricultural Marketing Corporation via their respective service cooperatives before being allowed to sell their produce in the open market. According to the Council of Ministers' policy statement, the quota of an individual resident is determined by considering farm size, total output, seed and home consumption requirements. However, our analysis indicates no significant relationship between any of these variables. The policy statement is not really taken into account when it comes to quota size determination at the local level.

The peasants we interviewed consider the AMC grain price to be exploitative. To a peasant, a "fair price" is the one he is offered in the open market. As an example, the AMC prices for a kilogram of horse beans, millet, barley and teff in 1989 were 0.25, 0.20, 0.25 and 0.47 birr respectively, while open market prices for the same items at Debre Sina market in April were 0.80, 0.65, 0.50 and 0.90 birr.

Open Market Sales

Ethiopian peasants are also exposed to unfair terms of trade. While they are forced to sell at fixed prices, non-agricultural products get more expensive from year to year. Peasants sell and deliver their produce at cheap prices and in turn buy non-agricultural products at exorbitantly high and inflated prices. Since tax collectors frequently oblige the residents to pay their taxes between January and early February, that is in the immediate post-harvest period, peasants are forced to dispose of their products at a time when grain prices and returns are at their lowest. It is only when the residents have a surplus above quota and subsistence requirements that they may be able to buy industrial and urban goods.

Even the service cooperatives which are supposed to deliver basic industrial goods to the peasants after obtaining them from the Ethiopian Domestic Distribution Centre (EDDC) are in most cases empty shelved, offering little or nothing of the basics to the population.

Seed and Consumption Requirements

The 26 residents in the study area give priority to seed reserves over consumption. Seventy per cent of the residents regularly keep an average of 80 kg of grain as seed reserve, the remaining 30 per cent produce far too little to think of reserves. When it comes to home consumption, only ten of the residents in the study area were able to tell us that they keep some amount of grain for themselves (an average of 232 kg). The remainder said that they ran out of it so fast that they were forced to buy grain from the market by selling their livestock and other assets.

ConsequencesPricing Policies

Over the past fifteen years, the performance of the agricultural sector has been very disappointing. Food production has consistently lagged behind population growth due to a host of environmental and policy factors. In spite of all these, the bulk of what is produced by peasants is, in one way or another, drained out to fulfil the imposed quota and other state and local obligations. Over and above this, the peasant is exposed to "unequal terms of trade" whereby he is forced to buy the much needed items from the uncontrolled urban markets at prices that are inflated.

In marketing, the major problem facing agricultural products stems from the quasi-monopoly position of the AMC. This obviously poses a number of problems. Not the least is the bureaucratic decision making process, which renders the task of obtaining permits Herculean and open to abuse because of its arbitrariness. This problem would be more tolerable were the AMC at least able to satisfy the needs of consumers in the different parts of the country.

Concluding Remarks

In Ethiopia, a policy of protecting agriculture, in the way that Western market economies do, is impossible. There is just no state income from other sectors which the state could use to subsidize agricultural prices. Extraction from agriculture is thus necessary to some degree. Introduction of a free market economy would not change this basic necessity.

But at present, the expressed goal of the government, that surplus from agriculture should finance industrialization, is far from being achieved. Pricing and marketing policies contribute to this failure, because they curtail production rather than stimulating it.

Objectively, if extraction is enforced up to a point where prices are below production costs, producers have no choice but to withdraw as much as they can. Poor peasants cannot afford to lose out on their sales. Compulsion through obligatory quota is certainly discouraging their interest in production. Higher producer prices may give the state less income per unit, but more total income because of production growth.

Subjectively, as long as there are large differences between official prices and free market prices, peasants will feel forced deliveries at low prices as unjust. Current free prices may be inflated to some degree because of artificial scarcity. Peasants could not expect to get such prices for all their produce if quotas were abolished and a free market established.[*]

Apart from the dual prices creating hopes which may be unrealistic, peasants calculate not in money, but in terms of what money can buy. A good market supply of consumer goods at prices which the peasant can afford could be the best stimulus to production. The consciousness that with good work he can buy goods worth an effort is more important than the absolute price level. A peasant, irrespective of where he lives, also needs access to those food items he cannot produce himself, in exchange for his own crops.

Marketing and price policies are needed which:
(a) take care of the productive capacity of peasants,
(b) offer a reasonable reward for work, and incentives for more effort,
(c) supply food where it is needed at reasonable prices.

Ethiopia badly needs a general agricultural policy which should consider a host of other factors including a rational marketing and pricing policy in order to revive and regenerate the agricultural sector. The overall policy should incorporate rationality in extraction based on contribution capacity, in addition to market liberalization and price incentives to peasants.

NOTES

[*] In March 1990, the government abolished the fixed price and quota system, turning the AMC into a state marketing board competing with private traders on the open market. Initially, open market grain prices fell, and then settled at a level between the former private trader price and the old AMC price. How the state will use the AMC, the biggest single operator on the

market, and which new pricing instruments will be applied remains to be seen. So far (October 1990), no other marketing policies have been established. (Editorial footnote)

1 On this and the broader issue of livestock products, see Australian Agricultural Consulting and Management Company, **Livestock Marketing Projects**, Report submitted to the Ministry of Agriculture, in two volumes.

2 This part of the paper is based on information obtained from Coffee Marketing Corporation.

11 Resettlement: Policy and Practice

Alula Pankhurst

Historical Background[1]

Prior to the Ethiopian revolution, resettlement was carried out on a small scale, as a result of individual initiatives by local governors and aid agencies with a variety of motives and objectives. No centrally coordinated planning was involved, and individual schemes were set up and implemented on an ad hoc basis. A few projects were also started by the Ministry of National Community Development. With the creation of the Ministry of Land Reform and Administration in 1966, and the drawing up of the Third Five-Year Plan (1968-73), an interest developed in resettlement planning, as a means of rectifying population imbalances and increasing productivity. However, proposals by several consultants were rejected because they were seen as too costly. Moreover, given the interests of the landed gentry, the will to address land issues was lacking in practice. By the time of the revolution, a mere 7,000 household units had been established in 20 settlement sites at a cost of US $ 8 million. This represented less than 0.2 per cent of rural households, 5 per cent of which resettled spontaneously during the same period.

During the first decade following the revolution two developments facilitated a dramatic increase in resettlement. Firstly, the Land Reform Proclamation nationalizing all land in 1975 paved the way for state intervention in land re-allocation. Secondly, the new government created various agencies with responsibilities for resettlement. The RRC was set up in 1974 in response to the Imperial Government's neglect of the famine. However, little organized resettlement planning occurred until the establishment of the Settlement Authority in 1976. This body took over existing schemes run by other agencies, and proposed settling 20,000 settlers annually. Three years later a new RRC was set up merging the former RRC, the Settlement Authority and the Awash Valley Authority.

Resettlement was seen as a means of addressing a range of issues. From an ecological perspective it was seen as a way to redress population imbalances and reduce population pressure in the highlands; from an economic standpoint it was believed that resettlement could help to increase productivity and make use of supposedly under-utilized fertile lands; and from a social point of view resettlement was seen as a way of providing land to those without it, to settle pastoralists, and remove unwanted urban unemployed.

By the end of the first post-revolutionary decade, some 46,000 households, comprising 150,000 people had been resettled on 88 sites in 11 regions.[2] This represented 0.6 per cent of rural households. The resettlement was criticized for its slow pace, high costs and low productivity (Eshetu and Teshome 1988, Colaris 1985, Dessalegn 1989). On all counts results fell short of the objectives. The numbers resettled were too insignificant to affect population redistribution, the economic results were poor in terms of production, yields, and cost. On the eve of the famine, settlements had not become self-sufficient and still required food aid.[3] Moreover, the use of mechanization proved unsustainable. Socially, the results were disastrous. The settlement schemes paid no regard to the local population; the attempt to settle urban unemployed and pastoralists on agricultural schemes, often against their will, led to massive desertions, and the policy of settling men without their families proved unpopular and was abandoned by the RRC.[4]

The Emergency Phase (1984-89)

During this period resettlement was not the responsibility of any single government body and yet, in less than two years[5], at least four times as many settlers were moved as in the previous decade. At a time when resources were most stretched as the country was confronted with the second famine to afflict Ethiopia within a decade, the government embarked on a massive emergency plan to resettle one and a half million people in two years. While the implementation of resettlement policy prior to the revolution was criticized for being too slow, the emergency phase was characterized by undue haste, which inevitably resulted in poor planning, all kinds of mistakes and unnecessary excesses.[6]

The Rationale

From a minor aspect of relief and development activities, resettlement was thus turned into a matter of national salvation referred to in the Constitution.[7] In the face of the crisis, resettlement was seen as a way of moving beyond immediate relief and addressing the longer-term root causes of the famine. Resettlement was portrayed as a purposive and hopeful bright spot at a time of gloomy forecasts of widespread famine and economic bankruptcy. Most importantly resettlement came to be seen as a nationalist option for development, by helping to escape humiliating dependence on external aid. In the words of the President introducing the Action Programme drawn up to address the crisis, resettlement was a way "to resolve the riddle of how it is that while we have we lack and when we could be lending we are beggars". The boycott organized by Western nations therefore simply served to strengthen the government's resolve to proceed with the plans at any cost.

The fresh start which resettlement required was perceived as an opportunity to introduce social and economic change in three major respects. Firstly, an essential component of the plans was to establish settlement villages linked in complexes. Resettlement was thus in some senses the precursor to the massive villagization which altered the physical appearance of most of the Ethiopian countryside between 1986 and 1989. Secondly, resettlement was

RESETTLEMENT - ETHIOPIA

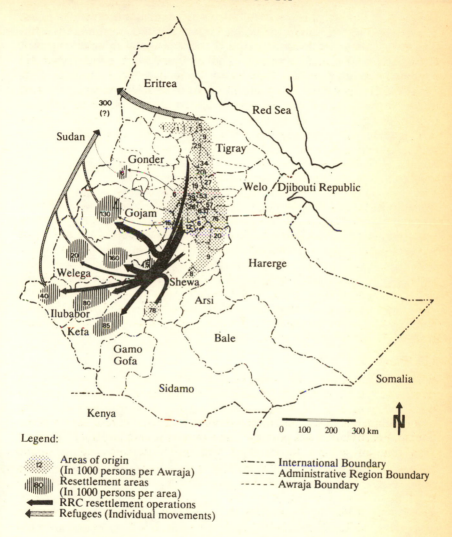

Legend:

- Areas of origin
  (In 1000 persons per Awraja)
- Resettlement areas
  (In 1000 persons per area)
- RRC resettlement operations
- Refugees (Individual movements)

- ---·--- International Boundary
- ---·-·--- Administrative Region Boundary
- ------ Awraja Boundary

Source: Stefan Brüne and Volker Matthies (eds), *Krisenregion Horn von Afrika*, Hamburg, (1990:99)

© Hans Hurni

seen as offering a chance to introduce settlers to improved forms of technology and thus liberate peasants from "backward" agricultural practices. Thirdly, and despite the experience of former settlements, more than half the settlements were planned as producers' cooperatives, with minimal private holdings of 0.1 ha.[8] Settlements were thus expected to cut out the first stage of collectivization and move directly to the second welba stage (ONCCP 1984b: 23-31). Resettlement became thus part of a package of increased state control over the peasantry, involving state farms, pricing restrictions and villagization.

Resettlement was not merely seen as one way of solving the crisis in the north. It was perceived as a way of putting to greater use areas which were assumed to be fertile and were presumed to be under-utilized, both of which assumptions were accepted without question or study. In fact in many cases neither assumption was well founded. Some resettlement areas (such as Gurra Farda in Kefa Region) and several villages within settlement complexes had to be abandoned after considerable labour and capital inputs, owing to poor soils, water shortages and water-logging. In the lowlands, settlements displaced minority groups practicing ecologically sustainable modes of subsistence. (Dessalegn 1988, 1989: 84-94). Faced with settlements, about which they had never been consulted and could seek no redress, these marginalized groups seem to have in the main opted for a strategy of withdrawal. In the highlands, where population density was greater, antagonisms and clashes with the local population occurred. Disputes have been reported over land use and demarcation, and some conflicts have arisen over resources, notably over coffee and bee-hives. On the other hand, local people in some areas have derived some benefits from being able to buy aid items, such as blankets, clothing and utensils at cheap prices from settlers, and sell them livestock and cash crops, such as the stimulant chat. The settlers' presence has also brought about some development of services and expansion of markets.

Resettlement Planning

Resettlement was the largest and most complex operation in the history of the state, requiring the coordination of almost a dozen government ministries and authorities. An action programme to resolve the crisis resulting from the famine was formulated by the Political Bureau of the Central Committee of the WPE. The resettlement component accounted for 123 million birr, or a quarter of the planned expenditure on emergency development (ONCCP 1984b: 23-31).[9] A committee comprising high-level officials selected settlement sites on helicopter tours often led by the Head of State. The whole venture was organized with great haste on a campaign-basis by the newly formed Workers' Party of Ethiopia which took over direction of the programme, and sent out cadres to organize the settlements, much in the same way that a decade earlier students were sent to the rural areas to spread the messages of the nascent revolution.

Conventional and Integrated Schemes

The level of government intervention in resettlement schemes has been the subject of several classifications, all of which hinge on the extent of governmental or non-governmental inputs and personnel.[10] In the emergency phase, the distinction is between so-called "conventional" and "integrated" schemes.[11] Most settlements established during the present phase fall into one of these two types.[12] Conventional settlements represent 53 per cent of the total, and are located mainly in the lowlands of Gojjam, Wellega and Illubabor. Integrated settlements represent 44 per cent, and are mainly in the highlands of Illubabor, Wellega and Kefa. There is also a third type of settlement, those which are "integrated within already existing settlement sites", and which account for the remaining 3 per cent, some 16,000 people. Conventional settlements involve mechanized agriculture and the linking of settlements into complexes located mainly in the sparsely-populated western lowlands, requiring land clearance and disease and pest control. These conventional settlements are in the process of becoming producers' cooperatives. Integrated settlements were more scattered, mainly in the western highlands;[13] they are subject to minimal directives, and tend to show a preponderance of private agriculture.

Three main differences between these two types of resettlement may be distinguished: scale, concentration, and inputs. In theory, conventional settlements are made up of villages of 500 households, while integrated settlements vary in size, with an average of about 50 households. Conventional settlements are organized in complexes which comprise between 10,000 and 20,000 households, normally within a radius of 100 kilometres. The concentration justifies expenditure on mechanized agriculture and facilities such as schools, clinics, mills, cooperative shops, and campaigners living on site. Integrated settlements, in contrast, are relatively inaccessible and are often quite far apart.

Conventional and integrated settlements received the same food ration in the initial stages of resettlement, but the former also sometimes obtained salt, pepper and a greater variety of food more regularly. In the conventional settlements, there are resident campaigners such as WPE cadres, health workers, agriculturalists, literacy campaigners and RRC food distributors, while the integrated settlements have no on-site extension staff. Instead, they receive visits from extension staff each of whom supervises several sites. Both types of settlement are provided by the RRC with agricultural hand-tools and by the MoA with seeds, but conventional settlements receive tractor services, while integrated settlements are provided with oxen[14] (Dessalegn 1989: 61-62). Both types have grain stores and buildings for literacy and health care, but conventional settlements have been provided by the government with better health and educational facilities since several sites may share facilities. Two or more conventional sites are linked and share a cooperative store and a grinding mill. Feeder roads are built, as well as offices for the peasants', women's and youth associations, craft workshops, model houses and cultural centres. In the case of integrated settlements, on the other hand, it was the local PA who were responsible for preparing provisional housing before the settlers arrived, and for ploughing land for them in the first year. In many cases the PAs did much more, providing food, cooking and household utensils and water carriers, providing seed and loaning oxen for ploughing and treading in the teff after sowing. In some places, close links developed between the local PA leaders and the settler executive committee.

The Implementation of the Plan

The haste with which the resettlement was carried out left little room for careful planning. There was no attempt to assess detailed resettlement needs or numbers wishing to be relocated on a regional basis, nor to estimate the capacity of reception areas to accommodate settlers. The only clear patterns that emerge are a tendency to move settlers from more easily accessible areas, rather than from areas where geography and warfare impeded recruitment, and a tendency to relocate settlers in less densely populated areas. No consideration was given to settlers' preferences, nor was any attempt made to relocate settlers from one area together. Settlers were taken from famine shelters as well as from peasant associations. The transit shelters became overcrowded, and there was no consistency in planning the journey. Some settlers spent weeks in shelters in the north, while others were not even given the time to dispose of assets and say farewell to relatives. Coordination between the "sending areas" and the receiving areas was almost non-existent. Some settlers made the journey in a matter of three or four days, while others had to wait for a month or more in transit shelters, where poor sanitation resulted in the spread of epidemics and unnecessary mortality.[15]

A number of changes occurred in the implementation of the plan. Firstly, the size of the operation was scaled down. Some 200,000 households were resettled instead of the planned 500,000. Moreover, the household size, instead of the estimated five members, consisted of an average of three, so that some 600,000 people representing 1.6 per cent of the country's rural population were resettled instead of the anticipated 1.5 million. Secondly, the plan concentrated on Wello, Tigray and Gonder.[16] Target figures for Shewa were not provided and certainly no plans existed to settle people from southern Shewa.[17] In fact after Wello, Shewa became the largest source area for settlers. Thirdly, the resettlement was halted earlier than planned in January 1986, probably not, as some commentators have assumed, because of external pressure, but for internal reasons. With the onset of the rains in the second half of 1985, willingness to resettle decreased among peasants who regained hopes of being able to subsist on their land. As the crisis subsided, the government also became less preoccupied with famine, and the strains on the economy caused by the disproportionate expenditures on resettlement became hard to justify. Resettlement was resumed when a new crisis seemed likely in late 1987. However, as the drought proved less severe than anticipated, and few peasants were willing to leave, the plans were scaled down.

The implementation of the resettlement programme was criticized on the grounds that it involved coercion, and resulted in excessive mortality and family separation. The controversy exploded in the international media as the French agency, *Médecins sans Frontières*, denounced the programme as a mass-deportation campaign. The government responded first with silence and blanket denials, and then by expelling the agency. These events obscured any attempt to understand the reasons for the use of force, which occurred at three levels. Firstly, at the regional level resettlement was sometimes used to further local policies other than the settling of famine-victims. These included moving people off slopes designated for reforestation, "disposing" of urban unemployed who were suspected of being trouble-makers, and sedentarizing pastoralists. Secondly, at the local level during the later phase of the programme when the rains had arrived and willingness to move had decreased, regional targets were turned into quotas. Thirdly, at the peasant association level, resettlement was used against people who were unable to pay taxes, and to "solve" disputes arising from land re-allocations. A few cases of discrimination and corruption were also reported.

Nonetheless, most of the resettlement was voluntary. In fact, the settler population was not composed merely of famine-victims. Large numbers of young people decided to leave their own areas, like migrants the world over, out of a combination of "push factors" in their homeland and "pull factors" in the resettlement areas. Among the former were land shortages, disputes with family and the lack of opportunities to become self-sufficient producers; among the latter were aspirations to become independent, to see the world, and also to become soldiers. Moreover, government propaganda suggested that the famine might continue and that aid would be targeted only to the weak and elderly. A glorified vision of fertile plentiful lands awaiting potential migrants was painted. Settlers were told that the land would be cultivated for them by tractors, that the houses would be built, and that they would be provided with food, clothing and equipment. Social pressures also affected the decisions of most settlers. Many who could have relied on relatives chose not to in order to remain independent, stating: "We won't beg from their hands". Some showed signs of great altruism. As one young man who left his father and sister succinctly explained: "What I eat could be for my sister". Others left for the sake of a relative, as expressed in the oft-heard saying: "Let the kite that eats him eat me". Large numbers resettled in response to peer and community pressure; as one man put it: "The torrent drove us". Others responded to the fear of a worsening situation; one man who still had reserves of food explained: "I had sold my oxen and heard that those who had done so should resettle; when you say 'wush' to a donkey all the others' ears stand up".

Official selection criteria included willingness, ability to partake in agricultural work, physical fitness and age limits for household heads. The resettlement of entire households was also a stated objective. These criteria were not always adhered to, presented dilemmas, and were sometimes mutually contradictory. The resettlement of urban unemployed and pastoralists was as unpopular and unsuccessful as earlier attempts. Many who were not fit moved all the same, often out of a fear of being separated from family. Some young people below the age limit still wanted to resettle.

The most problematic guide-line, however, was the recommendation that families be settled as units. In practice, settlers were separated from close family members due to a variety of factors, including the strategic choices of individual settlers themselves, the chaos and disruptions of the famine, and poorly designed and implemented government policies, all of which partly explain the small resettlement household size. Some decided to split their family, so that those who remained had a better chance of surviving without selling all their assets, notably plough oxen. The remaining family members could thus also retain their land holdings. Some of those who had sons with jobs or daughters married elsewhere where conditions were not so dire decided to remain behind. In many cases household members did not wish to pursue the same options; in particular the elderly often preferred to remain and be buried in their homeland. The decision to leave often involved painful choices and inevitable separations. Peoples' allegiances to parents and spouses were put to the test. Sometimes a spouse would refuse to go, deciding to remain to look after an elderly parent, or a wife would leave her parents to go with her husband, while others would leave their husbands to go with their parents. As one woman commented: "You can always find another husband, you can't find another father". Other settlers were separated from close kin when they pursued different famine survival strategies; men would often seek wage-labour while women sought aid. When assistance could not be obtained many had no option but to join the resettlement, and left before their spouses returned. Others were separated in the confusion of the shelters and transit camps, and during the journey. Some left sick relatives so as not to be separated from the rest of their departing community. Daughters who had married in a neighbouring peasant associations to their parents' found themselves moved to completely different regions.

Assessments

Paradoxically, settlers have been a favoured section of Ethiopian society, while at the same time they have been treated as second-class citizens. State intervention has had two aspects, care and control. On the one hand settlements have received a greater concentration of assistance than any other group. Settlers have been over-privileged in a number of ways. Large amounts of the country's resources, in terms of land, labour and capital, were put at the disposal of settlements. The number of agricultural and health extension workers in resettlement areas is far in excess of any other sector. Settlers have received free tractor services and medical facilities. They have also been exempt from taxes. Clearly such a situation is unsustainable and will require policy changes.

On the other hand settlers have been subject to greater restrictions than other groups in society. Firstly, collectivization has been forced upon them, while other cooperatives have been formed voluntarily as a matter of policy. Settlers' labour time is strictly controlled according to the points system of reward devised for producers' cooperatives. The system is poorly understood by settlers, cumbersome and bureaucratic to administer, and does not provide people with incentives. The settlers' freedom to engage in sales of their crops is also curtailed by market days sometimes being defined as work days. In practice the paucity of local markets and restrictions on private traders resulted in a situation where settlers until recently were selling their grain for half the already low prices set by the Agricultural Marketing Corporation.

Secondly, settlers do not have the same religious freedom guaranteed other Ethiopians.[18] A restriction on the building of places of worship was imposed on conventional settlement sites (Council of Ministers 1988a: 76, 80; MoA 1989: 3), and Sundays were often defined as work days. Traditional religious practices such as prayer gatherings and forms of healing practices were also discouraged by the WPE cadres.

Thirdly, settlers do not have the right to travel (Council of Ministers 1988a: 64, 80; 1988b: 173), even though it is guaranteed to every Ethiopian in the Constitution.[19] Only those in positions of leadership can obtain passes to travel. This misguided policy, which aimed at restricting defections, was not only ineffectual but also counter-productive. It gave resettlement a bad image, and has not deterred most of those who wish to leave from doing so, using either old or forged documents or taking a chance in the hope that they will not be stopped. Most of those who leave manage to get through;[20] those who are stopped are returned to their villages where they face up to a fortnight of hard labour or a fine. Many of those who leave do not in fact return to their homeland, and a few of those who do, return to the settlements. This is partly because of restrictions on returners in their homelands: having lost their land, they can only become dependent on relatives or seek wage-labour (Council of Ministers 1988a: 81). Other factors are continuing unfavourable climatic conditions and warfare. Many of those who leave therefore look for wage labour in the west. Women work in bars and in rich peoples' houses; a few marry locals. Men work on seasonal labour during peak agricultural periods, notably the coffee-picking season. Some also find work as share croppers in areas where there is a labour shortage.

The costs of the resettlement programme will never be fully known. Some aspects such as the human suffering involved cannot be computed, and most of the economic costs remains hidden since land was appropriated by the state and labour was mobilized in a series of campaigns, at all levels of society from local peasant associations to university staff and students.[21] Capital was diverted from other sources: busses from the transport system, food from relief, agricultural machinery, oxen and seed from Ministry of Agriculture allocations, household equipment, clothing and medicines from national and international donations, as well as from RRC and Ministry of Health budgets. The full extent of yet other costs, such as environmental damage, will only be felt in the long term.[22] Nonetheless some attempts at estimating the costs have been made. A report concentrating on agricultural expenditures submitted to the Council of Ministers estimates government expenditure at 564.5 million birr from 1985-88 (Council of Ministers 1988b: 125). An estimate produced by the Central Planning office suggests a figure of 471 million birr (ONCCP 1988a: 114). Actual government expenditure was probably at least 500 million birr.[23] Foreign assistance may account for as much again, in spite of the boycott by most Western countries, following the lead of the USA. The largest bilateral contribution was the Italian Tana-beles project. Government assistance also came from the Soviet Union, Canada and the German Democratic Republic. In addition a number of NGOs, religious organizations and international organizations have also assisted resettlement projects, as part of their country-wide programmes. The total cost may therefore be in excess of half a billion US dollars.[24]

In agricultural terms the results of the settlement schemes show that although land under cultivation, production and yields have increased over the past four years, the results are poor compared to what the settlers used to produce (Dessalegn 1989: 5), and to what can be expected with appropriate agricultural practices. Moreover, a number of problems have resulted from the way the settlements were organized. The policy of mechanization presents serious difficulties in working out sustainable forms of production. So far the costs have been hidden and borne by the state, but now that resettlement has fallen out of the limelight, the commitment to fund unsustainable projects has waned. Currently, attempts are being made to revise the system. Inputs of seed, fertilizer and pesticides by the MoA are gradually being phased out.[25] The settlers will have to pay for tractor services from 1992. However, given the virtual monoculture of maize and sorghum, and the low prices set for the cereal crops produced, it is difficult to see how a self-sustaining system can be established. Moreover, the experience of earlier mechanized settlements gives grounds for pessimism. After more than a decade, most have not achieved full self-reliance, and cannot buy spare parts or replace tractors.

Two options can be pursued: moving towards producing more cash crops or converting to oxen as a means of traction. The former course of action was indicated by Chairman Mengistu in his report to the Sixth Plenum of the WPE Central Committee in 1987, and began to be put into practice in some settlements, such as Gambella and Metemma, where production of cotton, sesame and groundnuts has increased. However, the processing of such crops, the transport requirements, and the dependence on market prices will increase the settlers' dependence, and continue the resented process of transforming peasants into wage-labourers. Moreover, mechanization is perceived by the settlers as an alien form of technology of which the settlers are not the masters. Training settlers in tractor driving and maintenance may be one way of addressing this problem. The other option, namely moving towards greater reliance on oxen, has been experimented with in two settlements, Jarso and Qet'o. However, the trypanosomiasis threat rules out this option in lowland areas, and requires careful monitoring and costly vaccinations in altitudinally borderline areas.

Policy Changes

There are two major policy changes that have had a dramatic effect on the settlements over the past few years, and a third planned change could have important consequences for existing settlements and for the future of resettlement in Ethiopia.

A significant development from the point of view of settler households was the policy of liberalizing trade. In 1987 grain prices were half of those set by the Agricultural Marketing Board or less, and settlements were grateful for the tardy intervention of the AMC which guaranteed them set prices. In 1988, the involvement of private traders led to a dramatic increase in prices and consequently settlements became reluctant to sell to the AMC. Settlers converted the money they obtained from higher grain prices into investments in small-stock, which has resulted in a visible increase in prosperity within a period of a year.

Secondly, a move away from collectivization has occurred, coinciding with the decrease of WPE involvement in resettlement and the corresponding increase in the MoA's role. Initially settlers had only 0.1 ha of private land. Gradually, changes were introduced. Settlers were given small additional plots on the edges of the communal fields, the rationale being that they could guard the collective harvest while working these plots. In 1987 an increase in private plots was introduced on an experimental basis in Gambella settlement. In 1988 the Ministry of Agriculture settlement division decided as a matter of policy to extend this experiment and introduce increases in private holdings in all settlement areas. Half a hectare of private land per household was allocated from collective fields for private use, providing that not more than half the settlement's land holdings were redistributed. The decision came too late in the season to affect the 1988 harvest, and it is too early to judge the consequences on 1989 harvests. However, it is clear that the settlers resented enforced collectivization (Council of Ministers 1988b: 73, 85; 1988a: 167; MoA 1989b: 33), which transformed them from independent producers into an agricultural proletariat, and the new measures have been welcomed by the settlers. The settlements have also moved over largely to a piecework system of labour whereby small groups of settlers are allocated tasks on a daily basis and are allowed to work on private land once the task has been completed. This has introduced incentives to work harder and an element of competitiveness.

Thirdly, a new government body with responsibility for resettlement has been in the planning stages for over three years. Pursuing a resettlement policy reliant on campaigns was recognized as unsustainable in 1987. In his speech to the Central Committee of the WPE in March 1987, Chairman Mengistu stated:

> We have learnt a lot in directing this programme from our past experience... Since it is not possible to direct this vast and continuous programme through temporary committees and campaigns, a special

government institution will be set up from next year which will lead the resettlement programme in a coordinated manner.

Over two years have passed since the statement was made. To date this decision has not been implemented and resettlement remains the Cinderella of government policy-making. Several recent official reports and studies continue to emphasize the need for action on this front (Council of Ministers 1988a: 91-92; MoA 1989b: 3, 33; 1989c: 79; Dessalegn 1989: 76), so that conservation and development of existing settlements can be planned, and future policies can be worked out to prevent the repetition of mistakes made in past resettlement policies and practices.*

Resettlement in Ethiopia still lacks a government planning agency, as it did prior to the revolution. Nor have the lessons of two decades been absorbed. Reports have repeatedly suggested that low-cost and small-scale settlements achieve greater production and yields, and are more likely to become self-reliant. Such schemes also seem to be more acceptable to settlers, who are therefore less inclined to abandon these sites. However, there has been a tendency to opt for large-scale and high-input projects. The bias in favour of high-profile schemes may be explained as an attempt to attract foreign investments, and as a result of the tenacious belief in the need to change the peasant mode of production by introducing mechanization and cooperativization. The fresh start that resettlement required was seen as an opportunity to rapidly bring about such transformations. However, after more than a decade, the earliest mechanized schemes are still not self-reliant, and after two major campaigns, cooperatives were tacitly acknowledged to be unsuccessful, and were scaled down.

Resettlement in Ethiopia has been characterized by over-zealous and paternalistic state policies. This has resulted in settlers becoming over-privileged in some respects, receiving too much unsuitable assistance. At the same time, settlers were discriminated against. Their rights to determine their own pace of agricultural and social development were usurped, and their freedoms of belief and travel were constrained. The challenge ahead will be to formulate measured and sensitive policies, and to work out a sustainable resettlement programme, which gives settlers more say in determining their future.

NOTES

* The policy changes announced in March 1990 did not mention resettlements. As in other fields, no major new steps have yet been taken (October 1990). However, there is a widespread expectation that settlers will be allowed to leave freely, and some may already be doing so (Editorial footnote).

1 This chapter is based partly on reports and government documents, and partly on fieldwork in western Wellega from October 1986 to June 1988, and a visit in April 1989. The

research was made possible by a grant from the Economic and Social Research Council of Great Britain. Thanks are due to the Ethiopian Government Relief and Rehabilitation Commission, to Addis Ababa and Manchester universities, and to the aid agencies Irish Concern and **Secours Populaire Francais**.

The chapter deals with resettlement policies, their implementation and consequences without raising the principal question whether resettlement per se is relevant to pressing economic and ecological problems.

2 Colaris 1985:51, quoting RRC Department of statistics, January 1985.

3 Some 74,000 settlers were receiving food aid in 1984 (ONCCP 1984c:57).

4 Colaris 1985:53.

5 In September 1984 the RRC was proposing to settle 14,000 people annually.

6 See Council of Ministers 1988a, 1988b, MoA 1989b, Dessalegn 1989.

7 Article 10.2.

8 The RRC had responded to the 1979 Proclamation concerning the development of producers' cooperatives with a plan launched in July 1981 to transform large-scale settlements into producers' cooperatives. By 1984 the RRC came to the conclusion that these ventures were unworkable and a new approach was proposed in September 1984, in which the lessons of the earlier decade were incorporated. Emphasis was placed on small-scale projects and oxen as the means of draft power. Existing mechanized cooperatives were to be scaled down and gradually phased out.

9 This figure does not include an estimated 2.3 million birr for tractors to be diverted from MOA allocations.

10 Simpson (1975) distinguishes between high inputs (full-time on-site extension staff), medium inputs (part-time staff), and low inputs (no resident staff). The RRC made use of two different sets of distinctions: firstly "low cost" (labour intensive) as opposed to "special" settlements, and secondly resettlement schemes "under budget" as opposed to those "under technical assistance" (RRC 1985: 160).

11 See also Alemneh Dejene in this volume.

The Amharic terms used are **kuta gettem**, or **medebegna** for conventional, and **sigsega** for integrated.

12 The Ministry of Agriculture distinguishes a third type called intermediate settlements, in the middle altitude range (1,000-1,500 m) in Kefa region which account for some 23,500 settlers (MoA. 1989a:7), and are composed of three to ten linked villages with a population of 1,000 to 5,000 households (Essaias 1988:7).

13 For a discussion of integrated sites see UNESCO 1988.

14 However, there are exceptions. At least one conventional complex has already successfully moved towards reliance on oxen. Conversely, a few integrated sites have benefited from tractor services loaned from nearby conventional settlements.

15 No accurate data are available; a government report suggests a figure of 6 per cent until 1987, excluding deaths in transit. (Council of Ministers 1988b:251). This is too low; data from Qet'o suggest figures of 12 per cent for the first four years.

16 Half of the 300,000 households were to be moved from Wello, a third from Tigray and the rest from Gonder (ONCCP 1984b:25).

17 Some 10,700 settlers were moved from November 1987 to May 1988 (RRC figures).

18 Article 47 of the Constitution.

19 Articles 49.1 and 49.2 of the Constitution state: "Ethiopians are guaranteed freedom of movement. Every Ethiopian has the freedom to change his place of residence within the territories of the PDRE."

20 One report estimated a rate of 14 per cent desertions from 1985 to 1987 (Council of Ministers 1988b:251). Data for Qet'o provide a rate of 15 per cent over four years. Detailed data for Village Three suggests a rate of 20 per cent for the first four years.

21 Over 25,000 workers from government and mass organizations were mobilized to take part in the Action Programme (Clarke 1986:63).

22 See Alemneh Dejene in this volume.

23 Dessalegn (1989: 54) estimates costs at 600 million birr.

24 For details of assistance provided see A. Pankhurst 1989.

25 In 1985 and 1986 the MoA provided full seed requirements; this was reduced to 50 per cent in 1987 and 1988, and was stopped in 1989. Fertilizers and pesticides were reduced to 25 per cent of settlement needs from 1988.

12 Villagization: Policies and Prospects

Alemayehu Lirenso

Villagization is a process by which rural households are moved from scattered dwellings into villages, as part of a governmental attempt to modernize rural life and agricultural production patterns. Since the first villagization campaign was launched in Ethiopia in 1977, one third of the country's rural population, over 12 million people, have been "villagized". The ambitious villagization campaign was the biggest such programme ever carried out on the African continent. Official documents and government statements portray it as a prerequisite for the more efficient utilization of national resources and an appropriate and adequate approach to rural development. The new villages are seen as a means to remedy the shortcomings of traditional farming and dispersed settlements, and to provide better services to rural Ethiopia (NVCC 1987a, 1987b).

However, many critics have voiced considerable misgivings about the programme. In marked contrast to the government's demonstrative optimism, they recall the disappointing experience of African countries like Tanzania with similar schemes, and express concern about the impact the programme might have on agricultural production and the rural environment in general (Kjekshus 1977, Hyden 1980, McCall 1985). There are few empirical studies on the implementation of the villagization programme in Ethiopia so far (Cohen, Isaksson 1987, Berihun 1988, Alemayehu 1988), but these seem to bear out such concerns. They criticize the government for too hastily implementing the schemes, with little knowledge of local conditions, a lack of professional planning, and disregard for peasant attitudes.

Commentators and close observers of the villagization programme often raise the following issues:

- The peasants will need to rebuild their houses in the new villages. This is likely to contribute to production shortfalls at a time when the country is already suffering from food deficits and regional famines.

- When peasants have to travel further from the villages to their fields, this may well impair agricultural production.

- Smaller plots may not allow peasant households to grow garden crops, raise small animals and perform side-line activities which augment their income and satisfy consumption needs.

- Without adequate planning and land use plans, the concentration of people in the new villages may contribute to overgrazing and soil degradation.

- Without adequate health care, sanitation and hygiene, the concentration of many people in a small area may increase the danger of epidemics and other health risks.

- The increased use of wood for house construction may accelerate deforestation, unless massive reforestation programmes compensate for the losses.

- Villagization will increase state control over the peasantry and at the same time pave the way for collectivization of agriculture and monopolization of rural trade.

The state lacks the resources necessary to supply the new villages with those services which peasants have been encouraged to expect. If at all, health stations, schools, water supply systems, electricity supply etc. can only be built in cooperative action by the peasants themselves. But observers doubt whether the present level of surplus extraction would allow peasant cooperation to mobilize the amount of resources needed for such development efforts (Cohen and Isaksson 1987). Without these, however, one of the major objectives of villagization appears not forthcoming. When such expectations are disappointed, one can hardly expect much peasant motivation for further development efforts.

Instead of discussing in abstract the pros and cons of villagization in Ethiopia, we will look at what has happened, and how the programme worked where it was implemented. We will present and evaluate, in the light of these issues, empirical findings from field surveys conducted by the author and others in Shewa and Hararghe between August 1988 and January 1989.[1]

The Emergence of Villagization as a National Programme

Villagization in Ethiopia began as a regional operation in Bale during the Ethio-Somali war in 1977-78. One of the main objectives of the programme at that time was to guarantee the safety of the local inhabitants from invading Somali troops. Six years later, in December 1984, the programme was extended to the adjoining region of Hararghe, again chiefly for security reasons. Within six months, about one million rural households were moved into the new villages (NVCC 1987c:40).

In July 1985, the scheme was extended to eight of the remaining 12 administrative regions, based on the experience from Bale and Hararghe. Interestingly this process was initiated by means of an internal memorandum and not as one would have expected through a public decree. By 1986, 15 per cent of the country's total rural population, about 5.5 million people, had been villagized. In the following years villagization proceeded at a rapid speed, and another 7 million people were moved between 1986 and 1988. Thus, 12 million Ethiopians were living in newly built villages by mid-1988, about one third of the rural population. The highest number of newly established villages was built in Shewa and Hararghe administrative regions, the lowest in Tigre, Gamo Goffa and Wello.

At its inception, the programme was neither well-planned nor well-coordinated. There were no feasibility studies available, and implementation was enforced under time pressure. Local bodies were left with much of the responsibility for implementation, and had a largely free hand. Consequently

VILLAGISATION - ETHIOPIA

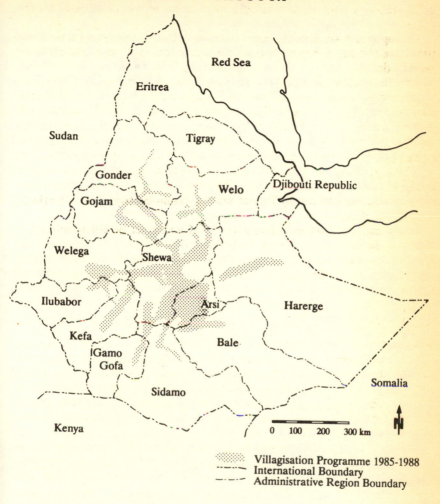

Source: Stefan Brüne and Volker Matthies (eds), Krisenregion Horn von Afrika, Hamburg, (1990:99)

© Hans Hurni

the *woreda* committees, consisting of party secretaries, local government officials, peasant association chairmen and officials of the Ministry of Agriculture, faced major operational problems.

To begin with, the local authorities had to overcome the shortage of trained surveyors. In many instances peasants were recruited and trained at the *woreda* capitals for a maximum of three weeks. There was also a considerable shortage of labour, though all able-bodied men, women, and even children were mobilized for building houses. While the men were doing the actual construction work, women and children were engaged in transporting materials and plastering the walls with mud. In some *woredas*, for example in Akaki, where authorities found not enough people for building houses, additional labour had to be brought in from the towns. As a consequence, many of those houses built with urban imported labour lacked strength and quality.

To alleviate the shortage of building materials, peasants were instructed to use wood from their old houses as well as stones and other materials. Thus in Welmera and Dalocha *woredas*, stalks of sorghum, wheat and barley were used for thatching the roofs, materials which were not strong enough and often made repairs necessary within a year. In Hasalisso peasant association in Dire Dawa *woreda*, peasants had to cover the roofs with soil and mud, since thatching grass (*eleusire jaegeri*) was not available locally. These roofs proved not tight against the rain, and some dwellers faced the prospect of their houses collapsing. Occasionally the government also attempted to supply corrugated iron sheets to those peasants who could not afford them. But demand, estimated at 10 million sheets in 1986/87, exceeded annual domestic production by more than 300 per cent. Efforts to ease the situation by importing corrugated iron had to be dropped due to lack of foreign exchange earnings.

In order to cope with these problems, local implementing bodies tried to learn from the experience of other resettlement projects and producer cooperatives. Visits were also made to some villages in Hararghe. But the problems remained. In many cases, local committees continued to enforce the construction of too many houses in too short a time, often without an adequate assessment of construction materials and labour available. Some people were even forced to move into their new dwellings before kitchens, pit latrines and stables had been built.

Additional problems occurred in the choice of sites for new villages. Houses were built on marshy land, water-logged plains or near the habitat of wild animals. Inexperienced authorities failed to allocate sufficient land for schools, shops and health centres. Some local committees even raised funds from the peasants without the knowledge or consent of central government (Shewa Regional VCC 1986). Regardless of such mistakes and shortcomings a number of party secretaries, cadres and *awraja* and *woreda* administrators received rewards from the government for their demonstrated enthusiasm for the programme.

The Villagization Guidelines

When widespread inconsistencies in local decision making became apparent, and the discontent of peasants became difficult to ignore, the government centralized the villagization programme. In June 1986, a National Villagization Coordinating Committee (NVCC) was set up. The Prime Minister was appointed as chairman, the Minister of Agriculture as secretary of the committee. Most of the fourteen members came from the ministries concerned with rural development programmes: water, education, health, energy, domestic trade and housing. The national peasant associations, trade unions, women's and youth associations were also represented. Shortly after the establishment of this central body, Villagization Committees (VVC) were formed at local level.

The first task of NVCC was to set out policy objectives, and these were soon published in its official organ *Mender* (The Village). Major objectives were to provide social services for the rural communities; to promote cooperative work; to raise the level of consciousness of the people; to improve village security and defence; to plan a more rational land use; to develop natural resources and increase agricultural productivity by introducing modern techniques.

In January 1987, the Ministry of Agriculture (MoA) issued "Villagization Guidelines" for the implementing bodies. It was decided to give priority to villagization in areas producing mainly annual crops, while permanent crop areas (ensete cultivation, coffee areas etc.) should be villagized at a later date, and nomadic areas at a third stage. A set of directives was issued on the criteria for site selection, the number of households per village (from 30 to 500), the size of compounds to be allocated to households for private use (between 1,000 and 2,000 m^2), and the design and layout of houses and communal facilities. According to these new guidelines some of the newly established villages had to be moved to more appropriate sites, and some settlements too close to the main roads were moved back some 400 to 500 metres.

It soon became clear that even these new guidelines alone could not solve all the problems. The guidelines instructed the implementing bodies to pay special attention to farmland, pasture land, water sources, roads and existing social infrastructure when selecting a village site. But in reality, all these things are rarely found close together in a rural setting. Building a village closer to fields often means moving it away from important facilities. Moreover there were no criteria for non-farming activities. In Welmera *woreda*, for example, it was found difficult to villagize potters because the new site was too far from the sources of clay. Attempts to introduce villagization in ensete-growing areas created other problems. Due to the high population density in many ensete regions it was difficult to find unused land for the new villages.[2]

Significant increases in distance between the fields and the new homes of peasants created another problem. In Welmera district the average distance between the fields and the homes grew from 1.6 to 2 km. According to officials from the Ministry of Agriculture in Dalocha, some peasants living more than 3 km away from their farms started renting them to peasants living closer. In Hasalisso the distance between the fields and the new villages was estimated to be over 6 km.

Every second household interviewed had lost a significant part of their crops and roots, being effectively unable to protect their fields from wild animals, pests and thieves from such a distance. It had also become difficult to carry manure to the farms and use it as fertilizer (Berihun 1988, Alemayehu 1988:54). Many peasants had to leave straw to decay, which could have been used to feed cattle in the dry season or to plaster walls, had their threshing grounds not been so far away. Increased distance to grazing land had reduced grazing time by 20 per cent, and livestock mortality increased significantly.

The guideline on the size of plots was not practical everywhere. Our survey showed that plots ranged from 500 m^2 in Hararghe to 2,000 m^2 in Shewa. Significant differences in plot sizes were also observed between villages formed before and after 1986 within the same locality. This is important as there is a significant difference between rural households having less than or only 1,000 m^2 and those having up to 2,000 m2. Peasants with smaller plots were disadvantaged as they do not have the space to grow vegetables or raise small animals and poultry, to keep bees or dry manure, or attempt other side-line activities to earn an additional income. In some *woredas*, the VVC were told to allocate up to 2,000 m^2 to each household. But though there was sufficient land, they feared to create unmanageable villages. The field survey showed that peasants generally wanted bigger compounds, and that a large variety in plot sizes is conceived as a problem.

In Dalocha and Welmera districts, many peasants complained that they were no longer able to grow vegetables and perennial crops like ensete and chat,[3] since the size of individual plots was reduced by up to 95 per cent. Peasants complained they had no space to dry the cow dung they needed for fuel and for manure in their mixed subsistence farming. Baked and dried cow dung is one source of cash income for the peasants, who often sell it in towns.

Problems were also created by the standard construction plans of the Ministry of Agriculture which were included in an appendix to the national villagization guidelines. Houses in the new villages were supposed to have standard sizes, say 30 or 40 m^2, regardless of household size. These compact and standardized dwellings were not sufficient for families with over 10 people. Sixty per cent of the peasants interviewed in Welmera district reported that their new houses were on average almost 20 per cent smaller than their former homes. Similarly, many people were not content with the standard division of dwellings into three rooms (living-room, bed room and store) as this limited the width of the rooms and made them dim even in day light. Moreover, the separate kitchen and stable required more than one kerosene lamp at a time. The fact that kitchen and stable were separate also raised the cost of construction. In the surveyed areas the average cost of construction for a house and auxiliary facilities was estimated at 1,500 birr in Welmera and 2,500 in Dalocha *woreda*. Even with a separate stable, many peasants still preferred to keep some of their animals, as calves or horses, either in the kitchen or in the house itself.

Another weakness in the guidelines concerned the time set aside for house construction. The government felt that the "slack" season between December and March was ideal for this purpose. A varying crop calendar, different cropping patterns and diverse religious customs made this impractical in some areas. In the surveyed areas, most peasants who are growing cereals during the summer use December to March as the peak season for planting maize, sorghum and ensete. Other studies have also revealed that peasants are rarely idle, even working on holidays, although they do not plough on these days. It is therefore not true that peasants are free between December and March or that they can devote their time fully to house construction in the "slack season" and on holidays.

As a result of all these shortcomings, there were quite a number of petitions from villagers during 1987. They asked the government to postpone the programme in perennial crop growing areas, to improve site selection practices, to reduce the number of people in new villages, and to allow more space for private household gardens. Peasants voiced considerable discontent about the widespread lack of professional planning and the poor performance of the programme. Many peasants had only moved reluctantly into the new villages and now wished to go back to their original settlements. In Welmera and Hasalisso peasant associations an alarming 50 per cent of the new villagers are reported to have requested to return to their original sites or to be allowed to establish satellite villages. Peasants often felt that even a brief stay in their original sites would save them the travelling time from the new villages and help them to tend their crops and feed their animals better.

Many village committees did not take peasant appeals seriously, but rather rejected them as counter-villagization moves. This shows the urgent need to involve local people in the process of change. In theory, mass organizations and peasant associations were expected to actively participate in local decision making. In practice, this was not the case in the surveyed areas, where government and party officials took most decisions on their own. Attempts to apply standardized solutions to different local conditions aroused widespread dissatisfaction among peasants. Empty promises provoked further distrust. In Welmera district, for example, people are still waiting for the electricity supply which they had been promised in 1986-88.

Achievements and Shortcomings

It might be too early to talk about the long term effects of villagization in Ethiopia. But an appraisal of short term effects can be attempted.

Contrary to what some people thought, villagization has so far not served as a prelude to cooperativization. So far the major gains of the programme are social and political. From the government's point of view, villagization has helped to strengthen village security and the control of contraband trade, particularly in Hararghe. Villagization has also made it easier to hold peasant association meetings, and has improved the access to social services in rural areas. Two thirds of the interviewed peasants in Dalocha and Welmera said that travel time to various service centres had been reduced, because the new villages are closer to roads, local markets, service cooperative shops, grain mills, schools, churches, and water sources. The programme has also facilitated reforestation efforts and extension services to peasant households.

Against this it must be said that economic gains have at best been negligible. Indeed, the villagization campaign has often lead to losses, as reported in Shewa administrative region. As the building of new houses absorbed much of the peasants' time, they were prevented from harvesting and threshing the *meher* (main season) crops in time. Many peasants were also unable to grow belg (short season) crops due to lack of time (Shewa Regional VCC 1986). Crop losses due to distance from the fields, and the loss of income from coffee and chat are other examples.

The choice of sites has allowed social and political gains and made the villages easier to defend. Pipe water and electricity have been installed in many places, and people are living closer to schools and health posts. But there was no parallel economic benefit for peasants. Economic constraints sometimes prevented the villagized households from exploiting the new services to the full. This points to a lack of overall coordination. It is therefore suggested that economic factors should be given higher priority in future when selecting settlement sites. Above all new villages should not just be tailored to the existing infrastructure, but preferably be located where it makes economic sense.

The effectiveness of a villagization policy depends largely on how the programme is implemented on a local level. A more flexible approach, taking the diverse social and physical conditions of rural Ethiopia into consideration, could alleviate some of its problems. Above all, local participation should be encouraged and enhanced. Villagization can elicit popular participation only if it responds to the needs of the people, who are after all supposed to be the ultimate beneficiaries of the programme. If the programme fails to appreciate the pressing problems of peasants or to respond to them, it must fail to promote rural development.[*]

NOTES

[*] The policy changes announced in March 1990 did not mention the villagization programme. As in other fields, the government has taken no new major steps to date (October 1990). Peasants in new villages now feel particularly insecure about their future. While they have been given a theoretical claim on a permanent holding, and on private ownership of their crops and trees, as well as free access to the market, they are not sure whether they are allowed to return to their former homesteads. This makes it difficult for them to take advantage of their new freedom. The government declaration stabilized land holdings as they were at the moment the declaration was made. Peasants unable to claim back the land they held prior to villagization

will not find it easy to return. A common agreement to return to the status quo ante may be even more difficult to achieve, given the legal ambiguities created by the new policy. As a result, few people have left the villages permanently so far, although equally few have settled permanently. At present, peasants are adopting a "wait and see" attitude, trying to strengthen their position for the time when the villages are dissolved, something most peasants expect to happen. (Editorial footnote)

1 In Shewa, field surveys were conducted on the basis of questionnaires. In Dalocha **woreda** in the former **awraja** of Haikotch and Butajira, and in Welmera **woreda** in Menagesha **awraja**, in-depth interviews were conducted with 40 randomly selected household heads. In Hararghe, representatives of peasant associations, members of local Villagization Coordinating Committees and officials from the Ministry of Agriculture were interviewed, and additional information was gathered in Dire Teyara and Hasalisso peasant associations (formerly Harar Zuria and Dire Dawa **awrajas**).

2 Ensete is a perennial root-crop which resembles banana trees. It is sometimes referred to as false banana. In Ethiopia some 12 million people depend on ensete as a staple crop which is considered to be a security crop against drought with a high land/yield ratio. With a density of over 150 people/km2 ensete growing **awrajas** in Shewa (viz. Chebo and Gurage, Kembata and Hadiya, Jibat and Mecha, and Haikotch and Butajira) belong to the most densely populated **awrajas** in the country. This is the main reason why villagization was, after some unsuccessful attempts, postponed in the ensete- growing regions.

3 Chat, a mild drug which is common in many parts of Ethiopia, is harvested twice a year. In many new villages the planting of chat was prohibited in favour of growing food crops. Farmers on Chercher Highlands claimed to have earned over 1800 birr per year from a chat field of 0.25 ha.

13 What Change and for Whom? The Case of Women in Menz

Helen Pankhurst

Introduction

For women, more than for men, tradition[1] plays a predominant role in behaviour and action. In an androcentric society, change is captured by men and tends to work through them first, before reaching women.[2] This has important implications for rural development and for state-peasant relations. In the following, questions of continuity and change are analysed in the world of women from Menz, northern Shoa. Costs arising from the lack of change in women's lives have to be set side-by-side with the social and economic price that may have to be paid when change is introduced which is not sensitive to women's needs. Four sections in this chapter deal with production, modern structures, reproduction, and cultural beliefs. Under each heading, only a few key questions can be pursued, the aim being to give an impression of the complexity and the dilemmas faced by women in rural Menz - a complexity which development programmes must acknowledge and attempt to evaluate if their aim is to improve rather than disrupt a way of life.[3]

"Women" is by no means a homogeneous category in terms of social and economic position, experience and status. Differences set them apart from each other and often bind them more to men in the same household or kin-group than to other women. *"Nuro assir now"*, "life is of ten kinds", was the response more than once when people were asked to generalize about the position of women.

Women and Production

The assumption that for rural areas, crop cultivation is the dominant, if not the only activity and source of livelihood, is incorrect in the mixed-farming systems characteristic of northern Ethiopia. It is an androcentric assumption since it places ploughing, a male-only activity, as the pivotal productive activity in the society.[4]

Livestock

Livestock plays a central role in the society and is closely linked with agriculture through such factors as fodder, the use of oxen or pack-animals for ploughing, and the use of dung as fertilizer. Either production system is untenable without the other. Furthermore, the livestock economy is also bound up with the third component of rural livelihood in Menz, namely wool processing. It could, in fact, be argued that livestock, around which both agriculture and manufacturing revolve, is the more pivotal resource base.

Livestock is usually held communally within a household. Women are as involved as men and children in herding. Which member of the family is allocated this task depends on household composition and on other work to be done. Sexual division of labour operates only in making butter and forming fuel-cakes from the dung.

Underlying the household joint economy, however, are individual rights which come to the fore when the household disintegrates, e.g. in case of a divorce. For most marriages,[5] animals produced or bought during the life of the marriage are divided equally, whilst livestock brought into the marriage is returned to the initial owner or to the individual it was given to.

This is the theory. In practice the rights that women have are often not activated if they cannot voice and protect their claims. Women usually manage to retain rights to some of their own animals and part of the joint wealth, though rarely an equal share. Thus, both men and women own livestock, although animals are more likely to be controlled by men, a generalization that can be made about most goods, and notably productive goods in the society.

There are exceptions to the story of greater male control. Chickens belong almost exclusively to women. The income from the sale of eggs, chicks and chicken is therefore conceived of as women's money, whilst looking after poultry is firmly set in the female sphere.

Wool processing[6] provides most households with a regular source of cash as well as some blankets for home use. On almost every day of the year women process wool. It is either bought or shorn from their own sheep, and, once spun, may be sold directly or accumulated and woven, by a male weaver, into a blanket. Women tend to contribute more, and more constantly, to household income through wool processing, though the work and income of a minority of men is significant in shearing wool and weaving it into blankets.

The importance of livestock and wool helps to explain why women have a greater say in the household than might be expected from a plough-agriculture based economy (Boserup 1970). Men undoubtedly have greater entitlements than women, but the latter are rarely powerless[7] and there is a sense in which the female contribution to the household economy is taken as an indisputable half. Yet this position at the domestic level is usually not carried through to the societal level, as will become clear in the discussion on modern structures, though it is not completely absent in traditional culture, as will be shown in the section on cultural beliefs.

Land

Women are not involved in ploughing in the rain-fed agriculture dominating in highland Ethiopia. They are little involved in other crop-production work, though at peak seasons they sometimes contribute alongside men in households with labour shortages, to such activities as weeding, harvesting, and transporting crops. On the other hand, processing grains is almost exclusively a women's activity. The tasks include: drying, washing, pounding, grinding and in general the production of "food".

The importance of rights to land lies not only in its value as a source of income and an asset, but also as a proof of rights to residence and shelter. There is considerable variation and it is impossible to make a straight-forward assessment of an individual woman's entitlements. Where women have rights, these can be either active or latent; they may be held by women as minors or as adults, and even where women have active rights as adults, they may be paying the full tax, half, or, officially, none of it. The categories below list some of the relationships between women and land:

- *Women with complete land-use rights* are often widows who inherited land from their husbands. If the woman has moved to join the household of one of her children in another Peasant Association, she will have less immediate control over the land. Other women may have inherited land from parents or other kin for a number of reasons, such as the departure or death of the initial male land holder.

Whether a woman's land is ploughed by her relative, friend, ex-husband or present husband will affect the control that the woman has and the amount of yield she gets.[8] Other important variables include whether the woman is living in the area where she has rights to land, how long she has been resident in the Peasant Association, and, if she has left, whether or not she has retained links in the area. The longer her connection with the place, the more secure her rights, *ceteris paribus*. The presence of children is also an important element, as children often reinforce a woman's rights to a share of the land.[9]

-*Some women have inherited half-shares to land rights* with an ex-husband, the land having been divided officially and each partner paying the full tax. The land is often ploughed by the woman's present husband who might or might not have land-rights of his own.

-Women who have been married for a number of years, have usually *latent rights to a share* of their husband's land should they divorce, but, in the meantime, the land remains in the husband's name. This is always the case if the marriage pre-dates the revolution. Potential rights can be transformed into direct ones in case of a divorce, providing the woman can argue her case or find people to do so for her.

-Young women, who were minors at the time of the land reform, might retain a *latent right to a minor's share* of land with the household they were living in at the time of the reform. This minor latent share is not always lost when the woman is allocated an adult share with her husband.

-*Women may have no active or latent land-rights*, because rights were ignored at the time of the land reform, because they were lost along the way,[10] or because the woman was born after the land reform.

The degree of control that women have over land-related production is highly variable and difficult to quantify. Any confusion in terms of men's relationship to land is negligible in comparison. Women's rights cannot be ensured by slogans of equality; there is as yet no clear governmental policy towards women's rights that tackles the reinforcing biases inherent in the social structure.

Women and Modern Structures

Modern services in Ethiopia are almost exclusively channelled through the state. The only exceptions are those provided by capitalist ventures which are essentially urban phenomena, and those connected with aid agencies which are piecemeal in nature, and even then usually in some way linked to the state.

Modern services providing water, mills, and afforestation programmes are major areas of change that reduce the burden of work for women, given the sexual division of labour. However, the fact that these changes reduce women's work is almost incidental to the rationale behind the policy. Afforestation became a policy due to soil erosion and environmental fears. Water and milling services were expanded because these were perceived as major constraints on the rural population, rather than because of the burdens they imposed specifically on women. The organizational structures of the state continue to focus on men, thereby perhaps inadvertently reinforcing the age-old androcentrism of power. This can be seen by considering the activities of the state as they impinge upon the daily lives of the rural population.

The peasant association is currently the most fundamental structure in the society - the administrative unit within which people now define their locality, their "country". Leadership is almost exclusively male. Men are the most numerous and most visible members, have the most secure rights to resources and in particular the most direct rights to land use. The same applies to service cooperatives and producer cooperatives.

However, this story of modern structures reinforcing gender inequality has to be seen in the context of the fact that the state still has only a small role in the society, one which is particularly weak in terms of direct access to women.

Surprisingly, given the on-going nature of the Ethiopian revolution, the Menze peasantry has few permanent links with the state. Campaigns (e.g. land reform, literacy, villagization) seem to engulf and alter the society, yet the changes become absorbed and the old way of life is, as far as possible, resumed. Production is still peasant-based and the economy remains predominantly subsistence-oriented. Sales to the Agricultural Marketing Corporation rarely take place, though there are annual and occasional extractions including the collection of taxes and recruitment campaigns for the army.

In general, few on-going extension services reach out convincingly to the peasants. In the area researched, literacy classes are poorly and irregularly attended, less than 5 per cent of the young attend school, and the majority of the population is unable to write their names. Clinics are usually located in towns and rarely visited, and though an infant vaccination programme exists, it is often interrupted and visits to the peasant associations are rare.

For women, almost all contact with the state is mediated through men. The major exception would at first sight seem to be the women's association, operating at the peasant association level, with links right up to the Central Committee of the National Revolutionary Ethiopia Women's Association, REWA. However, at least in this region, the impact of the association on the society is minimal: it is limited to sporadic, unsuccessful attempts to introduce a few women to income-earning skills (sewing, pottery), and an annual membership fee, perceived as a tax, collected usually only when action is taken by the peasant association leadership to ensure payment.

The fact that modern structures deal more directly with men than with women does not necessarily mean that women are thereby deprived. This is clear in particular with respect to the extractive arm of the state. For example, military service, perhaps the most feared connection between the government and the people, is restricted to male conscription.

Finally, *corvée* labour, *Sera Zemecha*, can be taken as a symbol of the relationship between state and people. It is a form of extraction since labour is often used to reinforce the position of those representing state authority. In addition, it can result in a direct income to the state through "donations" of agricultural yield. However, *corvée* labour is also channelled towards the community and local "capital" investment, when it is used on programmes such as afforestation, terracing, etc. Regardless of who the beneficiaries are, in *Sera Zemecha*, the majority of the work force in Menz is male. The direct costs are therefore borne by men and not women. In addition, the household becomes more dependent on women's contributions, since male labour is syphoned off for *corvée* outside the household. Women's income earning, in particular from the spinning of wool, therefore becomes more visible and valued.[11]

The central argument being put forward is not new, namely that women's contact with the state is usually mediated through men on whom it has a more immediate effect. Women are not, however, immune from feeling the impact of these changes. For example, military service syphons away the mother's labour to "produce" the country's soldiers.

Women and Reproduction

The state has few direct links with women and impinges little on them. The criticism of omission is nowhere clearer than in the lack of a general policy or even of campaigns around reproduction-related issues.[12]

Yet in the society, the role of wife and mother is taken to be an unquestioned progression in women's life-cycle. In the peasant association under consideration, there are no cases of women reaching old age without having been married, usually more than once, and sometimes as often as ten times. Whilst there are a few cases of women not giving birth, this is never by intent.

Many of the experiences specific to women are not discussed openly, nor are provisions made to improve their lives, despite the costs and discomforts that they bear. Poor sanitation and nutrition, together with lack of medical attention, results in high infant,[13] child and maternal mortality.

In Menze society there are few taboos associated with menstrual blood. In practice women continue with their tasks.[14] However, the physical discomforts from menstruation are great. Women, as elsewhere in the world, tend almost universally to complain about pain before the start of the cycle, as well as irregular and heavy flows. Furthermore, most women have no protection, at best absorbing some of the blood with old rags, but more often than not, doing nothing, "letting it drop to the ground". This is not only uncomfortable and unsanitary, but also a source of embarrassment.

Marriage should and usually does occur just before menarchy, which, in the area, starts as late as between fifteen and eighteen - undoubtedly a reflection of poor nutrition. Blood from loss of virginity is often not differentiated from menarchy. In fact the start of menstruation is culturally interpreted as connected with intercourse.[15] Turning now to some of the conflicts resulting from change, it can be seen that with development and nutritional improvements bringing forward the age of menarchy, the age at which a woman is expected to get married will be lowered. This can lead to a series of detrimental effects: increased constraints on young women, population increase etc.

This is a culture in which, in bad times, people want fewer children, whilst good times are greeted by an increase in procreation. This situation should act as a warning against the view that development is a simple, straight line trajectory towards Utopia. Traditional forms of contraception are limited to "long-term" breast-feeding. Though there is a knowledge of the existence of modern contraception, in the rural areas at least, its use is frowned upon and it is only very rarely practised, and then usually by women with urban links.[16]

It is being suggested that the reproductive burdens of women are generally not addressed, that economic growth does not necessarily reduce these, whilst traditions that contribute to the high burden cannot easily be altered. This is not to say that the social structure is totally oppressive. There is a tradition, in many parts of Ethiopia, of ensuring that after childbirth the mother is looked after, usually by her closest female relative, for a convalescence period.[17] In Menz, this used to be forty days. It is now twenty days, though some women return to their duties after ten, probably because of increased nuclearization of the family, looser kinship ties, and increased impoverishment which make it difficult to find and finance the extra female labour for the full forty days.

In general, in many reproduction-related spheres, changes are inevitable if development is to take place. In particular, life-cycle events, such as pregnancy, birth, the post-partum period, circumcision and marriage, have to be discussed in this context. The welfare challenge is to avoid the conflict and outright condemnation of traditions surrounding women's life-cycle. It is not easy to distinguish the admirable from the abominable,[18] to know where practices are best maintained, adapted or rejected.[19]

Women and Cultural Beliefs

In Menz, most cultural prescriptions are religious in nature. Of these, the most visible and tangible to outsiders are based on Ethiopian Orthodox Christianity. Parallel, and often indistinguishable from this "Christian" conduct,[20] lies one which is an expression of a number of different spirit-belief systems.

The actions of individuals[21] conforming to the "Christian" culture include abiding by the restrictions against certain types of work on saints' days, fasting, food taboos, vows, pilgrimages, etc. Life cycle events are also predominantly expressed and celebrated through religious rituals. These include baptism, christening, marriage,[22] funerals and post-funeral remembrances.

Under the imperial *regime*, Orthodox Christianity was the state religion, the culture supporting and legitimating the power of the ruler. In socialist Ethiopia, Christianity has been down-graded at the national level and given a status equal to Islam. Early on in the revolution there were attempts to discourage fasting and the honouring of saints' days through work prohibitions. At least in Menz, the attempt to reduce the role of Christianity in society had few successes. At the same time, five of the thirteen official holidays are still Christian in nature. A church tax has been established, legitimating and perhaps even strengthening the role of Christianity in the community. The peasant association leadership remains closely in touch with the Church and is in the forefront in all religious ceremonies. It can, therefore, be concluded that, though uncomfortable about it, current "Marxist" power structures defer to Christianity.

Spirit beliefs were never legitimated by the state, have been discouraged as backward, and have unhesitatingly been subject to attack by both the previous and the present regimes. In post-revolutionary Ethiopia there have been campaigns to encourage people to throw away the trappings of spirit-beliefs: beads and other spiritual paraphernalia.

The importance of spirit-belief systems is sometimes hidden from view because it is known to be frowned upon, almost forbidden by the priests of the "legitimate" Christian religion. It is also invisibilized by the very nature of the beliefs, dealing with uncertain relationships between humans and spirits. Finally spirit-belief systems are under attack by forces of modernization, and scientific explanations of phenomena. Though many of these changes also undermine the Christian component to the culture, spirit-belief systems are more vulnerable because their religious prescriptions operate to a greater extent in terms of secrecy and individual rather than group identity, and because they have never been structured into a doctrine, let alone used as a force legitimating state authority. They are also operating in a sphere of culture in which women predominate, and perhaps, therefore, function as an alternative, a culture in opposition rather than in power.

Women are more involved than men in this spirit culture - not just as worshippers, for in this role they also predominate in the Christian scene, but in the more interactive role as communicators with, and "embodiments" of the spirits. This is in contrast with the menial role women are given in the Church hierarchy.[23] Spirit-belief systems form a culture in which women can express themselves and which can sometimes provide them with material benefits. However, this culture is also one which in many ways binds them to traditional behaviour patterns that some of them might wish to alter.[24]

The power of these spirit systems and their hold on individuals and especially on women in Menz society spills over into the Christian religious culture, despite the Church's attempts to avoid "contamination". For example, the ritual slaughtering of livestock which is then consumed, is part of the Christian culture for celebrating Christmas. The slaughtering inside the hut when it is part of a ceremony, the prohibition against entering the huts for three days which applies to all those not present at the time of the slaughtering, and the specificity of colour and sex of the animals are part of the spirit-belief system which colours traditions celebrating Orthodox Christianity.[25]

Spirit-belief systems are a key component of women's lives - central expressions of belief and action. Spirits can be interpreted as sources of support to the extent that they present an explanation of women's world view, and represent practically the only public sphere in which women have power. Spirit manifestations also serve as a way of justifying celebrations and consumption of the society's luxury goods.[26] At the same time, these beliefs are perceived, from within the society, as a source of oppression and fatalism. For these reasons, the direction of change towards eroding these beliefs tends to be looked upon favourably by most women. The researcher has often heard them comment that villagization has had at least one good result - it has released them from subservience to the "place" and its "habits"; from the *Timbuho* and the "Blood".[27]

Conclusions

Questions of culture, modern structures, production and reproduction have been considered, to give an overall impression of women's lives rather than to examine any single issue exhaustively. No aspect can be understood in isolation from the others. Women's lives are characterized by an interplay between possibilities and constraints that are rooted in economic, cultural and biological factors.

In the household, men's production, ploughing and harvesting, are the most visible and valued activities. Yet the involvement of women in the livestock economy and in wool-work, as well as in crop processing, is no less important, and helps to explain their power at the domestic level.

The most active external agent is the state. Its involvement is androcentric in practice, even if sometimes couched in an idiom of equality. The state is active in maintaining gender inequality through its focus on male spheres of production, through ambiguous policies, e.g. on the issue of land-tenure rights, through an almost exclusively male political structure and through inaction in areas deemed to be "women's", e.g. in reproduction related issues. However, and ironically, since the state is essentially extractive, the costs borne by women are perhaps lower and more indirect than those shouldered by men.

The gender hierarchy has its source in the traditional dominant culture. However, there exists an alternative, almost a "mirror" culture in which women are more central than men, though it has always had a negative image and is in the process of being eroded. Spirit-belief systems can be seen in contradictory ways, as constraining women's choices and actions, or as providing them with security, influence and material benefits.

Women's lives in northern Ethiopia are dominated by a peasant economy and culture - the state or other external agents provide few inputs and have little impact. Change is captured by men and only indirectly trickles down to women. This is not to say that there is no change, no dynamism, in the economy and culture that jointly provide the guide-lines for women's thoughts and actions. Nor is this suggesting that women have no interaction that empowers them in society and in production.

The overall conclusion is that external agents of development have had a more marginal effect on women than on men because of a patriarchal structure in which change is captured by men whilst continuity is embraced by women, as a reaction against androcentric development. The implication of this situation for policy makers is that intervention in society must be gender conscious, rather than gender blind, since in this context blindness implies male bias. Furthermore, the token and segregated policy on women will not on its own create egalitarian forces in state and society.

NOTES

1 Many terms will be used without being defined or discussed. These include "modern", "tradition" and "culture". Though such a treatment might seem highly unsatisfactory, it has been resorted to because of the restriction of space.

2 This is well documented in the literature on gender relations, e.g. Afshar 1987, Croll 1981, Molyneux 1981, Rosaldo and Lamphere 1974.

3 The scene is set in the material sphere of production, where the importance of livestock is stressed and the heterogeneity of women's position vis-à-vis access to land is noted. The section on the provision of modern structures and how they affect the gender divide, focuses on the state, since it is the channel through which inputs are made and extraction occurs. This is followed by a discussion of the issue of reproduction, an area rarely broached save in the context of population growth. Some of the conflicts attendant to change are mentioned. Finally, the section on cultural beliefs focuses on religion and the existence of a spirit-belief system which is central in particular to women's conception of the world.

4 For a comparative view on the devaluing of women's economic activities, see Bradby 1976 and Young 1984.

5 This is not the case for example in **demoz** marriages, which are based on the payment of a salary to the wife.

6 There is also cotton processing going on, though this is usually on a smaller scale and, on the part of the woman, exclusively for use-value.

7 The role and impact of trade has not been discussed. This is another area where, in traditional markets, women have an important economic role. However, the sexual division of labour is still such that the larger transactions are usually undertaken by men.

8 "Women's" land is likely to be ploughed after the male plougher's own land and at his convenience, making it more vulnerable to bad timing and resulting in poor harvests. This is one of the additional costs of women's inability to work on crop-production.

9 Other factors enter the equation, such as the extent of corruption or social conscience of the peasant association leadership, and other groups involved in land redistribution.

10 E.g. because the woman left the area.

11 Another example of the state's greater involvement in the "male only" areas of the economy is that, to date in Menz, the state's extraction is focused purely on land and agriculture, i.e. in the area of production in which women's labour is insignificant.

12 The term "reproduction" is highly unsatisfactory since much more than procreation is at issue. The effects of menstruation and cultural expressions associated with the women's life cycle, such as circumcision, are not discussed in the section. It is often the case that the division of production and reproduction into separate sections contributes to a mental classification system which perpetuates the hiving off of women's issues. If nothing else, women's role in giving birth to "labour", points to the problems with the production/reproduction dichotomy. See Roberts 1987, Croll 1981, Beneria & Sen 1981.

13 It is not unheard of for a woman to give birth to ten children and lose more than half.

14 There is talk that it is "bad" to grind etc, but most women continue with their tasks for "who else is there to do the work?" The only active taboo seems to be against intercourse and going to church.

15 That the two phenomena are not distinguished, or rather only reluctantly accepted as separate, is suggestive of the prevalence of marriage and intercourse prior to the start of the menses.

16 There is also knowledge that pills have side effects, suggesting a need to study these in the context of local conditions.

17 The new mother gets special treatment in a number of other ways, including the slaughtering of a chicken, primarily for her consumption, and the fencing of an area of the hut to allow her some privacy.

18 This is not to say that the welfare effects are never clear. An example of a tradition, clearly detrimental to women is that of female circumcision. The effects of "Amhara" circumcision need more analysis. However, it is clear that the practice is both dangerous for the infant and a cause of problems for the mother during pregnancy.

19 For example, it is difficult to react to the tradition of women reducing and excluding the intake of some foods in the late stages of their pregnancy. This practice is sometimes seen as a prohibition, though women argue that they do it because they feel unwell if they eat certain foods. At the same time a poorer nutrition results in a smaller baby, and hence in an easier birth. The dilemma for external developmentalists is whether or not to speak out against this tradition which might result from a complex internal knowledge and from a reaction to the difficult conditions women face or, on the other hand, might be part of a patriarchal environment that subjugates women.

20 Although it probably both pre-dates and has subsequently borrowed from it. In Menz, there are hardly any Muslims in the peasants association studied, only one out of 423 households.

21 The outward show or visible side of culture could, for analytical purposes, be divided into two. In the first, the individual stands alone, her or his actions and beliefs being a manifestation of the society. In the second, it is the joint actions of groups of people which defines the event or belief, and hence gives a label to the culture of the community.

22 In Amhara Ethiopia, the Church is not involved in most marriages: hence the possibility and frequency of divorce. Why this pattern developed (see Weissleder 1974), when so many other ceremonies are religious in nature, and given that marriage is the one area where in many other societies the Church plays a central role, needs further investigation.

23 Their only official role in the Church is as "servers" helping with food preparation, a role that can be taken up by "nuns", i.e. old women who have declared their commitment to the Church. As worshippers women have to stay on the outer edge of the church, without entering the inner sanctum, coming near the **tabot**, or symbolic Ark of the Covenant, etc.

24 These points can be illustrated by removing the abstraction with which spirit-beliefs have been discussed so far, and by describing how they are manifested in the society. Some of the main spirit systems are:

The **Abdar** is a spirit associated with a specific area, referred to as the place, **bota**, or country, **ager**. As well as an annual celebration of the spirit, usually in May, actions are taken daily in order to appease the spirits. These include spilling the coffee dregs at a certain spot outside the hut, burning tobacco leaves, **timbuho**, outside the hut on Wednesdays and Fridays, and annual events such as the ritual slaughtering of livestock.

Wik'abi and **Zar** are similar spirits. Both are internalized, part of the individual rather than a separate being, expressed in terms of a benevolent illness. **Wik'abi** could be seen as a milder form of **Zar** and affects a majority of women. The **Wik'abi** spirit comes in the form of ill-health and discomfort and needs to be pampered, usually with coffee, and a particular piece of clothing, a special neck-scarf, or **angel-libs**. However, the spirit of some women can be more demanding, asking for such items as a complete dress, honey, and the slaughtering of livestock. The **Zar** spirit takes possession of people in a more dramatic way, resembling an epileptic fit. Pacifying the spirit involves a greater amount of ceremony, with chanting, incense, a variety of luxury foods and drinks.

Ch'ele is similar to **Wik'abi** and **Zar** in that offerings are made to an internalized spirit - offerings consumed by the individuals themselves. However, the **Ch'ele** spirit manifests itself at a particular time, often in July. A basket containing beads (hence the name, **Ch'ele**, the Amharic term for beads), perfume and other goods is opened, and women dress up for the occasion with their finest clothes.

Ginn, Aganint, Aynet'ela and **Buda** are all externalized. **Aganint** is a water spirit, purportedly the cause of most deaths anywhere in the vicinity of rivers. **Ginn** is a general evil spirit, likely to be encountered on the road, which disconcerts people since it appears as human and promptly disappears; it also has evil intentions. **Aynet'ela** and **Buda** are both forms of the evil eye. Outsiders and people involved in crafts or trade are most likely to be identified as the ones inflicting the evil.

25 To give other examples, **T'enk'way** sorcerers, who can be male or female, offer predictions, advice and amulets and legitimate their knowledge by weaving it into Orthodox Christianity. Priests themselves are not averse to delving into the "opposition" system of beliefs in spirits for a greater influence on people's actions and beliefs. People explain births and deaths, health and illness, wealth and poverty, temperament, and many other things besides, in terms

of spirit "interference", often in the same breath as making reference to the will of God and/or the Satan of the Christian belief system, and only rarely seeking explanation in material terms.

26 E.g. coffee, butter, honey, meat, perfume, beads, clothes.

27 **Timbuho** is tobacco, the blood is that from slaughtering sacrificial animals. See note 24.

14 Population Issues in Rural Development
Markos Ezra

Development planners, policy makers and scholars have begun to recognize that Ethiopia's development problems are at least in part associated with prevailing demographic trends and the resulting population structure. Rural development demands, among others, a thorough understanding of the complex relationship between population growth, declining per capita farm land and growing ecological degradation and agricultural stagnation.

Population Size and Growth Rate

Before the 1960s, there was no coherent set of demographic data on Ethiopia. Demographic information still remains poor and the coverage is always far from complete. Even the most recent 1984 Census of Population and Housing, which is considered the most reliable source of demographic data to hand, is far from complete. It covered almost all the urban population but only 85 per cent of the country's rural population (CSO 1984). Despite their limitations, sample surveys and the census have been instrumental in providing estimates of basic demographic parameters necessary for development planning (CSO 1964, 1974).

In the First and Second Round National Sample Survey, the population of Ethiopia was estimated at 22.5 million and 24 million respectively for 1967 and 1970. The 1984 Census of Population and Housing gave a total population of 42 million for May 1984. These surveys permit only a crude approximation of the actual increases of the population. The actual numbers are much higher than reported.

In May 1984, 46.5 per cent of the population were below 15 years of age and only 4.2 per cent 65 years and older.[1] This is a typical shape for a population with a very high dependency ratio, suggesting a high reproductive potential and a continuing high growth rate for some time to come. In view of this relatively young population, it was estimated that the growth rate would increase from 2.9 per cent in 1985 to 3.0 per cent in 1994 and that there would be 56.4 million people in Ethiopia in 1994 and about 67.4 million by the turn of the century (CSO 1985).

Population Distribution and Density

In studying the population problem in Ethiopia, it is necessary to look not only at the size but also at the spatial distribution of the population. In 1984, only 11.3 per cent of the population were reported as living in urban areas (CSO 1984). Although Ethiopia still remains largely an agrarian country, net migration from rural to urban areas increased rapidly since the 1960s. Migra-

Table 1
Population distribution
May 1984

Region	Population			Per cent Urban	Area km² (000's)*	Density
	Total	Urban	Rural			
Arssi	1,662,233	133,135	1,529,098	8.01	24.6	67.6
Bale	1,006,491	77,207	929,284	7.67	128.3	7.8
Gamo Gofa	1,248,034	73,253	1,174,781	5.87	40.1	31.1
Gojjam	3,244,882	263,387	2,981,495	8.12	64.4	50.4
Gondar	2,905,362	223,562	2,681,800	7.69	73.4	39.6
Eritrea	2,614,700	407,095	2,207,605	15.57	91.6	28.5
Hararghe	4,151,706	314,601	3,837,105	7.58	254.8	16.3
Illubabor	963,327	66,171	897,156	6.87	50.8	19.0
Kefa	2,450,369	150,839	2,299,530	6.16	53.0	46.2
Shewa	8,090,565	749,262	7,341,303	9.26	85.3	94.8
Sidamo	3,790,579	249,178	3,541,401	6.57	116.7	32.5
Tigray	2,409,700	198,034	2,211,666	8.22	65.7	36.7
Wollega	2,369,677	143,376	2,226,301	6.05	69.8	35.5
Wello	3,609,918	250,143	3,359,775	6.93	79.0	46.1
Addis Admin.	89,300	31,037	58,263	34.76	25.8	3.5
Addis Ababa	1,412,575	1,412,575	-	100.00	0.2	7,062.8
Country	42,019,418	4,742,855	37,276,563	11.30	1,223.5	34.3

Sources: CSO, Census Preliminary Report 1984
*CSO, People Democratic Republic of Ethiopia, Facts and Figures, 1987 pp. 24.

tion slowed down following the revolution of 1974. In 1971, for example, about half of the population of towns with more than 20,000 people consisted of rural migrants (CSO 1975). The average growth rate for urban centres was 6.3 per cent during the 1960s and mid-1970s, but declined to 4.0 per cent in the 1980s. The growth rate for Addis Ababa alone declined from 7 per cent to 4.3 per cent during the same period (Bariagaber 1987). The 1975 Rural Land Proclamation, which gave the great majority of the peasants access to rights of land use, is cited as the major factor in the reduction of the urban growth rate.

The population distribution in the country is also uneven, as shown in Table 1. The most outstanding fact is that the overwhelming majority, 88 per cent of the population, lives on the highlands (FAO 1986:59). This high concentration of population on 44 per cent of the land area of the country reflects the close relationship between physiography, climate, economy and population distribution. The average population density in the highlands is about 61 persons per km^2. This figure is almost double the national average and eight times more than that of the lowlands. In general, the density is highest in the north-central highlands and lowest in the western and eastern lowlands (CSO 1987:23).

Morbidity and Mortality

Data on mortality in Ethiopia are very limited. Using the 1981 demographic survey, CSO estimated that the crude death rate for 1980/81 was 18.4 per cent, while the infant mortality rate was 144 per thousand births. Life expectancy at birth was estimated to be 46 years. The current estimate by the United Nations, however, put the crude death rate for 1975-80 at 21.5 per thousand and life expectancy at 42.0 years for the same period (UN 1989a). These estimates correspond to the data collected by the Ministry of Health (MoH 1985).

The level and trends of morbidity and mortality in the country are still considered as unacceptable. This situation is attributed mainly to widespread communicable diseases such as malaria, tuberculosis, measles, diphtheria, poliomyelitis, and pertussis and parasitic diseases which include schistosomiasis. Other serious health problems are malnutrition and trachoma. The quality of maternal-child health services is also extremely poor (UN 1984b).

The official policy of the government has been to provide health services to the rural population, to attain an equitable distribution of health services between rural and urban areas and to improve the nutritional status of the population. It has adopted the objective of "health for all by the year 2000" through the use of a primary health care strategy. Particular attention is given to the eradication of communicable as well as parasitic diseases through a programme of immunization and environmental sanitation which includes water supply protection, insect and animal control, waste disposal and food hygiene.

The effort to improve the health situation in the rural areas is hampered by the absence of an adequate health infrastructure. In the last few years, most government measures have focused on the construction of new health centres and increasing the capacity of existing hospitals. The number of health stations and centres increased from 649 and 93 respectively in 1973 to 1,761 and 131 by 1982. The government is also expanding training institutions by enlarging the existing nursing and medical schools (UN 1984b:4). In addition, the government aims to train 31,500 community health agents in the years to come with the objective of providing one health worker for each Peasant Association and Urban Dwellers Association (ONCCP 1984).

Fertility: Levels and Trends

As is the case with mortality and morbidity, fertility data in Ethiopia vary from one source to another. The First and Second Rounds National Sample Surveys conducted in 1964/67 and 1968/71 respectively were the first demographic data sources that collected information on fertility. Fertility estimates using these sources were, however, low by African standards. The reported crude birth rate for 1964/67 was 44 per thousand while the general fertility rate was 190 per thousand. Similarly, the gross reproduction rate and the total fertility rate were reported as 2.8 and 5.6 per cent respectively.

Realizing the deficiencies of data, adjustments were made using different methods to estimate the most plausible levels. Accordingly, the reported fertility measures in 1964-67 were adjusted to provide a crude birth rate of 50.0 per thousand, a general fertility rate of 221 per thousand, a gross reproduction rate of 3.3, and a total fertility rate of 6.7 per cent (CSO 1971:24).These figures are almost similar to Bariagaber's estimation made eight years later where he found the crude birth rate to be 50.4 per thousand and the general fertility rate at 231.9 per thousand (Bariagaber 1979b). He gave a total fertility rate of 6.9 and a gross reproduction rate of 3.5 using the 1977/78 Agricultural Sample Survey conducted by the Ministry of Agriculture.

The results of the Second National Sample Survey showed fertility levels relatively lower than those reported in the first survey: 44.7 for crude birth rate, 6.2 for total fertility rate, 188 for general fertility rate and 3.0 for gross reproduction rate (CSO 1974:65). Once again, these figures almost correspond to the 1981 demographic survey conducted almost seven years later. The 1981 survey provided a crude birth rate of 46.9 and a general fertility rate of 211 per thousand, while the total fertility rate and gross reproduction rate were estimated to be 6.9 and 3.4, respectively (CSO 1985). Other reports mention a crude birth rate around 50 per thousand corresponding with a crude death rate of about 20 per thousand, implying a natural increase of about 3.0 per cent per annum (Bariagaber 1979, CSO 1985).

Some fluctuation may be explained by differences in time, data source and data quality. The high level of fertility is expected to continue for some time because there are no indications of change in the factors that influence fertility. The rate of urbanization, literacy, parents' attitude towards children, economic and social values of children, age at marriage, and the status of women in the household are still conducive to high fertility rather than reducing it.

Population Density and Land Availability

Ethiopia, with a population of 48 million, is the third most populous country in Africa. The current growth rate of 2.9 per cent is expected to continue for some time to come given the persisting high fertility and declining mortality rates. If the trend continues, the population will more than double within a quarter of a century and this is expected to have a serious impact on agricultural productivity and the supply of energy.

Official estimates put the total land mass of the country at 122 million hectares. Of this, 79 million ha (64 per cent) is classified as agricultural land (cultivated, forest and grazing land). Of the 70 million ha, only 9.3 million ha are under cultivation, 3.1 million were fallow and the rest is given over to pasture (World Bank 1986a). Taken at face value, these figures imply that the country has a good agricultural potential. But the situation is quite different when one looks at the uneven spatial distribution of the population by agro-ecological zones. The highlands in Wello, Tigray, northern Shewa, Eritrea, eastern Gonder, and parts of Hararghe and Bale regions have suffered from serious ecological degradation and their carrying capacity of people and animals has been severely undermined mainly due to high population densities.

Population densities are higher in the highland areas than in the lowlands and plot sizes allocated to farm families vary greatly by location, as shown in Table 2. For example, in the south eastern highlands and southern Rift Valley ecological zones, cultivable land per household has increased in spite of massive population growth. In the northern zone, on the other hand, the decline in cultivable land was relatively small (from 0.44 to 0.42 ha) in relation to the increase in population, which went from 4.5 million to 8.2 million. However, there has been a larger decrease in cultivable land per household (from 0.70 to 0.67 ha) in the south eastern highlands zone where population has practically stagnated between 1970 and 1988. It may therefore seem premature to conclude that food production declined because of the fact that peasants operate small plots, a phenomenon caused by high population growth. There are countries in Africa where agricultural production has not been constrained despite high population growth and limited cultivable land.

However, as long as peasants lack access to technology and investment, increased area productivity can not cope with population growth. And as long as peasants cannot find alternative employment, expansion of cultivated land cannot keep pace with the number of new families demanding land. Thus, resettlements and opening up of new land notwithstanding, on average plots get smaller with fast population growth. While peasants may increase output per hectare, all other factors remaining equal, production per head is bound to decrease. This will reduce the marketable surplus, or, if quota regulations

Table 2
Population and Cultivated Land

Ecological Zones	1970				1988			
	Est.Pop. in (000)	%	Density (persons per km²)	Cult.land (ha. per household)	Est.pop in (000)	%	Density (persons per km²)	Cult.land (ha. per household)
Ethiopian Highlands								
Central	11,500	39	68	0.83	15,310	32	91	0.74
Northern	4,500	15	21	0.44	8,160	17	39	0.42
S. Western	4,000	14	42	0.70	4,090	9	43	0.67
S. Eastern	2,500	9	35	0.40	5,540	11	78	0.49
Eastern Highlands								
Arsi Bale	1,250	4	17	1.60	2,510	5	34	0.92
Haraghe-Bale	2,130	7	12	0.94	4,360	9	25	0.42
Southern Rift Valley	3,380	8	45	0.42	6,520	13	123	0.62
Lowland regions	1,250	4	3	-	2,160	4	6	0.35
Country	29,510	100	24	0.69	48,650	100	39	0.60

*The population for 1970 has been adjusted upwards from its previous estimate of 24.5 million on the basis of 1984 Population Cencus data.

Source: Solomon Bellete, 1989. Population Growth and Agricultural Development in Ethiopia; Paper Prepared for the National Conference on "Population Issues in Ethiopia's National Development", Addis Ababa.

enforce deliveries, it will reduce the food available to peasants for home consumption. In any case, rural poverty grows with a declining ratio between land and agricultural population - unless productivity grows even faster.

There is a growing disharmony between the present demographic trends and the trends in economic growth and development. A review of the current status of the agricultural sector made by the World Bank in 1987 reveals a picture of virtual stagnation. While the economy grew at around 2.5 per cent during the last decade, agricultural GDP growth averaged only around 1.1 per cent per annum during the same period (World Bank 1986). The shortfall in food production has led to rapidly increasing dependence on food aid and imports, resulting in a drain on scarce foreign exchange resources.

Growing Ecological Degradation

Deforestation, land and a soil degradation have reached catastrophic levels in Ethiopia. The forest cover is currently about 3.6 per cent of the total area of the country. This is roughly 4.5 million ha. Less than a century ago, about 40 per cent of the country is believed to have been covered by forest (ONCCP 1984). It is estimated that over 200,000 ha of forest land are lost annually. The destruction of trees and shrubs for fuel wood, construction, agricultural implements and other uses sets the pace for accelerated soil erosion and progressive deterioration of the productive capacity for food and energy supply. In most parts of highland Ethiopia, deforestation has been almost complete (Tadesse 1989, FAO 1986).

According to the Ethiopian Highlands Reclamation Study, the ecological and economic costs of land degradation and soil losses are tremendous. Degradation is estimated to cost Ethiopia over 15 billion birr in the next 25 years, or about 600 million birr per annum. This is equivalent to 14 per cent of the contribution of agriculture to GDP in 1982/83. In terms of cereal production, the losses would amount to about 120,000 tons annually in the early 1980s (FAO 1986:7-8).

These losses, when viewed against a background of stagnating development and technological inputs, and increased population, are likely to lead to a grave displacement of population. The Highland Reclamation Study estimates that by the year 2010, over 10 million people of highland Ethiopia would have to derive their livelihood from sources other than cropping their own land. They would have to be absorbed elsewhere in the economy.

Conclusion

Rural stagnation in Ethiopia is a structural problem. The degradation of the environment, the decline in agricultural production, rural underemployment are problems that need to be addressed on a high priority basis. Unfortunately, the government's approach to the population issue is far from satisfactory. In fact, it does not have an explicit policy aimed at modifying fertility or population growth, although in recent years, it has acknowledged that these rates are too high. Therefore, the most important option to be suggested is that the government should adopt an appropriate population policy aimed at reducing fertility and ultimately the population growth rate. Equally important is the need to improve the quality of life of rural residents by expanding social services and other economic opportunities. This could have a direct impact on family decisions to limit the number of children they want to have. In the absence of radical transformation in rural areas, the next drought will produce a holocaust the like of which the world has never seen before.

NOTES

1 Compared to UN estimates, the CSO estimates of growth rates are far too high. The UN put the birth rate at 43.0 and the death rate at 23.5 per thousand, arriving at a growth rate of 1.74 per cent in 1980-85. Projections for 1985-90 are 2.01 (BR: 43.7, DR: 23.6), 2.66 per cent in 1990-95 (BR 46.5 and DR 21.5) and 2.74 per cent in 1995-2000 (BR 46.7 and DR 19.4). Consequently, the UN projection of Ethiopia's population growth is much lower, arriving at 53.383 million by mid-1995 and 61.528 million in 2000.

15 Environment and Mass Poverty
Daniel Gamachu

Introduction: Developing Hunger?

In Ethiopia, as elsewhere in the tropics, rural people are highly dependent on the exploitation of the natural environment. Rural producers knew how to conserve soil moisture where it is scarce, and how to drain land when it gets waterlogged, long before "development agents" tried to teach them that water flows downslope and carries some dirt. They knew what kinds of crops to grow on which types of soil before the pedologists came up with "soil order" classes. They rotated cereals and legumes on their fields, long before scientists started advertising the significance of nitrogen "nodules". Wherever appropriate, they intercropped their fields, long before agriculturalists woke up to the importance of crop "rooting depth" in land use.

By all accounts, however, rural people in Ethiopia remained poor. Production was seldom above mere subsistence level. When disasters have struck, peasants have rarely been able to ride out over even one cropping season. In many parts of the country recurring starvation and famine are still part of rural life today. Indeed, the last famine was the worst known both in dimension and intensity.

Can the problem of environmental degradation be cured by proper conservation measures and land use management? Can the problem of population "explosion" making ever more people compete for the diminishing land resources be overcome by proper birth control and family planning? Can the problem of technical backwardness be solved through judiciously measured modern agricultural inputs? Can the result of social and economic problems be remedied through realistic legislation and other forms of government intervention?

The following discussion concentrates on problems of environment and renewable resource use in rainfed food crop production, and does not deal with cash crops and irrigation. It reflects problems of the rural rather than the urban poor. Because the problems of poverty, underdevelopment, environmental degradation and the related social, economic and political issues are so complex and intertwined, no attempt is made to discuss the issues separately.

The endemic nature of mass poverty in Ethiopia, and the alarming rate of environmental degradation and natural resource depletion are closely related, a vicious circle, where people are forced to over-exploit their environment because they are too poor to protect their resources, and where they get poorer because the environment is degrading. The tragedy lies in a set of interrelated problems linked to a rapid population growth, estimated to be close to 3 per cent annually, while neither economic nor natural resources can be developed at the same pace, leading to mass poverty which in turn reinforces environmental hazards and accelerates degradation of natural resources.

Blaikie (1985:9) sees environmental degradation, at least in poor countries, as a *result*, a *symptom* and a *cause* of underdevelopment (and poverty). "Poverty is invariably associated with forces which bring about environmental degradation"; although it may not always "explain resource losses" (ADB/ECA 1988:69). This problem became the focus of attention of both Ethiopian and international scholars and politicians as a result of the 1972-74 mass starvation and famine. That crisis gave impetus to the rapid, revolutionary and socialist-oriented political change in Ethiopia in 1974.

Famine struck the country again in 1984/85, on a wider geographical area and with unprecedented intensity, though basic revolutionary changes had been implemented, and the social and political turmoil had subsided. This compels scholars and politicians to re-examine the nature and causes of mass poverty and food shortages in this country, and also to evaluate in this context the achievements, the problems, and the mistakes of the revolution.

Population Explosion: A Problem of Procreation ?

Chambers (1983:35-40) divides analysts of poverty and development into two major groups: a "physical ecology cluster" (mostly ecologists and conservation practitioners) and a "political economy cluster" (mostly social scientists and economists). "Physical ecologists" explain rural poverty mainly in terms of what may be called the "population explosion scenario": As a result of rural population growth, farm holdings get progressively smaller and production even at subsistence level becomes untenable. Intensification of land use and shortening of fallow periods leads to further deterioration in soil fertility. Ecologically marginal and fragile environments are occupied and farmed. Biomass is removed through land clearing for cultivation, overgrazing, and gathering of wood and shrubs for fuel. Shortage of wood fuel supply leads to the substitution of natural fertilizers, such as crop residues and animal waste, for wood fuel; which in turn leads to further deterioration in soil fertility and low productivity.

Low and declining agricultural production per capita leads to malnutrition, disease and physical weakness, and a further decline in labour productivity. Where droughts are frequent, processes of desertification and environmental degradation are intensified. Estimates show that Ethiopia is one of the 14 sub-Saharan African countries where present population exceeds land carrying capacity[1] (ADB/ECA 1988:63). At an annual growth rate of nearly 3 per cent, the population of Ethiopia is fast striding towards the fifty million mark. Nearly one person per hundred on the globe is now an Ethiopian.

According to the "physical ecology cluster" of scholars, solutions to these problems lie, among others, in making soil, biomass, and water conservation measures part and parcel of land use management and economic planning for "sustainable development", coupled with programmes of human and animal population growth control measures.

However, measures to bring human and livestock population growth under control may be considered only as long-term objectives in rural development. Peasants in general see children as future labour for the family and security in old age. Traditional Ethiopians say they need more children *le mogn, le mot:* for (security against) imbecility and mortality. Similarly, peasants tend to see livestock not only as an important source of income but also as an investment and security against crop failures. It is thus difficult to convince peasants to reduce their livestock herds to save the environment.

Exploitation: Policing the Policy Makers ?

Political economists and social scientists in the main explain rural poverty in terms of what may be referred to as the "exploitation scenario": the suppression of the poor reduces their incomes, their incentives, and their ability to increase their production. Unfavourable terms of trade between rich and poor nations and the debt burden may force poor nations to exploit their natural resources at unsustainable levels to increase their food supplies. At national and local levels, terms of trade which favour urban populations at the expense of the rural poor (a point which the urban poor in Ethiopia are likely to dispute vehemently) and unreasonable levels of surplus extraction from peasants (which may also be disputed in the case of Ethiopia), may force peasants to intensify the exploitation of renewable natural resources of soil and biomass at their disposal, if they have to maintain their standard of living. Unfavourable terms of trade and unreasonable levels of extraction may also act as disincentives to increase agricultural production (Chambers 1983, Blaikie 1985, ADB/ECA 1988).

The "political economy cluster" of scholars recommends equitable terms of trade and government policies which favour poor peasants and provide incentives. Easy access to modern inputs in agriculture, including mechanization and fertilizers, are expected to enhance productivity, but also to make peasants less dependent on over-exploitation of degraded soils and marginal, fragile areas. The problem remains: how to assure that policy makers feel obliged to give proper attention to the interests of poor peasants?

The Rural Poor: Too Many or Too Weak?

There is no doubt that the rural poor are vulnerable. They are exposed to diseases due to malnutrition and physical weakness. They have limited assets as a buffer against natural or man-made disasters. They are isolated from the mainstream of national economic, social and political life, and powerless against the powerful political and economic forces that affect their lives (Chambers 1983:103-104). Is it their number or is it their weakness that makes them vulnerable?

There is a big variation of agricultural production in different parts of Ethiopia, and levels of peasant production and poverty are highly variable from region to region and from one ecological zone to another. The Ethiopian Highland Reclamation Study documents indicate that the highlands of Ethiopia (above 1,500 m) host about 88 per cent of the total human population, 60 per cent of livestock, and account for about 90 per cent of the land suitable for rainfed agriculture (Hurni 1985). The High Potential Perennial (HPP) highland zone in the south and west has high rainfall and high potential for perennial crops like coffee. The High Potential Cereal (HPC) highland zone in central Ethiopia has medium rainfall and the most fertile soils. The Low Potential Cereal (LPC) zone in northern, north central and eastern parts has low rainfall, is drought prone, has the most degraded soils and is most deforested.

What the highland peasant household grows is determined by the ecological zone it occupies. Crop production covers between 0.85 and 1.40 hectares of land and produces in average between 740 and 1160 kg of grain a year. Averages of animals per household vary between 1.7 and 6.2 cows, 1.6 and 8.8 goats and sheep, 0.1 and 3.1 equines, and between 0.4 and 1.6 oxen. Annual income from crops is between about 330 and 640 birr, and from livestock between 70 and 125 birr. Crop production demands some 16 to 45 ox-days and 70 to 125 person-days of work. Monetary costs for seeds, animals and other inputs are about 90 to 190 birr a year. Net farm income varies between the regions at averages from 270 to 620 birr. These figures may not be very reliable in absolute values, but give an indication of the broad patterns of variation between different regions, and in the level of peasant poverty.

The area cultivated by a peasant household appears not very variable from region to region, probably indicating the technological bottle-neck for a peasant to expand cultivated area even where land is not in short supply. Basic food grain production per household does not vary much either from region to region. Incomes vary, however, depending on the types of crops grown - whether staple or cash crops - and the number of livestock owned. The latter may indicate real income differences among peasants: livestock is to the peasant what a bank account is to the urban middle class. It may therefore be difficult to convince peasants to reduce their livestock in order to save the environment. Stocking rates are most critical in the LPC zone where the actual rate is some 11 to 34 per cent above the carrying capacity (Constable 1985).

In those zones where environmental degradation is serious, there is obviously a need for protective measures, because otherwise, production might be reduced as much as 2 per cent per year due to soil degradation (Constable 1984, Hurni 1988). But even for other regions, poverty will remain endemic unless technological changes improve production. Conservation of natural resources, their rational use, and investment in their further development have to be seen together. There is no "trade-off" between natural resources and development: one can not pay for improvements in living standards and production by depleting some of the natural resources. Only their protective development can allow Ethiopia to overcome both poverty and the vicious circle of growing depletion because of population growth.

Vulnerability: A Side-effect of Development?

Drought years have indeed been a regular feature in peasant life in Ethiopia. Peasants know about it, and know how to protect themselves against drought. Under normal conditions, subsistence includes sufficient reserves to give security even in years of bad harvests and of drought. Mesfin Wolde Mariam (1984) demonstrated that social conditions are decisive mediators which can turn a drought into famine and mass starvation. Drought is a natural disaster, which affects agricultural production and the bearing capacity of the natural environment. But famine is a social effect, caused not necessarily by the drought, but by social conditions which force the "normal" precautions of security and solidarity of subsistence peasants to break down. Such social factors may be a degree of inequality within the rural population which creates mass poverty, and / or extraction of resources, be it through landlords or the state, through unequal trade relations or through other mechanisms of resource transfers.

One might add that natural environments are also more or less vulnerable to droughts dependent on the same factors. "Normal" drought years have in historical times worked as a corrective mechanism to prevent human and animal populations from growing too large. But social organization and technical developments allowed human interference to upset this balance, keeping a growing human and animal population alive. This led to over-exploitation of some natural resources, and gave nature no chance to regenerate after a drought period.

It is not possible to return to a natural state in which droughts reduce populations and re-establish the old natural balance. Once modern medicine is available, it cannot be justifiable to let people die of easily curable diseases. Having developed mechanisms to break the limitations of natural cycles, society has the responsibility to refine its tools to re-establish an ecological balance on a new level. It will not be possible to achieve such a new balance by just one line of action. Neither will population control in isolation achieve a new balance, even if population growth rates are reduced to zero or below. Nor will environmental rehabilitation solve the problem, as long as people demand improved standards of living; nor even would fairly equal distribution, economic development and improved agricultural productivity help, as long as other factors continued to upset the balance anew. Only an interplay of determined and closely adjusted measures in all four areas - environmental rehabilitation, population planning, economic development and a social order of equality in the distribution of resources and rights, finely tuned to each other, can achieve a new, but dynamic balance.

We are far from such a new ecological equilibrium, and we will never reach it completely. All we can work for is a better understanding of why poor people accelerate environmental degradation, and how environmental degradation makes people poorer. Hopefully such knowledge will help to increase human capacity to react to major disturbances in the ecology, and to act before natural variations result in human and ecological disasters.

The Good Old Days: How Bad Were They?

Before the revolution, land ownership in most parts of the northern highlands of Ethiopia was communal *rist* land shared for use by kinship groups. In the Southern half of the highlands, most land was privately owned *gult* land. Most of the land of pastoral nomads in the lowlands was owned by the state.

The former *rist* regions of Ethiopia seem to be the core of the problems associated with population pressure on land resources, desertification and land degradation, rural poverty and vulnerability to natural and man-made crises. These regions are in general drought-prone areas with low and variable rainfall. The geographical areas where these problems are felt have in historical times expanded southwards from the Eritrea and Tigray core into Wollo, Hararghe, northern and parts of southern Shoa, and eastern Gondar, and are now also threatening the Gojam highlands (McCann 1988). Today, the northern and northeastern regions of Eritrea, Tigray and Wollo have acute shortages of land with deep soils, forest land, and land areas with reliable rainfall and sufficiently long growing seasons, relative to their rural population. The central highlands of Arsi and northern Shoa are highly deforested and have acute shortages of grazing land.

McCann points out that the northern highlands have the longest sustained settled agriculture in Ethiopia, which has eventually led to unsustainable rates of land exploitation, as population increased. Population varied, depending on natural and man-made disasters, but in general population growth had an upward trend throughout this century, and accelerated after the war during the last three or four decades. People migrated up the steep slopes of the mountains and down to climatically marginal lowlands and the Rift Valley escarpments, and southward as share-croppers on private land, or as daily labourers or petty merchants. Land degradation accelerated as the size of holdings declined, fallowing periods became shorter, and grazing areas shrunk.

It may be difficult to ascertain today whether the *rist* system of land tenure originally allowed population growth, because it had a mechanism of equalizing distribution of land within villages, and of population between villages. This might imply that population growth eventually exceeded natural limits, so that it destroyed the basis for the very social system the mechanism was built on. Another hypothesis would argue that the disturbance of a delicate social balance in rural culture and society, through the centralization under Emperors Menilek and Haile Selassie, is responsible for growing disasters, ecological degradation and famines, in the second half of this century.

Documents from the former Ministry of Land Reform and Administration indicate that in most parts of the "privately owned" land in the southern half of the country, 40 to 70 per cent of the farmers were tenants who had to render from a quarter to half of their produce to the landlords, in addition to taxes and other contributions; and 10 to 50 per cent of the total area under private ownership was owned by absentee landlords residing in urban areas (Tennassie 1988). These figures also indicate that 30 to 60 per cent of the farmers in the *gult* land areas of the south owned land privately.[2]

The "archaic" land tenure system in the pre-revolution period is often blamed as one of the major factors for agricultural underdevelopment in Ethiopia:

> The major obstacles to the development of the (agricultural) sector included archaic, inequitable and complex systems of land tenure, technological backwardness, poor infrastructure, and a government policy that was at best lukewarm to agricultural development. (Eshetu 1988:27)

Other writers single out the role of traditional, backward looking and conservative Ethiopian peasants as the major bottle-neck in agricultural development, and their inability to adopt new technologies and take initiatives and risks:

> An important dimension of vulnerability in Ethiopia's rural economy has been the failure of smallholders to adopt innovation in design, materials, or application of technology in either farm equipment or the technologies of application (irrigation, mechanization, agronomic techniques) over the past century. Crises in climate and food resouces, far from stimulating innovation, appear to have drivn smallholders further into conservative risk aversion strategies. (McCann 1899:12-13)

Again, it appears an easy way out to blame peasants for causing environmental destruction and perpetuating underdevelopment by their fear of taking risks. After all, their only chance of survival may be to avoid risks that would prove fatal in case of a disaster. To save trees for the next generation may be important; but if this generation does not survive, there won't be a next one at all. It is hard to distinguish, on the basis of scientific experience, to what degree risk aversion is a reason for poverty, or on the contrary a reaction to it.

Post-Revolution: Proclamations and Disincentives?

The 1975 land reform proclamation and subsequent legislation laid the foundation for a socialist agriculture. Peasants were given a chance to share land on the basis of equity. Each peasant association member received his share of different quality soils. Each one cultivated therefore several scattered small plots. As population increased and the young came of age and claimed their share of land, the size of holdings diminished further. Equity was an important consideration in land distribution in the *rist* system also.

But it was modified by other social concerns, which were largely abolished and discredited during the land reform. The idea of equity is now so ingrained in the minds of peasants that not only crop land but even grazing land is in many parts of the highlands allotted equally to each household. The adverse ecological consequences of such fragmentation are visible in the highlands today.

A key problem in land use that the land reform could not solve is the problem of land fragmentation. To the contrary, other concerns being reduced in importance, equity has become an overshadowing concern, which demands frequent redistribution of land, and consequently creates insecurity of holdings. Fragmentation and insecurity became a major disincentive which prevented peasants from embarking on conservation measures and other investments. As long as peasants are not assured how long they will be allowed to keep a plot allotted to them, they are necessarily reluctant to invest work and time in long-term improvements. The land reform has also significantly curtailed the free out-migration from problem areas to other parts of the country which historically had helped to some degree to diffuse the pressure on land resources.

Government policies attempted to correct such problems by bringing unviably fragmented plots together in producer cooperatives which would have allowed more rational land use and modern mechanized cultivation techniques. But peasants were not enthusiastic about producer cooperatives, which brought more restrictions than advantages for their cultivation and their family economy. In spite of many incentives to cooperative members, resistance of peasants continued, and only about 4 per cent of the peasants had become members of some 2,900 producer cooperatives by 1988 (Tenassie 1988). The privileges given to the new cooperatives must appear as disincentives to those peasants who decide to stay outside. Where peasants know that private traders offer far better prices, but are prevented from making use of such offers, the marketing arrangements and the quota deliveries to AMC must appear as disincentives.

In spite of such problems, the organization of peasant associations has greatly enhanced possibilities for soil conservation and afforestation efforts. Such measures were unknown to many peasants before the revolution. Planting of trees and construction of soil and stone bunds against erosion have become known throughout the country, through substantial government and international financial inputs and mostly through the voluntary work of peasants. A first step has been taken towards a "greening" of Ethiopia. But deforestation rates are still much above afforestation. Some estimates show that at present rates, it would take over 70 years before all land that is today already in need of conservation measures was treated (Hurni 1988a). Hurni claims that current soil conservation and afforestation programmes would have to be increased fourfold over the next 50 years to attain sustainability - an increase which is not achievable with the limited financial and technical means available (Hurni 1988b). The only way out is, as Hurni sees it, an integration of conservation and afforestation in normal cultivation cycles and land use practice.

This demands that the knowledge of peasants about conservation and natural cycles is given its rightful place again. If peasants understand that their knowledge matters, they will themselves find ways of adapting conservation techniques so that they become cheaper, can easily be applied by peasants, and offer immediate benefits, making conservation attractive to the peasants. In such an environment, there would be no need to demonstrate to poor peasants that conservation-related efforts pay, not only in the long run, but immediately.

Future Prospects: Central or Local Knowledge?

The following five recommendations are based on the conviction that economic development heavily depends on increasing agricultural production, at least in poor countries. Production depends on the quality and quantity of government services offered to peasants, as much as on natural environments. Environmental rehabilitation programmes cannot succeed unless the whole spectrum of social and environmental rural development problems is tackled at the same time. This complex entity is essential in concepts like "sustainable development", "integrated rural development" and "conservation-based development".

A simple recommendation of one strategy for "sustainable development" would be too simplistic, and create new problems. Any solution must be adjusted to local conditions and tuned to peasant culture and self-understanding to have a chance of success. However, the following principles should be useful as guide-lines for their discussion:

1. Environmental policies and regulations should be based, as much as possible, on scientific assessments of current land use practices and accessible natural resources. Government institutions currently engaged in such activities, such as the Land Use Planning and Regulatory Department (LUPRD) of the MoA, ought to be strengthened. Geographical information systems should be created, to generate a reliable data base on environmental resources and problems such as "forest cover, soil erosion and soil capability, desertification risks and the distribution of human and livestock populations" (ADB/ECA 1988:81-82).

2. Environmental policies and regulations should take into account that nearly all areas of economic activity have environmental dimensions. Policies and regulations ought to be comprehensive and include all sectors of the economy. National and sectoral plans and project designs should incorporate environmental considerations. An institution which can act as a "environmental watch-dog" should be given a mandate to oversee and monitor the implementation of such policies and regulations.

3. Problems that have arisen through the land reform of 1975 have to be critically examined and flexible and socially acceptable solutions sought. In particular, issues related to land fragmentation, security of holdings, use of

community forests, cooperative efforts, land leases to private farmers, and the employment of labour on private farms have to be reconsidered.

4. Environmental conservation and rehabilitation plans should be sufficiently detailed to include specific plans for different ecological zones and farming systems. The basis for the plans should be ecological zones rather than administrative units.

5. National environmental policies and regulations should be general and comprehensive rather than specific and restrictive. They must provide sufficient scope for local adaptation and modification, depending on local culture, history, farming systems and ecological conditions. The administration and implementation of environmental policies and regulations should be highly decentralized and build on local participation and self-administration, not on execution of central decisions.

NOTES

1 "Over-population" is of course a relative phenomenon, and if new technologies and resources are put in use, it may cease to exist. Nevertheless, one may speak of over-population relative to the existing natural and social conditions, capacities, and distribution patterns.

2 These figures were published in official reports from the ministry in 1965-71, but are based on questionable assumptions. At that time, a majority of peasants in the south were still convinced that they "owned" an unquestionable claim on their land, while in legal terms they were already reduced to tenants, without knowing it themselves. The figures collected, based on surveys in which peasants were asked how much land they owned, do thus reflect subjective peasant claims, but not the objective legal situation. Questionnaires did not consider the implications of an abstract (European) concept of "ownership". Asking a peasant how much land he has would give totally different results from asking a landlord the same question. See Chapter 3 in this volume and footnote 5 in Chapter 2 (Editorial footnote).

16 Peasants, Environment, Resettlement
Alemneh Dejene

The movement of people from the densely populated northern highlands to the central and southern regions of contemporary Ethiopia, where land and opportunities were better, dates back to the 18th century. During the period of Ethiopia's expansion under the Emperor Menelik (1855-1913) such movement of people became more common. North-south migration was mainly undertaken by initiative of individuals and accelerated under Haile Selassie's rule because of imperial land grants, the expansion of trade, communication, population growth, shortage of land and drought in the northern highlands. Figures are difficult to cite but millions of people had voluntarily resettled shortly after the Italian occupation in 1940, until 1970 (Wood 1977:84). There was little government involvement; all of this movement took place quietly without the label of resettlement.

This changed when the 1973/74 Wollo famine claimed the lives of 200,000 people. The imperial regime's futile attempt to cover the Wollo famine aroused the indignation of many and contributed to the overthrow of the monarchy.[1] When it came to power in 1974 one of the most pressing concerns of the new military government was to figure out how to deal with the still lingering famine and its victims. It immediately established the Relief and Rehabilitation Commission (RRC) as a means to deal with the emergency situation as well as to coordinate relief and rehabilitation projects in a systematic way. The RRC was also entrusted to undertake resettlement activities which the government saw as a major option in reducing recurrent famine in the north. Between 1974 and 1984, during the first ten years of the military government 45,849 families (most of them from the drought-afflicted areas of the Wollo and Tigray regions) were resettled in various regions of Ethiopia under the auspices of the Relief and Rehabilitation Commission (Samuel 1985:16).

A decade later, in 1984/85, a devastating famine had once again struck Ethiopia. The scope of the population affected by famine is unparalleled in this century. At the height of the famine eight million people were affected. The worst hit regions were Wollo and Tigray. In Wollo, 2.6 million people were affected out of a total population of 3.6 million and in Tigray 1.4 million people were affected out of a population of 2.4 million (Jansson 1987:XII)

While the world's attention focused on Ethiopia, the government once again found itself under enormous pressure. In the central administration's view, resettlement became the most immediate and viable option in order to deal with the emergency situation. Referring to the famine victims as "environmental refugees", the government, in November 1984, announced an "emergency resettlement programme to resettle 1.5 million people from the famine affected areas, particularly from Wollo and Tigray, within a year (Samuel 1985: 50). Indeed, from November 1984 until March 1986, 594,190 family members were resettled in Illubabor, Wollaga, Keffa, Gojam and Gondar regions.[2] The largest number of settlers, 374,432, came from Wollo region. The second largest group, containing 107,230 settlers, came from Shoa region, while the third largest group with 89,716 settlers came from Tigray region. The majority of the settlers (81 per cent) went to the south western regions of Wollaga, Illubabor and Keffa. Most of the remaining (17 per cent) went to the Italian assisted resettlement scheme in Metekel in the Gojam region, while about 2 per cent settled in Gondar region.[3]

Government action to resettle such a magnitude of people may be dramatic but the rationale for the resettlement on environmental grounds is supported by the Ethiopian Highland Reclamation Study which is financed by the United Nations Food and Agricultural Organization. According to this study the Ethiopian highlands occupy 44 per cent of the country's 1,251,282 square kilometres (CSO 1987:1) and include about 80 per cent of the country's 47 million people (CSA 1988:10) and two-thirds of the 77 million ruminants (MoA 1984c:12). The highlands suffer from massive land degradation due to soil erosion. It is estimated that 1,900 million tons of soil is eroded annually from the Ethiopian highlands and this severely reduces soil fertility and crop yields (MoA 1984:23). The 1985 estimation indicates only 20 per cent of the total area of the highlands, i.e. 10 million ha, has relatively minor problems of erosion; 76 per cent (41 million ha) is significantly of seriously eroded and 4 per cent (2 million ha) has outstripped its capacity to be of value for production. If this trend continues, 18 per cent of the highland will be bare rock by the year 2010 and 10 million people will not be able to produce food from the land (MoA 1984:29-48).

This severe level of land degradation is largely attributed to the enormous pressure exerted on the ecosystem by human activity including intensive cultivation, overgrazing, over-population and deforestation. The major rationale for the resettlement programme is to reduce the human pressure on the land and thus to avert the accelerating loss of productive land. The magnitude of this problem is visible in many parts of the highlands including Wollo, Tigray, and northern Shoa regions. In Wollo, where most of the field work for this study has been carried out, a number of peasant associations confront slopes exceeding 30 per cent, high population and livestock density and little vegetative cover. The rugged Gale Giorgis peasant association in Yeju *awarja*, for example, has 450 ha of which 320 could be cultivated. This cultivated land which has numerous and expanding gullies has to support 458 heads of household (1,323 family members) and 2,061 livestock. In this peasant association the average holding is below 0.5 ha. Thus, in principle, the relocation of farmers from these highly degraded highlands seems legitimate. It would be futile, however, to implement such a programme without careful planning as attempted by the government during the "emergency resettlement" programme.

Peasant Views on Resettlement

The government resettlement programme has focused in Wollo because it is one of the most severely damaged areas due to land degradation and recurrent drought. The following paragraphs will examine the issues of resettlement based on a field investigation that was undertaken from October 1987 until March 1988 both in Wollo and the south western regions of Ethiopia. A follow-up field study was conducted between November 1988 and February 1989. In Wollo interviews were conducted among randomly selected farmers covering 9 *Awraja*. The sample consisted of 230 households from 46 peasant associations. Five farmers were selected from each peasant association for an interview. As a questionnaire survey alone is of limited value in providing insight into the conditions of the rural poor (Chambers 1983: 49-64), an "in depth study" of a limited group of farmers, and discussions with extension agents and local officials helped to complement the survey questionnaire method in generating the data.

The study specifically examined peasants' views towards resettlement in Wollo. It looked at the experiences of Wollo peasants who have settled in the relatively fertile western regions of Ethiopia, and the environmental impact of resettlement in both Wollo and the settlement areas.

In Wollo, nearly all of the peasants interviewed were emphatic in their response that they did not wish to be resettled. Peasants' views on resettlement have been partly influenced by their previous experiences. According to eyewitness accounts of relief agents, the 1984 resettlement was chaotic. This chaos was due primarily to the massive number of people pouring into relief centres everywhere. In the process of travel, some families were separated and sent to different destinations.

A considerable number of peasants who left for resettlement were unhappy about the conditions in their new homes and have returned to Wollo. Forty-eight per cent of the respondents knew someone who had returned to Wollo after resettlement. The government agencies in Wollo, although secretive about this affair, have acknowledged that 15,047 formerly resettled peasants have returned due to favourable weather conditions in Wollo.[4] In our estimation, the real figure is likely to be at least three times higher than officially admitted. However, it is difficult to obtain exact figures, as most of the peasants live as fugitives, fearful of being caught and sent back. Returners are not entitled to land in a peasant association. One of the few places where these returners actually identified themselves and informed us about their plight was in the Kello peasant association (02), located 5 kilometres from the town of Kemise in Kalu *Awraja*. In this peasant association, 68 heads of households left for resettlement in 1984/85, 30 of whom have returned. Reasons for their return included serious health problems, the death of a family member, poor working conditions and harvests on huge farms, poor health, a desire to reunite with family members, hostility among natives, and homesickness.

The 1984/85 resettlement in Wollo was not entirely undertaken by brute force, despite some media coverage in the west to that effect. Most peasants had left voluntarily, seeking, under the circumstances, the only available alternative for survival. But peasants' attitudes towards resettlement have dramatically shifted from ambivalence in 1984 to defiance in 1987. Among the most important reasons for this shift were horror stories that most peasants have heard about what had happened to those who left for resettlement. Many of those first-hand stories were told by their fellow peasants and relatives, who are now among them. Many of them have also mourned the death of a relative or a friend in the resettlement area. Peasants are also deeply attached to their community and have an unwavering loyalty to their birth place. A familiar response they give for not wanting to resettle was that "they would rather die in a place where their umbilical cord is buried". Some fear that their families would not be able to adjust in the new environment; and many feel that they would be able to grow enough food at home for their families during normal years.

With these sentiments in the background, the government plan called for the resettling of 50,000 heads of households (209,000 family members) in one year's time beginning in October 1987. To implement this plan, quotas of the number of families required are assigned to each *Woreda*. In return, each *Woreda* instructs peasant association leaders in the recruiting of a specific number of families. In spite of the quotas, recruitment for resettlement is to be pursued on an entirely voluntary basis. This guide-line became a puzzle to both local officials and peasant association leaders who were uncertain how they should interpret it.[5] On the eve of our interview, in the Ashinga peasant association (01) in Sayent *Woreda*, Borena *Awraja*, local officials and peasant association leaders rounded up to 40 heads of household along with their family members for resettlement. They were sent to Dessie (the capital city of Wollo), only to be sent back to their homes after they informed high level officials that they were forced to leave from their homes. Local party officials and administrators blame some zealot local administrators for these incidents. The pretext that led to such abuses was the quota for resettlement. If resettlement was to be on a voluntary basis, as the government had consistently asserted, then there would be no need for quotas.

The criteria for the selection of the *Woredas* and the peasant associations which would be included in resettlement were as follows:

1. a topography of rugged hills and slopes exceeding 35 per cent;
2. severe deforestation and / or severe erosion;
3. few natural resources and poor soils;
4. affliction by recurrent famine in the past 25 years;
5. population density to the point where average land size is too small to sustain a family.[6]

Meeting the quota for voluntary resettlement proved futile as it yielded about 1,785 family members as of March 1988.[7] In all parts of the country, peasant attitudes towards resettlement are decidedly negative. There have been attacks on peasant association leaders and extension agents who were involved in recruitment. For example, the Goshmeda peasant association (017) in Delanta *Woreda*, Wadela Delanta *Awraja*, meets every criteria identified for resettlement. It was affected by the 1987 drought. Nevertheless, to avoid hearing about resettlement, most peasants have paid their taxes ahead of time. The government, at least for the moment, has wisely abandoned obligatory quotas for resettlement in Wollo.

Given the depth of peasant resentment towards resettlement, whether the present resettlement programmes could bring an end to environmental degradation in Wollo is an important question. Firstly, resettlement could reduce the amount of human pressure exerted on the land. However, it does not deal with over-population which is a major cause of land pressure in the highlands. If we do not control the present trend of over 2.9 per cent population growth rate, Ethiopia's population will be three times greater (114.5 million) by the year 2015 (CSA 1988: 29). Thus resettlement can siphon a segment of the population, but it cannot slow down population growth. A decline in rate of population growth is essential in the attempt to arrest the massive land degradation.

Secondly, resettlement has created a great deal of uncertainty and insecurity among every peasant in Wollo. Thus, peasants, either individually or collectively, are not motivated to undertake conservation activities fearing that they will be forced to resettle any time. Among the interviewed farmers, 5 per cent indicated that they were not planting trees because they feared resettlement. Some extension agents entrusted to promoting conservation and afforestation publicly admit that the hysteria over resettlement has constrained peasant participation in these endeavours. Thus, resettlement, as being implemented presently, is detracting from the very objective it should promote.

Thirdly, one of the major sources of land degradation is livestock density and poor management of grazing land. The resettlement programme focuses only on humans and does little in addressing the role of livestock in the process of land degradation. The assumption that most erosion takes place on cultivated land may be true. It is also true that livestock roam freely for most parts of the year on the cultivated land and this results in soil crusting and compaction. This makes the soil vulnerable to erosion.

Environmental Impact in Settlement Areas

We shall now examine the environmental issues facing the relatively "fertile" regions of western Ethiopia, namely Illubabor, Keffa and Wollaga where most of the resettlement is taking place.[8]

The western part of Ethiopia has an area of 175,300 square kilometres of which the Wollaga region covers 41 per cent, Illubabor 31 per cent, and Keffa 28 per cent of the total area. This is one of the most sparsely populated regions of the country, containing 6.5 million people. The dominant ecological zones are a medium altitude zone covering 46 per cent of the area (1,500 to 2,500 meters above sea level), and a lowlands zone covering 45 per cent of the area

(500 to 1,500 meters). Only 4 per cent of the area is considered to be arid land less than 500 meters above sea level. It is estimated that half of Ethiopia's remaining natural forest (3.6 per cent) is located in these three regions.[9]

There are three distinct resettlement schemes under which peasants make their new homes: "large-scale", "low cost" and "integrated" (placement within existing peasant association) settlements.[10] The most significant schemes are "large-scale" settlements and "integrated" settlements where 224,576 people where 252,442 were settled respectively.[11] Only 26,888 people have settled under "low cost" settlement schemes.[12]

The "large-scale" settlement schemes were hastily prepared under the 1984 emergency programme by clearing a large amount of forest land in sparsely populated areas. In this scheme, a huge estate of 8,000 to 20,000 ha of land with 6,000 to 16,000 heads of households was broken down into smaller units of 1,000 to 2,000 ha, and about 500 heads of households. These units are further divided into villages. This scheme is highly mechanized, involving over 100 tractors and several combines and is similar to a state farm or commune. The peasants are transformed overnight into daily workers in a modern farm with little understanding of the modern farming involved. The management collects what is harvested and then distributes the products based on labour contribution. Peasant attitudes towards this collective system of production are clearly negative. This was also expressed by the Ministry of Agriculture staff and extension agents closely working in the resettlement areas who have advised on increasing the size of the individual plot in the large-scale schemes. The only individual land the peasants own under this scheme is a small plot (considerably lower than a half hectare) around their homestead.

All the "large-scale" settlement schemes are in Wollaga (Asosa, Keto, Jareso, Anger Guten) with the exception of the one in Illubabor at Gambela. The largest of the settlements in this scheme is Asosa which has 14,143 heads of households (47,079 family members) and 18,808 ha of land. Gambela is the second largest with 11,234 heads of household (44,664 family members) and 15,600 ha of land. Keto has 10,397 heads of household (37,024 family members) and 11,234 ha; Anger Gutine has 9,756 heads of household (29,217 family members) and 12,329 ha; and Jareso has 3,860 heads of household (13,528 family members) and 4,644 ha of land.[13]

Since soil fertility is a major factor in improving agricultural production in Ethiopia, the impact of "large-scale settlements" on the land has been devastating. The indiscriminate clearing of dense forest with bulldozers and other heavy equipment has removed the top soil to within 10 to 20 centimetres, a part of the soil which is crucial in maintaining soil fertility. This top soil is easily detachable and is irreversibly lost due to rain or wind erosion. Some extension agents assert that the relative decline in yields in Asosa after the initial year may be related to the removal of a large amount of top soil in the first year clearing of the forest for cultivation.

The "large-scale" settlements scheme is by far the most inappropriate and poorly functioning scheme for the peasants' conditions. The most formidable challenge a Wollo settler faces in this scheme is the physical environment.

Most "large-scale" settlements are located in very hot lowlands and semi-arid regions. In particular, the settlement in Gambela has a very harsh climate throughout most of the year. Those who came from the highland areas find it extremely difficult to cope with such a hot climate and many of them are reported as having serious health problems, particularly malaria and elephantiasis. The largest number of deaths reported is among those who have settled in this area. Compounding this physical alienation is the collective and highly mechanized system of production in the "large-scale" settlements. Consequently, a large number of the people who have escaped are those from the "large-scale" settlement scheme. According to one government report, about 52,000 heads of household (92,000 family members) who were settled under the "emergency programmeme" are no longer in this scheme. About 45,000 heads of household have escaped while 7,000 of them have died. Among those in the "integrated" scheme, about 4,000 heads of household are reported to have escaped while another 4,000 have died (Council of Ministers 1988 b: p. 18). Most Wollo settlers we have interviewed in the "large-scale" resettlement schemes do not feel at home and wish to return to Wollo.

In the "integrated" settlement peasants are placed within existing peasant associations and are allocated land to farm individually. The selection of a peasant association as well as the number of people who are located in one area is based on the size of the peasant association and on the number of households therein. Peasants under this scheme live similarly to the previous conditions and there is little social disorder. Here, peasants own their own land, keep bee hives in their back yards and, above all, are in control of the fruits of their labour. The climate where the "integrated" scheme is concentrated is suitable (especially in the medium altitude) and peasants under this scheme did not report having chronic health problems as did the peasants in the other two resettlement schemes. As of 1988, the number of heads of households under the integrated scheme in Illubabor is 89,849, in Wollaga 59.947, and in Keffa 46,247[14] (CSO 1986 (49): 30). A large part of these settlements are in the fertile and densely forested highlands of Illubabor. Illubabor has a little more than one million inhabitants and 4.6 million ha of land (CSO 1986 (49): 30). In this region, forest land is relatively plentiful. One Wollo peasant who has resettled said: "All we have to do is clear more forests if we need more land to cultivate".

The "integrated" settlements may also cause major land degradation. There have been many instances of peasants cultivating land of considerable slope without the necessary precautions. Contour ploughing is not widely practiced. There were hardly any terraces or soil binds on the hilly areas which are being cultivated by settlers as well as by the local population. As a result, many of the rivers and streams from these hills are carrying a massive amount of top soil to the neighbouring Sudan. This happens particularly during the rainy season when the rainfall intensity is high.

Crop rotation, which is one way of maintaining soil fertility, is distinctly absent in many of the settlement areas. The natives plant their staple food ensete once in every five to ten years and supplement it by cultivating maize, their main crop, each year. This farming system does not require the clearing of large areas of forest land for agriculture. The settlers (from Wollo and Tigray) strongly dislike ensete and are getting accustomed to having maize as their major crop. They use maize to make *injera*, the Ethiopian staple food. The Wollo settlers have made numerous attempts to grow teff but it gets waterlogged in most areas. Little attempt is made to introduce different kinds of cereals in settlement areas and settlers miss the variety of crops they used to grow in Wollo. As more forest land is converted for agricultural use, the absence of crop rotation in settlement areas has an adverse impact on soil fertility.

Another major problem is the deforestation taking place in "integrated" settlement areas. There is an increasing demand of wood for the construction of houses, fuel and farming equipment. In addition, the burning of forest, a common practice, is more detrimental now because of the increasing demand of land for cultivation. The settlers seem to be overwhelmed by the dense forest around them and often complain of wildlife destroying their crops and threatening their families. The settlers have a habit of cutting trees for many reasons. They are cutting the wood around their homestead to make chairs, tables and other household items, not only for their own use, but also to sell. Wood and wood products are becoming a source of cash to some settlers. This has intensified the destruction of the natural forest. In fact, the sight of "integrated" settlements easily stands out throughout Illubabor because they occupy bare land that is devoid of natural vegetation, and is in the midst of thick forest.

The third type of resettlement scheme is the "low cost" settlement. The difference between "low cost" and "large-scale" settlements is one of magnitude. The "low cost" settlements are usually established in smaller estates of less than 1,000 hectare and have considerably fewer numbers of tractors and modern equipment than "large-scale" settlements. They are also run on cooperative principles based on a point system. There are nine "low cost" schemes all located in the Keffa region. These are Gura Ferda with 4,121 heads of households and 2,323 ha; Milgawa with 344 heads of households and 304 ha; Arguba with 554 heads of households and 477 ha; Kishe with 891 heads of households and 883 ha; Miche with 666 heads of household and 1053 ha; Dedesa with 292 heads of households and 512 ha; Begi with 502 heads of household and 620 ha; Chunege with 570 heads of households and 481 ha; and Gale with 378 heads of households and 354 ha of land.[15]

The Kishe and the Miche settlements are established on a modern farm nationalized by the 1975 agrarian reform. The rest of the "low cost" schemes are built by clearing dense forest areas similar to the areas cleared for "large-scale" settlements. A major difference between "low cost" and "large-scale" settlements is that the operation of the "low cost" settlements is smaller and less mechanized. Peasants under the "low cost" settlements have more individual plots around their homestead and are given oxen to plough it. Most peasants assert that the bulk of their harvest is produced on their individual plots rather than on the modern collectives. The Wollo settlers in the "low cost" scheme do not appear to be as alienated as those in the "large-scale" scheme. In the Keshe settlement particularly, most of the Wollo settlers are well-adjusted. The soil in Keshe is fertile and most peasants feel they could produce a surplus if they could get more individual land and oxen.

With regard to environmental degradation, the "low cost" schemes present similar problems to those of "large-scale" settlements. Forest for these settlements are cleared in the same way as observed in "large-scale" settlements except that the amount of land being cleared is smaller. The heavy equipment employed in the clearing of the forest has had an equally destabilizing effect on the soil's fertility.

It is difficult to say which scheme presents the greatest risk of environmental degradation. One's immediate reaction is likely to be that of "large-scale" settlements when seeing the huge trees being devastated by bulldozers in large quantities. The "large-scale" settlements have an immediate impact on the land. In the long term, however, the "integrated" settlements could have a much more profound impact on land degradation. The present farming practices, and the indiscriminate clearing and burning of forest poses an enormous environmental threat. The Committee appointed by the Council of Ministers to investigate resettlement in the western regions gave one a blunt warnings regarding this problem. The Committee headed by Ato Aklu Girgire, the former head of the Natural Resource Department in the Ministry of Agriculture stated that if the present rate of deforestation and soil erosion continues, there will be a major imbalance in the ecosystem in the settlement areas within only eight years. This would be similar to the magnitude of the problems we presently find in the famine affected areas of the northern highlands of Ethiopia (Council of Ministers 1988). The Committee's assessment which exhibits a great deal of courage is not alarmist. It is based on field investigations and rather reflects the sober realities of the magnitude of the natural resource destruction occurring in the relatively fertile regions of western Ethiopia.

Perhaps one of the greatest contributors to environmental degradation, irrespective of the kind of settlement scheme, is the absence of a systematic way of assessing the land potential (land use planning) in both the selection and the implementation of settlement sites. Little attention is given to soil chemistry, land topography, slope gradient, availability of water, possibility of expanding land, suitability of livestock rearing, and the threat to natural forest and wildlife. Settlement sites were often selected by some of the highest party officials who have little understanding of agriculture. The advice of the Ministry of Agriculture staff and officials was often neglected. The prevailing sentiment of the party officials in charge of resettlement at that time was to establish settlements as quickly as possible. The common phrase used in promoting this goal was "saving lives is more important than trees". This statement has also put some of the Ministry of Agriculture staff who were advocating caution in the establishment of settlement sites on the defensive.

Shortage of land, particularly in the "low cost" settlements, has already been reported. The average holding in the "low cost" scheme is 0.96 ha and there seems to be little possibility of expanding land in the Chinega, Gale and Gura Ferda settlements.[16] Most of the settlers in the "integrated" settlements presently have adequate land. However, this situation could change drastically because of the high rate of population growth and because peasant associations could be overwhelmed by the influx of people into areas with a limited capacity to expand land in the fertile highland areas.

Soil analysis, which is an important indicator in assessing the land's suitability for cropping and the kinds of crops that are likely to give better yields, has been ignored in the selection of settlement sites. For instance, in most of Gambela the soil has a cemented layer which hinders water absorption and is believed to be deficient in organic content. Here the Ministry of Construction selected a settlement site in the Gilo valley and cultivated 8,000 ha of maize. As no yields were obtained since water could not penetrate below 35 centimetres because of the hard cement underneath it, the site had to be abandoned only a year later. The corn fields were drenched by water during the rainy season and by the floods from the nearby Gilo river. Even the settlement areas that have good drainage in Gambela, such as Abobo, have surprisingly low yields. Extension agents secretly admit that yields in settlement areas in Gambela are very low. They average about 5 quintals for maize and sorghum in spite of mechanization and the availability of fertilizer and improved seed. The "low cost" settlement in Dedesa valley and Miche in the Keffa region also suffer from poor water drainage which has adversely affected yields in those areas.

Other settlement sites were established in rugged terrain with steep slopes. A good example of these are the "low cost" settlement schemes at Gura Ferda and Gale. The roughness of the terrain in these two sites makes cultivation and the use of tractors difficult. The soil depth in these sites, particularly at Gura Ferda, is shallow. This fact is acknowledged by Ministry of Agriculture staff in Jimma who have recommended to the local party officials that settlers at Gura Ferda and Gale should be resettled elsewhere. Since its establishment, Gura Ferda and Gale have not produced enough food and their settlers are totally dependent on food assistance from the Relief and Rehabilitation Commission.

Settlement sites were also established in both the "large-scale" and the "low cost" schemes where there are serious shortages of water (in Gambela and Miche), where wildlife is threatened (in Gambela and Milgawa), and where there is a devastating livestock disease known as "Gendi" (in Gale and Chunege). Thus, the establishment of most of the settlement sites did not take into account the land potential needed to support the settlers in the long term.

In fairness, the highest level of the Ministry of Agriculture officials and its staff at the field level were often in conflict with party officials concerning the establishment of settlement sites under the "emergency resettlement" programme. The differences between the two were such that the Ministry of Construction was entrusted to establish several of the "large-scale" and the "low cost" settlement sites directly with little regard to the advice of the

Ministry of Agriculture officials and staff, who were seen as giving only lukewarm support to the resettlement programme.

How productive these schemes are is beyond the scope of this study. Yet, with the exception of the "integrated" settlements, they are generally not self-sufficient and depend largely on food assistance from the Relief and Rehabilitation Commission. The "integrated" settlement incurs the least cost when compared to the "large-scale" and the "low cost" settlements (Samuel 1985:38-47). Yet, the "large-scale" and the "low cost" schemes have not made the majority of settlers self-sufficient in food. This shows that the resettlement programme, by and large, has not attained its fundamental objective - the improvement of the productive capacity of peasants.

Conclusion

To minimize environmental degradation both in the highly degraded highlands of Ethiopia and the relatively fertile western region of the country, more emphasis should be given to programmes that would reduce the need for resettlement. The present resettlement programme has an adverse impact on the natural resource base of the western regions. If it continues there will be a dramatic decline in natural vegetation and in forest land. Land that was under dense forest became vulnerable to erosion, because of lack of careful farming practice. A more massive movement of settlers to the western regions (as intended by the government) coupled with the present high population growth rate, would mean the expansion of cultivable land, intensive cultivation, less fallowing and the drastic decline of the forest resources. This in turn would result in a substantial loss in soil fertility.

Moreover, one of the lessons learned from the resettlement experiences in western Ethiopia is that the land where forest flourishes is not necessarily suitable for cereal cultivation. A prominent example of this is the "large-scale" settlement in the Gilo valley (Gambela region) and the "low cost" settlement in the Dedessa valley (Keffa region) in which the soil looked fertile, but the forest and wildlife were adversely affected. Maintaining some of the forest resources in these regions could be both environmentally and economically sound. It is feasible that forest and forest products (under good management and incentive mechanisms) in many parts of western Ethiopia could have economic returns as good for the peasants as that of cereal cultivation.

Nonetheless, the Ethiopian government's major argument in favour of reducing the extraordinary pressure exerted on degraded land in many parts of the highly eroded highlands is legitimate. Wollo is a good example of this. But removing humans alone is not a viable solution. The pressure from both humans and livestock could be reduced, at a lower cost, without massive resettlement outside of Wollo. Resettlement should be an option available for anyone at any time, and the government should assist in such voluntary resettlement. The success of voluntary resettlement would depend largely on the participation of peasant association leaders and members. It would require a decentralized approach that would delegate more authority to peasant associations and less to the party and the Ministry of Agriculture.

In summary, resettlement could be one of the options in reducing environmental degradation in famine affected regions of the north and in improving the welfare of peasants if it is implemented strategically and voluntarily. It cannot, however, be a panacea for dealing with environmental degradation or famine victims as it is presently implemented. On the contrary, it is likely to result in a rapid degradation of land resources, and might well set the stage for the re-creation of the conditions we find today in the famine affected regions of the country. Above all, the government's effort should be to substantially reduce the root causes that have lead to resettlement, i.e. to reduce the need for resettlement by undertaking conservation and rehabilitation activities of the famine prone regions in the Ethiopian highlands.

NOTES

1 A good description of the Wollo famine is presented by Mesfin Wolde Mariam (1984:40-51).

2 Data obtained from an official Chart at the Relief and Rehabilitation Commission in Addis Ababa, March 1988.

3 Ibid. Similar figures are reported in a document on Resettlement Activities from the Sending Regions, prepared by a committee appointed by the Council of Ministers (1988: 20). Also the **Ethiopian Herald** (March 9 1988) reported that 360,000 families had been resettled from Wollo since 1984.

4 Regional Planning Office for North Eastern Ethiopia, A Special Planning Document Prepared to Deal With the 1987 Drought in Wollo, Dessie, Ethiopia, October 1987 :14. Document written in Amharic.

5 Reported in the Special Planning Document Prepared to Deal With the 1987 Drought in Wollo (Regional Planning Office for North Eastern Ethiopia), Dessie, October 1987:21. Document written in Amharic. These quotas are not set in Wollo but with the approval of the highest government and party officials in Addis Ababa.

6 Regional Planning Office for North Eastern Ethiopia, A Special Planning Document Prepared to Deal With the 1987 Drought in Wollo, Dessie, Ethiopia, October 1987, p.14. Amharic. pp.63 - 64.

7 This figure was reported in The Ethiopian Herald, Wednesday March 9 1989, p.1.

8 Some have been resettled in the Gojam region at Metkele which is not included in this study. The resettlement scheme in Gojam is highly subsidized by the Italian government and cannot be compared with others.

9 This figure was quoted in a document from the Regional Planning Office for Western Ethiopia, A Study of Resettlement Activities: 1985-1988, Jimma, August 1988, pp.4-6. Amharic.

10 Resettlement schemes have been subject to several classifications. See also Alula Pankhurst who, in his contribution to this volume, for the emergency phase (1984-89) distinguishes between "conventional" and "integrated" schemes.

11 According to the Regional Planning Office for Western Ethiopia, see their Study of Resettlement Activities 1985-1988, August 1988, p.4-6.

12 According to the Ministry of Agriculture Zonal Office for Western Ethiopia. See: A Study of Low Cost Settlement Schemes in Keffa, Jimma, January 1988, p.26. Amharic.

13 According to an Amharic document of the Regional Planning Office for Western Ethiopia, A Study of Resettlement Activities: 1985-88, August 1988, pp.11 and 42.

14 According to the Amharic document of the Regional Planning Office for Western Ethiopia: A Study of Resettlement Activities: 1985-88. Jimma, August 1988, p.10.

15 According to an Amharic document of the Ministry of Agriculture Zonal Office for Western Ethiopia: A Study of Low Cost Resettlement Scheme in Keffa Region, Jimma, January 1988, pp.26-43.

16 Amharic report of the Ministry of Agriculture Zonal Office for Western Ethiopia: A Study of Low Cost Resettlement Scheme in Keffa Region, Jimma, January 1988, p.43.

17 Data obtained at Ekuna Kijang and Baro Abol settlement villages in Gambela. These figures are also cited by unofficial report written by the Ministry of Agriculture Office in Metu, Illubabor.

17 Natural Resource Management and Rural Development in Ethiopia
Adrian P. Wood

Introduction

The natural resources of Ethiopia's rural communities are the basis for their development. To improve standards of living, which must be the major aim of rural development, increased production from the natural resources is required. This is necessary both to raise consumption levels, and also to permit capital accumulation. However, in many parts of Ethiopia, the natural resource base is currently being degraded. This is leading to lower levels of production and a deterioration in standards of living which threaten the survival of some rural dwellers.

Trends in Natural Resource Use

Over the last two decades increased awareness has developed of the serious environmental situation in rural Ethiopia. A number of studies have shown that present trends in natural resource use pose serious constraints to rural development (cf. FAO/UNDP 1984; FAO 1986; FAO/UNDP 1988).

Deforestation and Devegetation

The highlands, which occupy 43 per cent of the country and support 88 per cent of the population, produce the majority of the national product. Originally 87 per cent of the highlands were covered with broadleafed deciduous or coniferous forests. Over the last three to four millennia cultivation has expanded and the livestock population grown causing the forested area to decrease considerably. Deforestation has accelerated during the last 80 years: 40 per cent of the highlands were forested at the turn of the century but only 5.6 per cent by 1988 (FAO 1986; FAO 1988).

A major consequence of devegetation is increased runoff which leads to erosion and reduced infiltration. Erosion is especially severe where slopes have been cleared and when the removal of permanent vegetation from arable land creates longer uninterrupted slopes across which water flows build up. Increased runoff and reduced infiltration cause streams to become more intermittent and lower watertables, both of which increase the time required to collect water in the dry season.

Another consequence of deforestation is shortage of fuelwood. This is especially severe in the northern and eastern Highlands (Table 1). Fuelwood has increasingly been replaced by dung and crop residues which together provide up to 55 per cent of domestic energy and are the dominant fuel source for one third of the population (World Bank 1984). The burning of these sources of soil humus and fertility has led to a progressive deterioration in soil structure, infiltration capacity, moisture storage, and fertility. Burning dung reduces the nation's crop production by an estimated 10 to 20 per cent below its potential. The decline in the humus content of the soil causes a further cumulative fall in crop production estimated at one per cent per annum (Hurni 1988).

The present use of wood exceeds the rate of sustainable production from the existing forest areas by between 50 per cent and 150 per cent depending on the estimates used. Every year some 100,000 ha of forest are lost. At this rate, by 2020 the last highland forests will have disappeared. To meet rural fuelwood needs in 2010, and replace the use of dung as fuel, some 16 million ha of rural fuelwood plantations will be required, with another 1.2 million ha of forests to provide timber needs (Davidson 1988). The prospects for this are poor. Over the last decade only 300,000 ha of rural fuelwood and community forest have been planted (Hurni 1988).

Table 1
Distribution of Shallow Soils and High Forest by Region

Region	Shallow Soils			High Forest		
	Sq km 000s	%of Region	% of Country Total	Sq km 000s	% of Region	% of Country Total
Northern	83.3	62.8	48.0	1.8	0.5	4.1
Eastern	21.4	61.0	12.2	0.3	0.1	0.6
Central	21.7	30.9	12.4	1.3	1.6	3.1
Southern	25.9	25.7	14.9	16.9	5.5	38.4
Western	22.0	12.6	12.6	23.7	10.1	53.9
Ethiopia	174.9	35.4	100.0	44.0	3.6	100.0

Note: Shallow soils are within Highland above 1500 m only.

Northern	Eritrea, Tigray, Welo, Gondar
Southern	Arsi, Bale, Sidamo, Gamo Gofa
Western	Gojam, Welega, Ilubabor, Kefa
Eastern	Hararghe
Central	Shoa

Source: FAO/UNDP, 1984; Hurni, 1986.

Soil Erosion and Degradation

Soil degradation is the most immediate environmental problem facing Ethiopia. The loss of soil, and the deterioration in fertility, moisture storage capacity and structure of the remaining soils, all reduce the country's agricultural productivity. It was estimated in the mid-1980s that 3.7 per cent of the highlands (2 million ha) had been so seriously eroded that they could not support cultivation, while a further 52 per cent had suffered moderate or serious degradation. Almost 75 per cent of the Ethiopian highlands are estimated to need soil conservation measures of one sort or another if they are to support sustained cultivation (FAO 1986). While the areas in greatest need of conservation at present are in the northern and eastern highlands (Table 1), the major areas of current agricultural expansion in the south and west have the highest potential erosivity. Many of the soils in these areas are nitrosols which are prone to erosion and show a rapid decline in yields once erosion begins.

Soil erosion is greatest on arable land where the average annual loss is 42 tons/ha. This is six times the rate of soil formation, and causes an annual reduction in soil depth of 4 mm. In contrast, average annual soil loss from pasture, at around 5 tons/ha, is roughly in balance with the rate of soil formation, while under forests there is an accumulation of soil as formation rates exceed those of loss (Hurni 1987).

Shallower soils with lower fertility are less resistant to erosion and produce poorer crop cover to protect the soil. Thus soil erosion is a self-accelerating process. It reduces the country's food production by an estimated 1-2 per cent per annum (in addition to the 1 per cent decline due to the reduction in the humus content). Erosion and the decline in the humus content of the soil reduce both rainfall infiltration (from 90 per cent on uneroded soils to 20 per cent on eroded soils), and soil moisture storage. These problems undermine the ability of crops to withstand drought and so exacerbate variations in crop yields. Hence soil erosion contributes to the famines in the northern and eastern highlands and to the country's structural food deficit.

Pasture and Livestock Resources

Pasture land is under increasing pressure from a growing livestock population, which now exceeds 30 million tropical livestock units. The fuelwood crisis forces people to burn crop residues and dung which could be used respectively as livestock feed and fertilizer for the pasture. Overgrazing makes pastures deteriorate as less palatable species invade. The ground cover is reduced, and run-off and soil erosion increase. The large livestock population and its relatively free grazing also inhibit conservation. Trees cannot regenerate, and physical soil conservation works are damaged. Highland cultivation, which uses draught oxen, is seriously affected by poor dry season pasture as weakened plough oxen lead to later sowing on poorly prepared seed beds which can reduce yields.

Natural Resource and Production Scenarios

Scenarios based on these trends produce a depressing picture. Unless major changes occur in land use and erosion in the highlands, 10 million ha (or 18 per cent of highland crop land) will be unable to support cultivation by 2010. This will leave 10 million people, or 15 per cent of the highland population, destitute (FAO 1986). Another study using similar assumptions suggests that by 2010 almost three-quarters of the old highland *awrajas* (prior to the 1989 administrative reorganization) will be unable to support their population at a subsistence level (FAO/UNDP 1988). Detailed modelling predicts that, in the absence of technological change, by 2004

Average annual rainfall in Ethiopia

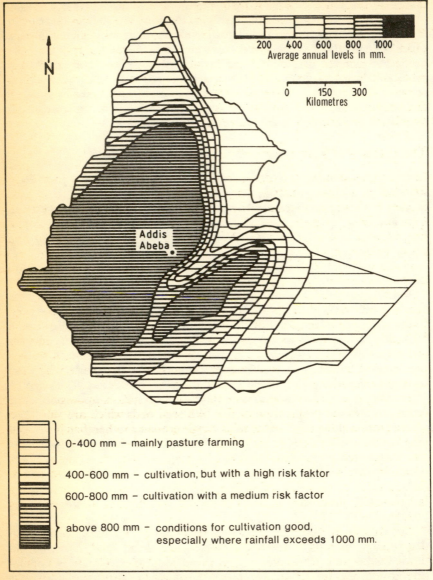

200 400 600 800 1000
Average annual levels in mm.

0   150   300
Kilometres

Addis Abeba

N

0-400 mm – mainly pasture farming

400-600 mm – cultivation, but with a high risk faktor

600-800 mm – cultivation with a medium risk factor

above 800 mm – conditions for cultivation good,
especially where rainfall exceeds 1000 mm.

Source: Walter Michler, *Weissbuch Afrika*, Berlin and Bonn, (1988:159)
© Verlag J.H.W. Dietz Nachf., Bonn

pasture land will be insufficient to maintain the livestock population, while arable land will be below subsistence requirements by 2018 (Hurni 1988).

The current environmental rehabilitation measures are gaining the country little time, and need a two to four fold increase to have a significant impact. Much greater efforts in improved management of the natural resources are needed to increase agricultural and livestock productivity, and to develop protective forms of land use. However even with such improved natural resource management it is suggested that to achieve an ecologically balanced and sustainable situation will also require the stabilization of the country's population at around twice its present size (Hurni 1988).

The Causes of Environmental Degradation

Interventions to improve natural resource management in Ethiopia must be founded on a clear understanding of the current degradation processes. Studies of these processes identify influences at a variety of levels varying from the field, through rural communities, and national policies, to the international political economy. These influences include soil physics and plant regeneration needs, household resource endowments and farmers's land management decisions, societal rules and crop pricing policies, and debt repayment and aid (Blaikie 1989).

In Ethiopia the intense rainfall and the dissected nature of the terrain, with nearly 70 per cent of the highlands having slopes in excess of 30 per cent, favour severe soil erosion once the vegetation is reduced. The soils in the highlands vary considerably in their resistance to erosion, with the nitosols and planosols of the southwest especially prone to rapid erosion. A further problem is a tendency for waterlogging in the valleys and plains which encourages cultivation on the more erosion-prone valley sides.

Farming practices also contribute to erosion. Emphasis upon small-seed crops requires the preparation of fine tilth seed beds which are subject to severe erosion at the onset of the rains. Single cropping rather than intercropping favours erosion as there are few permanent crops whose leaves and roots can provide protection and stability at the start of the rains. Growing crops on residual moisture after the rains also means that there is no protection of the soil at the height of the rains. The tradition in some areas of making the last ploughing downslope in order to reduce waterlogging also encourages erosion (FAO 1986).

Population growth is often thought to be the major cause of environmental degradation. To provide fuelwood, pasture and arable land, trees are cut down. Cultivation expands onto steeper slopes with high erosion risks. Population growth also reduces fallowing, which affects the structure and humus content of the soil. The situation is worsened where dung is burnt instead of fuelwood. When crop yields fall, more frequent cultivation of the land is necessary. This may lead to a breakdown in the crumb structure of the soil, reducing infiltration and resistance to erosion.

While the acceleration of population growth in Ethiopia to around 3 per cent per annum does create pressure upon the natural resources, similar population growth has occurred in comparable environments without producing the severity of erosion seen in Ethiopia today. Farming systems can be adjusted to meet the increased demands while also protecting the soil. This raises the question of why conservation oriented land management and farming practices have not developed in Ethiopia. The answer may lie in cultural preferences for small-seed crops such as teff, in poor communication of agricultural innovations and the absence until the 1970s of an extension service, and in the lack of appropriate research findings for dissemination. However, a crucial factor appears to be the socio-political environment for peasant farmers. They have little security of access to land, and have been impoverished by poor returns from farming and exploitation by elites and the state. Under such conditions farmers hardly have the resources needed for soil conservation and environmental rehabilitation, while the medium- to long-term returns typical for most conservation initiatives are discounted by farmers because they are uncertain about their access to land (Wood 1987).

Experience of Recent Years

Since 1974 the government has introduced a number of measures which show that it recognizes the serious implications of environmental degradation and poor natural resource management. However, as these were the first major conservation initiatives in Ethiopia, a number of problems undermined their adoption and effectiveness. Analysis of these difficulties is currently underway and some re-orientation of soil conservation and afforestation programmes will be necessary. Agricultural policy changes are also required to ensure the widespread spontaneous adoption of conservation-based farming practices.

Institutional Developments and Programmes

Since the revolution institutional structures have been established to address the previously neglected environmental issues. Within the Ministry of Agriculture the Natural Resources Conservation and Development Main Department was established in 1985. It has Departments responsible for Land Use Planning, Wildlife, State Forests, and Community Forestry and Soil Conservation. In the Office of the National Commission for Central Planning a Department of Natural Resources and Human Settlements evaluates the environmental implications of all government plans. Most recently the Ethiopian Valleys Development Studies Authority has been established, with a wide research mandate which includes introducing an integrated view of natural resources into regional planning.

There are now close to 1,100 staff working in field activities in either soil conservation or forestry. A package of conservation measures has been developped including terraces, bunds, tree planting, and the closure of grazing areas. These measures are mainly introduced through food for work programmes. This creates a close link between famine relief and environmental rehabilitation. Between 1976 and 1988, food for work programmes funded the construction of 600,000 kms of hillside terraces for afforestation of steep slopes, and 800,000 kms of soil and stone bunds for terrace formation on 350,000 ha of cropland. Some 500 million tree seedlings were planted covering some 180,000 ha. Another 100,000 ha have been closed for natural regeneration. These food for work conservation activities now cost US$ 50 million per annum, most of the funds coming from the UN World Food Programme (Hurni 1988, Belshaw 1988, Daniel Gamachu 1988).

Since the revolution the government has made a number of public commitments to improve the country's natural resources, and their management. The land reform proclamation made peasant associations responsible for the protection of natural resources in their localities. The 1987 Constitution requires the state to ensure that ecological balance is maintained and that natural resources are conserved and developed for the benefit of the population. The Ten-Year Perspective Plan (1983/4 - 1993/4) gives a clear commitment to improve the management of natural resources to prevent drought and desertification, while its fourth objective is "conserving, ... and exploiting rationally the natural resources of the country". Within the Ministry of Agriculture several departments have recently reviewed their activities and suggested policies to improve their impact upon the country's natural resource problems. Some of these ideas will be included in a Ten-Year National Forestry, Wildlife, Soil and Water Conservation Development Programme which is due to be launched soon.

Problems with Environmental Rehabilitation Initiatives

Experience over the last decade has identified a number of problems in conservation initiatives and the circumstances in which they operate.

Scale of the Rehabilitation Measures. A basic problem with the present conservation initiatives is their limited areal extent. Because of the link with food for work, most conservation activities are concentrated in accessible areas along major roads. It is estimated that over the last ten years only some 7 per cent of the highlands have been "treated" with conservation measures. The current annual rate of progress suggests that it will take some 70 years to provide a "first treatment" for the highlands (Hurni 1988). This is hardly commensurate with the problem, especially when the area in need of treatment is growing rapidly as a result of agricultural expansion in the south-west.

Approach and Quality of Work. The food for work approach has meant that conservation has been introduced as a subsidiary activity to relief food distribution. People have built conservation measures primarily to obtain food. This, combined with the lack of education about environmental degradation and conservation measures, has meant that there has been little understanding of the potential benefits from conservation and environmental rehabilitation.

Food for work programmes have often been planned in a top-down manner. Government officials tell the rural communities what they should do to obtain the relief food, and provide little opportunity for discussion and local participation in conservation planning. New conservation measures have not been linked to traditional ones nor integrated into the farming system. As a result conservation initiatives are often seen by farmers as measures which the government has imposed on them, and as additional tasks on top of their farming work (Yeraswork Admassie 1988).

Food for work as payment can make farmers see conservation measures as belonging to the government rather than the local community. Hence the quality of construction is often poor, while the maintenance of the measures is not important to farmers. Occasionally farmers even destroy the bunds and terraces in the hope of obtaining further opportunities for food for work. The low success rate in afforestation, around 7 per cent one year after planting (Daniel Gamachu 1988), is also attributable in part to the lack of responsibility which results from top-down planning.

Problems with the quality of conservation work also occur because the physical measures require supervision to ensure that they are constructed properly and retard, rather than accelerate, erosion. However, at present there are only some 1,000 field staff in the departments of Community Forestry and Soil Conservation and State Forests to supervise the 800,000 to 900,000 man-days of conservation activities which food for work finances each year (Brown 1989). Hence most conservation work is supervised by peasant association officials who have little training.

Nature of the Conservation Measures. The government's approach to conservation has focused upon physical measures, such as bunds and terraces, and tree planting. This has been partly due to the food for work link, which has required specific tasks against which food payment can be made. Also physical measures still dominated conservation thinking when this programme was designed in the mid-1970s. Biological and agronomic conservation practices, which have a potential to create attractive conservation packages, have been overlooked until recently.

Recent evaluations show that in the short term returns from the present conservation package are negative. The benefits of increased infiltration and reduced soil loss do not outweigh the loss of land to conservation works, and the reduced yields caused by vermin living in terraces, waterlogging and the disturbance of the soil profile. Yields improve little in the short-term, and may in fact decline, while there are extra labour requirements and maintenance costs. This is hardly an attractive package. Rather it is a source of negative attitudes towards conservation, which is now expected to involve extra work but produce little immediate return (Yeraswerk Admassie 1988). These conservation measures are also dependent upon external supervision and funds (food for work), hence it is unlikely that they will be adopted spontaneously.

Socio-political Environment. Research has shown that Ethiopian farmers are well aware of soil erosion and deforestation, and know that some action is necessary to arrest these processes before their agriculture is undermined. An adverse policy environment has been suggested, among other reasons, as discouraging farmers from adopting conservation measures.

Insecurity of access to land discourages farmers from making investments in physical structures, trees and even soil fertility, as returns accrue over several years, if not decades. Unless there are clear rights to trees, which ensure that the benefits accrue to those who plant and protect them, there is little chance that farmers will undertake afforestation spontaneously. In some cases conservation measures that produce reasonably quick returns may not be adopted because low agricultural prices make the returns unattractive (IUCN 1986).

Despite more than a decade of government initiatives in conservation there has been limited success. An attractive approach to conservation has not been developed, and the policy environment has discouraged farmers from adopting conservation measures except against food for work payments. As a result, there has been little spontaneous adoption of conservation. A further problem is the absence of an effective conservation approach for the food surplus regions, despite their growing erosion problems.

Towards a New Approach to Conservation for Sustained Agriculture

Characteristics of a New Approach

With the budgetary constraints in Ethiopia today, and the limited aid flows, a two to four fold expansion of the existing environmental conservation programme is impossible. Indeed in the light of the criticisms above, it is undesirable to follow the established emphasis upon physical conservation measures more than is necessary. While conservation initiatives must be the basis for agricultural development in Ethiopia, they should not be dependent upon government or external funds which can fluctuate from day to day, nor should they require a range of tasks and measures which farmers must undertake in addition to their farming. Instead, conservation must become part and parcel of the farming work cycle. Conservation-oriented crop combinations and land management practices must be integrated within the farming systems. Such crop and farming practices must involve few new inputs or extra risks. Above all they must also provide farmers with short-term economic benefits, so that conservation-based farming systems are adopted rapidly and spontaneously, with minimal external support (FAO 1986; Belshaw 1988).

The biological characteristics which such farming systems must introduce include a more vegetated landscape. Increased ground cover will protect the soil from erosion, improve infiltration of rainfall, and reduce runoff. Increased biomass production is necessary to meet food, fodder and fuel needs. Expanded fuelwood production is especially important as this will allow the use of dung as a fertilizer and so increase the humus content in the soil. In turn this will improve infiltration, reduce runoff, raise soil fertility and crop yields, and improve vegetative cover (IUCN 1986). Improved fodder production by reducing overgrazing can stem erosion on pasture land, and should improve agricultural production if the condition of draught animals is better at the start of the rains. Increased biological productivity must be sought not just to ensure rapid improvements in farmers' incomes, but also to provide flexibility in the land use system which will be necessary for the rehabilitation of degraded areas.

Farming Practices for Conservation

Farming practices which can help to conserve the natural resource base and raise productivity have received some attention from researchers in Ethiopia in recent years. A preliminary inventory of traditional practices has been made and a series of conservation-based agronomic trials is being introduced (Tahal 1988a, 1988b). Intercropping and relay, or sequential, cropping are valuable as they improve soil stability with their diverse rooting systems and increase the density and period of leaf cover which protects the soil from direct rainfall and the sun's intense radiation. Crop rotations which help to maintain soil fertility and greater integration of livestock farming with arable cultivation to improve the use of manure are other techniques whose application might be more widely tested. Undersowing of cereals with legumes can stabilize the soil and improve its fertility, as well as providing fodder after the harvest (Anderson 1989). The benefits are increased where such crops will self-seed or survive ploughings as they will provide leaf cover early in the next rainy season. Rotating, rather than resowing crops each year, is another potential innovation for crops such as sorghum and pigeon peas, as this leaves established root systems in the soil at the start of the new cultivation season and reduce the need for ploughing (Belshaw 1988).

Research by the International Livestock Centre for Africa (ILCA) has investigated the cultivation of the seasonally waterlogged vertisols through the use of an ox-drawn broadbed and furrow maker. Cultivation of vertisols, which are usually left for grazing, can reduce the cultivation pressure upon the slopes, and permit the reorganization of land use and the introduction of grass and shrub belts to stabilize slopes. However, some increase in fodder production is needed to replace that lost from the vertisols, while present trials show some increase in soil loss on the vertisols when broadbeds are made (Getachew Asamenew et al 1988). Single ox ploughing is another ILCA innovation with potential for reducing pressures upon pasture but has yet to prove viable in on-farm trials.

Other farming practices which benefit conservation include the cut and carry method of using degraded pasture which has been closed to grazing. Pasture productivity can also be improved by controlled grazing and tethering. This would help protect conservation measures, and facilitate pasture improvement with sown legumes.

Crops for Conservation

Crop changes could also make a contribution to conservation. While a shift away from teff and similar small-seed varieties requiring fine tilth seed beds is unlikely, more widespread use of semi-permanent crops, such as ensete and cassava, or self-seeding and volunteering crops, such as legumes and sweet potatoes, could help stem erosion by reducing the need for cultivation (Belshaw 1988). Some new legumes such as pigeon peas, Desmodium and Sesbania have been introduced in a few areas to stabilize physical conservation measures and provide improved returns from the land which has been given over for these works. These and other legumes are important for forage and can improve soil fertility and increase biomass production from degraded areas (Robertson 1989).

Agro-forestry, which integrates shrubs and trees into arable land, is of particular importance. In some cases shrubs and grass strips may replace physical conservation works. The most attractive shrub and tree species for agro-forestry are those which provide multiple benefits. Sesbania and Leucaena provide not only fodder, fuel and soil stabilization, but also improve soil fertility by fixing nitrogen. Traditional agro-forestry techniques are practised in some parts of Ethiopia, for instance with Acacia albidia in the Rift Valley. The wider application of these techniques must be tested. This is especially important as relatively few exotic species have so far been found to be suitable for agro-forestry in Ethiopia.

Cost-Benefit Analysis

A crucial point with conservation innovations is to ensure that not only do they meet environmental requirements, but that they are economically attractive, and fit into the existing farming systems with the range of resource constraints which farmers face. Hence on-farm trials are necessary once the efficacy of the innovations has been proved on research stations. As widespread spontaneous adoption is one of the crucial requirements of a new approach to conservation, it may be necessary to allow for some trade-offs between conservation benefits and economic attractiveness. However where the innovations meet specific needs, e.g. fuel or fodder, problems of attractiveness should be reduced.

Finally, it must not be forgotten that a more favourable policy environment will be required before these innovations will be attractive to farmers. Farmers need security of access to land and clear rights to trees, as well as agricultural prices which encourage investment in farming and the protection of the natural resource base. Secure access to arable land is especially important if agro-forestry methods are to be attractive. Crop pricing can also be used to encourage the adoption of new crops and rotational rather than mono-cropping practices.

Prospects

There is no reason why Ethiopia should suffer the present level of environmental degradation and her rural population face such poverty. By African standards the country has a favourable natural resource base. Other countries with similar resources and levels of population density have managed to achieve higher standards of living and restrict natural resource degradation to lower levels. Ethiopia has the potential to greatly improve food production and to rehabilitate her natural resource base so that rural standards of living can be improved. However, to achieve this within the medium term will require a more catholic approach to conservation, with more emphasis upon farming systems development and less reliance upon physical conservation works. Above all, conservation practices must be attractive so that they will spread spontaneously through the country and need only a few demonstration plots and limited extension by way of specific support.

18 Famine or Preparedness?

Dag Hareide

There are two traditions, two professions of people who fight famine in Ethiopia and elsewhere. The *relief workers* consider themselves most effective in saving lives wherever it is necessary. The *development planners* think they are most important because they will finally eradicate famine. Both are right. Both are important. But often they work as if they belonged to separate worlds. And because of this, they sometimes fail.

In Ethiopia they have failed. Twice in ten years shelters have been filled by hundreds of thousands of famine victims. The relief helpers came too late. And the development workers had to face the fact that all their work had been in vain, and that development had once again been set back for years.

The relief people are always rushing from one emergency situation to the next, to save more lives. They seldom get a chance to think about how one could intervene earlier in the famine cycle, how one could be better prepared to avoid the calamities which have already developed when they arrive at the scene. The people who work on development seem to try hard to keep away from any disaster or relief work, as if they fear it might steal their time from development. They plan for "normal" development, as if it was not the case that, every eight or ten years, a drought will recur. Often this can become a schizophrenic schism within governments, aid and donor organizations, with separate desks, separate budgets and training systems, separate organizations for aid and for relief.

There are, however, a few people planning ahead for a potential disaster in their area, who work on *preparedness*, who interpret the early signs of famine and act in advance. There is a need for contingency planning, to be able to intervene before it is too late. Preparedness cannot avert a drought, but it can cope with the effects of a natural disaster. It can meet food shortages so as to prevent them becoming a famine. Preparedness can, at best, eliminate the need for relief, and it can also save development from being destroyed by a famine. As long as development planning is not supplemented with preparedness, it will always be in danger of having to start all over again after a new disaster has destroyed what has been achieved.

The Need for Preparedness

Ethiopia has experienced more ravaging famines in the last two decades than any other country in the world. In one generation Ethiopia has seen four major famines, and the last one killed 800,000 people.[1]

The last famine broke out late in 1983. But it was only in late 1985 and 1986 that Ethiopia, with international aid, was able to feed all the 7 million people in need of relief food. This proved that the famine could have been avoided if the intervention had been in time and adequate in quantity. This fact shames everybody involved. The responsibility rests first and foremost with the Ethiopian government. The first and most important task for any government is surely to secure food for its population through normal production and distribution, and to ensure it has the capacity to prevent a food shortage from developing into a famine.

That this is possible is best demonstrated by the example of India. India had droughts more severe than Africa in the 1980s, which affected not tens of millions as in Africa, but hundreds of millions. The Indian countryside is not less stricken by poverty than Africa's. Some data indicate that India has less food available for its population than sub-Saharan Africa. But unlike Ethiopia and Africa, India has had no big famine since the Second World War. The classical land of famine during the 19th century seems to control famine at the end of the 20th century, without any radical change in the country's overall poverty.

There are of course several reasons. But the most important difference may be that India has developed famine codes and drought preparedness systems which have efficiently prevented serious food shortages developing into famines.[2]

Ethiopia has not yet developed a National Famine Preparedness Plan. But Ethiopia has, since the revolution, developed a highly regarded institution: the Relief and Rehabilitation Commission (RRC), which should, according to the laws, be able to do the same work. However, so far it has not done so either effectively or in time.

In December 1988, the Office of the National Commission for Central Planning arranged a big "National Conference on a Disaster Prevention and Preparedness Strategy for Ethiopia".[3] This was a good sign that famine preparedness might receive a high priority from the governnment.

A New Thinking in a Continuum

Traditional thinking about relief and development moves in phases: a disaster demands relief work; when the most immediate starvation is over, rehabilitation has to bring things back to normal, before one can start thinking about development again. Then comes another disaster which interrupts all the achievements of development and necessitates relief, and so on. As far as there is preparedness today, it is only forward preparation for efficient relief. It is like having a fire brigade, but no policy of preventing fires.

This could go on for generations if nothing new is done. Ethiopia is dependent upon food aid for many years to come. Trends in food production, rural income and vulnerability to famine show that this situation will not get better immediately. A vicious circle is developing, where crisis management will increasingly push aside any meaningful development effort.

A new thinking is needed, which sees this process as a continuum. Preparedness, development, relief and rehabilitation have to be integrated, to work simultaneously and relate to each other. The bridge between relief, rehabilitation and development is preparedness.

Preparedness: A Bridge between Development and Relief

Around $1.3 billion were spent on relief aid in Ethiopia in the famine year of 1985. This is more than four times the development aid the country received in any year before! What effect did this massive influx of resources have ?

An intervention with relief aid can:

a) increase the vulnerability of poor people to famine (especially in the case of pure relief supplies which do not consider rehabilitation and development);

b) get things back to "normal" (when rehabilitation measures seek to re-establish the status quo ante - which often includes a high degree of vulnerability to famine); or

c) decrease vulnerability (if relief aid is development oriented).

Most observers would agree that famine aid in Ethiopia in 1984-87 increased the vulnerability of large groups of people in the affected areas. The factor which could have made a difference is preparedness planning.

Preparedness planning can also be of help to development efforts. Famine preparedness can offer an *insurance* against disasters crushing the achievements of development work. Some agencies have realized this, and have built preparedness as a *component* into their programmes, a system of food reserves, early warning, and contingency planning.[4] Others also see the prevention of famine as a major *perspective* in basic development efforts.

Preparedness as a perspective of development planning allows one to give priority to efforts to reduce vulnerability to famine. It provides a better chance to mobilize the people involved, and hence a better chance to achieve positive changes.[5] This perspective also helps to finance development programmes, as famine is an issue which attracts attention and makes it possible to mobilize the will of rich nations to allocate money.

Famine preparedness can build a bridge over the schism between relief workers and development planners, making the development people aware of the likelihood of recurring droughts and natural disasters, and reminding relief people that their work is also part of a long term development effort.

Elements in a Famine Preparedness Plan in Ethiopia

A preparedness system has its own specific elements, giving it a substance different from both relief and development. I will mention ten such elements, and relate them to the state of affairs in Ethiopia:

1. An *evaluation* of past experience: there must be a political will and a capacity to critically evaluate what went wrong in past famines, and to draw the lessons necessary.

The Ethiopian Government has not made any comprehensive and critical evaluation of government efforts during the last famine, at least not publicly. This is a serious omission, as we can see in the example of India. Without their Famine Commissions and the public debates that followed, Indian authorities would never have developed their Famine Codes.

2. A capacity to *predict* future famines is needed, together with the capacity to communicate predictions to the people who will be involved in relief reactions.

Ethiopia does, in fact, have an Early Warning System. However, in the early 1980s, it had the image of "crying wolf", and donors only provided about 10 to 30 per cent of what the authorities asked for. This atmosphere of distrust for figures proved fatal in 1984.

3. A *public information* system which can alert and mobilize the people affected, and inform others involved during the operation.

A system with heavy press censorship is seriously handicapped in a famine situation (Hareide 1990, Sen 1986).

4. A capacity for *management* of food crises. Disaster units are needed with trained, qualified full time staff, working within the governnment system.

Ethiopia chose to build up a separate system for relief and rehabilitation, the RRC. When the crisis turned into a catastrophe in late 1984, this organization was "brought under the administration" of new superstructures by the party. This demonstrates that separate relief organizations are not effective in handling acute food shortages. In other countries, systems which are connected to the normal development power structure have proven more efficient.[6]

5. *Knowledge* about vulnerability and national capacities before and under a food crisis: vulnerability profiles and food information systems are essential as a basis for contingency plans and decision making.

The RRC knew the number of people in need in 1984. It had a capacity for "disaster need assessment", which is useful knowledge, but not sufficient for more advanced action. In 1986, the RRC came closer to adequate overviews of the aid flows and actual aid performance. But it still lacked any comprehensive data that could orient relief action towards development. In an emergency, it is not enough to be familiar with the road system and to know the number of people affected. Comprehensive knowledge of local conditions and past disaster history is essential. The first comprehensive vulnerability profile was drawn up in 1988 on Wollo (RRC/Hareide 1989).

6. *Contingency Plans* are needed for different areas of concern, like logistics; response to migration; health; water; agriculture; relief distribution; animal husbandry; market interventions; aid regulations; law and order; financial arrangements; emergency work programmes; operation plans for food and other reserves.

The only contingency plans available in Ethiopia concern food reserves. The RRC has its relief regulations, but no contingency plans for the other areas mentioned. The Office of the National Committee for Central Planning has repeatedly been forced to revise or scrap plans because of bad weather, war, or other contingencies. Several hundred experts have thus been preparing plans which never became operational, while less than a handful of people are involved in the most essential contingency planning.

7. *Reserves* of food, seeds, tools or whatever is necessary for a crisis response.

Food reserves in 1984 were less than 12,000 metric tonnes. This was less than a week's supply at the peak of the famine, and in fact the reserves were used for consumption in the cities. Since then, reserves have been increased, and in 1987/88 a famine was prevented thanks to food reserves. The work of building up seed reserves and other rehabilitation oriented reserves has not yet taken off.

8. The *logistic base* for a relief operation: transport, storage, communication networks, etc. are essential.

The UN organizations FAO and WFP predicted in their fatal report of 1984 that Ethiopia did not have the logistic capacity to handle more than 200,000 metric tonnes of food a year (Gill 1986). The following year, 800,000 metric tonnes were distributed ! Major improvements have been made in the logistics, but the present war situation has made it even more difficult to meet a crisis like the one in 1984.

9. *Cooperation* with international aid donors and non-governmental organizations needs practical arrangements.

The last famine strengthened or created several useful networks like CRDA, the informal Donors Committee, the UN - EPPG and others. However, even the best networks cannot function unless there is the political will and the mutual trust needed to support coordination.

10. *Decision making* procedures and policies within the governnment: there is a need for clear rules for the declaration and the management of a crisis, including the necessary legislation.

During the last famine, several peasants in famine areas had to pay taxes and deliver quotas to the AMC (Dessalegn 1987). This is one example of how one government authority can undermine the relief efforts of another. The necessary legislation is in place for the RRC to intervene in such situations, but it lacks the political power to do so.

Famine preparedness, then, has the following tasks:
1. It has to prepare for efficient relief, which saves lives.
2. It has to prepare for a development-oriented relief and rehabilitation work, which decreases vulnerability to famine in rural areas.
3. To achieve this, famine preparedness has to become an integrated component and a perspective in all development planning.

NOTES

1 On the history of Ethiopian famines in the last generation, see Mesfin 1984. Though his empirical concept of famine is somewhat vague, Mesfin's discussion of rural vulnerability has greatly influenced the discussion. For a definition of "famine", famine in world history, and a record on deaths in the last famine in Ethiopia, see Hareide 1990.

2 The best literature on Indian preparedness systems are the several Famine and Drought Codes from Indian State Governments. Analytic works are Jean Dreze: **Famine Prevention in India**, London School of Economics, Jan. 1988; Michelle B. McAlphin: **Famine Relief Policy in India - Six Lessons for Africa**, Brown University, Providence, 1985; and V. Subramaniam: **Parched Earth. The Maharashtra Drought 1970-73**, Bombay 1975. See also Amartya Sen: **Poverty and Famines. An Essay on Entitlement and Deprivation** Oxford 1981, and Donald Curtis, Michael Hubbard and Andrew Sheperd: **Preventing Famine: Policies and Prospects for Africa**, London and New York 1988.

3 The papers presented at this conference were mimeographed and distributed at the meeting, but are so far not published for a wider circulation.

4 Among others, the Norwegian Save the Children Fund and the Swedish SIDA have included preparedness components in development programmes.

5 One example is the primary health care programme run by the American Save the Children Fund during the famine in northern Shoa, which gave immediate results in low death rates.

6 Examples are India, Botswana and Kenya. Literature on India see footnote 2. Literature on Botswana: John Holm and Mark S. Cohen: "Coping with Drought in Botswana: An African Success", **The Journal of Modern African Studies**, Vol. 23, 1985, no. 3, 463-482, and Roger Hay: **Famine Incomes and Employment: Has Botswana Anything to Teach Africa?** Oxford 1987. Literature on Kenya: Michael Glantz: **Drought and Hunger in Africa**, Cambridge 1987.

19 Pastoral Nomadism and Rural Development
Fecadu Gadamu

The General Condition of Pastoral Nomads

Pastoral nomadism is a significant component of the rural socio-economic system in Ethiopia which comprises three distinct groups: a sedentary population engaged in peasant agriculture and animal husbandry, pastoral nomads, and shifting cultivators.[1] Pastoral nomadism accounts for less than 6-10 per cent of the Ethiopian population who occupy 61 per cent of total land area of the country, and produce close to 20-30 per cent of the livestock population. Shifting cultivators, on the other hand, occupy a vast territory and comprise only 0.5 per cent of the population.

The pastoral nomads, who occupy the peripheral areas together with the shifting cultivators, encircle the country while the peasants occupy the centre. The centre / periphery dichotomy begins with environment. The periphery consists of generally lowland plains, mostly below 1,500 meters in elevation and with a very low level of rainfall (400-700 mm). The lowlands have sparse vegetation composed mainly of grass, bushes, scrub and bare lands. There are no permanent rural settlements due to the low level of surface water and high temperatures. This contrasts to the environment of the central highlands where there is sufficient rain for crop production.

The two regions contrast in the mode of production as well. In the centre, we find peasant agriculture where crop production is much more emphasized than livestock production. As a result of greater interaction among ethnic groups and encapsulation by the state, there is a greater degree of integration among the population of the central highlands than in the peripheral lowlands. In the highlands, the state has established an extensive administrative super-structure and has a greater hold of every citizen. The state has built and provided physical and social infrastructure, thereby enabling the citizens to play a greater role in the national life.

In contrast to the central highlands, the peripheral lowlands suffered a paucity of infrastructure and social services and hence isolation from the centre and from each other in every sense of the term, which limits their participation in national development. The contacts of the pastoralists had been characterized by cattle raiding and sporadic fighting with each other, with the centre and with neighbouring states. The pastoralists are also accused of conducting illicit trade in the border areas.

Until recently, most policy makers displayed limited knowledge about pastoralists and their habitat. There are various misconceptions about the mobility and lack of crop cultivation of pastoral nomads. The widely held assumption is that the pastoralist lacks knowledge of crop production and that he does not farm and does not want to settle down in one place. Another misconception concerns the social organization and defensive action of pastoral nomads. It is often assumed that the pastoral nomad is devoid of any rationality concerning outsiders, that he attacks them without good cause. Lastly, there is the notion that the pastoral nomadic area is suitable for crop cultivation and, if and when it is so used, the pastoral nomadic group will not be affected. Hence, approaches to the development of the pastoralists often seek to settle them and to use their unused land as much as possible.

Intervention in the pastoral nomadic socio-economic system probably dates back more than half a century if we consider the colonial Italian attempt at integrating the Eritrean pastoral nomads (in Beni Amir, Tigre, Reshaida and Saho), by appointing clan leaders as district officers acting as intermediaries between the colonial government and the clans. This tradition continues up to the present time. Clan leaders were also given such a status in other parts of the country, in less formal ways.

Recent interventions began in the late 1950s when the Awash Valley Authority was established to survey the agricultural potential of the lowlands. This instigated the development and expansion of irrigated agriculture by private individuals and concessionaires who took little notice of the needs of the pastoral nomads of the area. The problem still lingers on today, and compensatory settlement schemes have met with very little success.

Beginning in the late 1960s, the then Livestock and Meat Board had prepared and implemented projects worth close to US $ 150 million. The Rangelands Development project, which went into effect in 1973, was the brain child of the Livestock and Meat Board. The project was intended to develop three range areas of the country: the Southern Rangelands Development Unit (SORDU), Jijiga Rangelands Development Unit (JIRDU), and the Northeast Rangelands Development Unit (NERDU).

The components of the development programme were the following: the development of ranches, demonstration of improved range management techniques to the pastoralists, the harvesting of water, the provision of veterinary services, the building of roads, livestock off-take and fattening, and training of pastoralists. These were implemented by and large in SORDU while security problems inhibited implementation in the other project areas. The SORDU and JIRDU projects are still in operation.

The Need for Development of Pastoral Nomads

The need for the development of Ethiopian pastoral nomads can be viewed from two perspectives: the condition of the nomads and the vital needs of the nation.

The Nomadic Condition

As it is generally true all over the world, the pastoral nomads of Ethiopia face an ecological and socio-economic crisis resulting from both desertification and encroachment upon their habitat by mechanized farming, game reserves, national forestry, and peasant farming. The pastoral nomads are peripheralized in terms of their social, economic and political relations to national life. The relatively stagnant nature of their economy, though wisely adjusted to its ecological niche, cannot cope with the modern economy with its superior technology and organizational efficiency. Limited interaction with the rest of the Ethiopian population and a lower level of political participation due to lack of education have hindered their integration into national life.

The Ethiopian nomads differ from each other in some of their basic socio-cultural features. They constitute some fifteen ethnic groups even though they have common and comparable factors. The major differences centre around their resource endowment, their mode of production, orientation to modernity and external relationships (i.e. trade, politics, and religion). These differences require variations in development programming, which in turn requires vigorous research, resources and organizations.

Pastoral Nomads and the National Interest

The nomads and their habitat comprise a significant component of Ethiopia's population, ethnic groups and territory. It is incumbent upon the government to make a significant effort to mobilize their energy and resources in order to alleviate the precarious conditions of such large numbers of its citizens, as well as to control and develop these resources.

In the formulation of national policy concerning organization and mobilization of the Ethiopian masses, two major socio-economic sectors (urban dwellers and peasantry) have been identified and accorded priority. Of equal magnitude and deserving the same degree of consideration is the pastoral nomadic sector. This sector is different from the other two sectors. The inherent qualities of nomadism must be taken as the kernel of development planning and mobilizing. This requires specialized institutions tailored to assist the development of the nomadic sector.

Economically, the pastoral nomadic sector raises a large portion of the total national livestock (i.e. 40 per cent of the cattle, 75 per cent of the goats, 25 per cent of the sheep, 20 per cent of the equines and 100 per cent of the camels). The greatest potential for irrigated agriculture exists in the areas occupied by pastoral nomads. The development, control, allocation and effective use of these natural resources calls for a vigorous organization and institution building.

The fact that Ethiopia is completely encircled by nomads and nomadic areas, the relatively isolated position of the nomads in national life, the fact that international boundaries do not conform to ethnic identity have all created a "push and pull" effect which in turn has a dynamic impact on Ethiopia's relations with neighbouring countries.

The government is committed to providing social services and cultural and economic development for all its citizens. However, it has not been possible to provide such services to these pastoral nomads, owing to their mobility and the inaccessibility of the regions where they live. There are no easy solutions to the mobility question. Overcoming such obstacles, in other words building environments conducive to the provision of both social services and development programmes presupposes an organizational capacity and effort of high magnitude.

Since activities concerned with nomadic development began quite recently, it is evident that there is no broad body of accumulated knowledge and experience of the nomads which can be used for development planning. This lacuna has to be compensated for by substantial research, experiments and follow- up studies. Knowledge gained from these efforts should be communicated to policy makers so that a correct policy for development can be formulated.

Ecological and Socio-economic Constraints upon Nomadic Development

The design and implementation of a development programme for pastoral nomads requires consideration of their specific environmental and socio-economic constraints and possibilities. The harsh climate, with low and unreliable rainfall and with all year round high temperatures, severely limits the potential for rainfed agriculture. An alternative land use pattern has to be adopted.

Pastoral nomadism is based on a livestock production system which is ecologically adjustable to the utilization of the meagre resources of the arid and semi-arid regions which are not generally suitable for rainfed agriculture. All necessary conditions are adjusted to making this mode of production viable. The techniques include, among other things, seasonal migration, herd diversification, as well as division of labour by age and sex in the production of various livestock types.

Encroachment into pastoral areas has continued unabated. The fact that the lowlands are under-populated has led to the erroneous notion that Ethiopia still has large land resources that could be used for large scale mechanized farming. As a result, highland crop cultivators have slowly been expanding their operations into these areas. Concession grants were given for the establishment and expansion of irrigated cash cropping. The state has continued such practices even after the nationalization of the companies in the mid-1970s. In addition, game reserves and national park expansion have often taken the best of the resource base which sustains the pastoral production system.

The establishment of all these projects was in a sense an encroachment upon pastoral rangelands, whether this was intended or not. Their negative consequences by far out-weigh their indirect benefits. This conclusion is not intended to suggest that the vast pastoral areas should be forever reserved for exclusive use by pastoral groups. Since the pastoral areas include the big river valleys of Ethiopia (The Awash River Valley, Lower Wabi Shebelle Basin, Lower Omo River Basin, Gambella Plains, Belles Valley and Dinder Shinfu Plains), one cannot advocate that these resources be reserved for the pastoralists alone. There is a need to exploit these areas by commercial farming, but the pastoralists should be among the main beneficiaries, or be provided with a viable alternative.

The general tendency of the pastoral nomads is to maximize their herd size on the communal grazing territory, in order to avert the risk associated with small herds. The belief is that owning a large herd provides a buffer stock when droughts or other calamities strike, not to mention the fact that it bestows high status on the owner. This economic strategy has resulted in overgrazing and destruction of the natural vegetation in some areas.

The social organization of the pastoralists is specifically adjusted to their production system. Since land is neither owned nor used individually, territoriality is not sufficiently significant to be used as a basis of social organization, except in a loose sense of the term. For many economic, social, political, judicial and defensive purposes, the social organization of the pastoralists, which is based on kinship, is highly cohesive. The problem arises when there is an attempt to reorganize the pastoral nomads, more or less on the basis of the model of peasant associations. Such attempts, for instance grazers' associations, have so far not been able to replace the clan system.

Since the pastoral nomadic groups have been isolated from the central highland peasant and government superstructure, there has been a much lesser degree of acculturation. Meaningful dialogue and commitment to implementation of development programmes is consequently more difficult. We also observe a lower degree of economic integration, transport and communication. Because of past educational neglect, it is difficult to recruit development workers who can act as "brokers of social change", not to mention the difficulty of finding sufficient numbers of representatives from among the pastoralists who could grasp the technical aspects of the operation as quickly as required. Provision of social services is also difficult when dealing with a mobile and scattered population.

A Development Strategy for Pastoral Nomads

Considering the magnitude and significance of the pastoral nomadic population and its areas, this sector merits special treatment by policy makers in Ethiopia. Priority must be given to the following:

Establishing a National Umbrella Institution

A national umbrella institution for nomadic development should be charged with the responsibility to:

*formulate appropriate legislation and policies regarding the status and rights of the nomads and their habitat;

*initiate and supervise the planning of development projects and programmes for nomadic development;

*create appropriate organizations for monitoring, administration and supervision of the implementation of nomadic development;

*create a mechanism for undertaking research and appraisal of the conditions of nomads and their development programmes, and based upon such findings, modify and improve development strategies;

*establish mechanisms for training of specialized staff for nomadic development;

*mobilize other government departments for the provision of social and physical infrastructures not covered by nomadic development programmes;

*solicit and channel funds coming from abroad to nomadic development and to mobilize, organize and orient the pastoralists for development activities.

Range Development Programmes

It should be clearly realized from the outset that, for various reasons, settlement similar to the one practised in central highlands is not the proper option for nomadic development. In the past, settlement for pastoral nomads was idealized by policy makers. However, it has proved impossible to implement due to the scarcity of land for rainfed agriculture and the lack of financial resources to develop river valleys for irrigated agriculture.

In contrast, there are more positive reasons for rationalization of the pastoral production system in range development programmes. The pastoral production system utilizes marginal resources for livestock production without requiring any financial input from outside. It is providing sustained employment, even though at subsistence level, for approximately 4.5 million people. It is also a major supplier of livestock both for external and internal demand.

Range management programmes involve very little financial input. They can be implemented through the existing socio-economic system of the pastoral nomads, using their present technology and knowledge. By resorting to local institutions and knowledge, the rangeland resources can be effectively preserved while increasing a viable livestock production to meet local needs.

A Minimum Package Programme

It should be quite clear from the outset that settlement for the Ethiopian nomads at present is out of question, for reasons outlined earlier. Of course, there is a limited possibility of combining irrigated agriculture with pastoralism, as observed in the Awash Valley and Kelafo in the Ogaden, which started mostly on the initiative of the pastoralists themselves, and gained some support from development agencies.

However, a realistic option for pastoral development which could be applied across the board for the foreseeable future is one which follows the current trend of the pastoralists. Specific interventions must be selective so as not to disrupt the pastoralists' way of life. The government should encourage the following actions:

1) Develop an extensive system of exchange between the pastoralists, the urban areas and the peasant areas. The Ministry of Foreign Affairs is already buying sheep and goats for export in the Ogaden and Afar areas in exchange for sugar and other commodities. Since almost all the pastoralists are in need of grain and other consumer items, such action would certainly contribute towards establishing a sounder ecological balance, by reducing the size of the herd in proportion to the carrying capacity of the grazing land.

2) If pastoralists are to play a vital role in the development of Ethiopia and their respective communities, it is imperative that the government provide education and health services. One obstacle for educational planners is the mobility of the pastoralists. There should be a way to circumvent this. Pastoralists have semi-permanent camps, and a schooling system which used this situation could be devised. Such a scheme could either use stationary or mobile schools, once the mobility pattern had been determined. Health programmes could be designed in the same manner.

3) Selective range management intervention is also necessary to make the pastoral sector more productive, while preventing adverse ecological effects. This would include primarily veterinary medicine and water harvesting.

4) In the light of recurrent droughts, schemes for crisis management and rehabilitation should be devised. Preparedness for drought situations should include the storage of grain and fodder.

5) Policies should be developed for the maintenance and provision of pastoral grazing land. Laws should be enacted and enforced to prevent encroachment upon the territory by mechanized agriculture without due compensation.

6) The present social system which is basically the clan system should be maintained, instead of attempting to displace it by newly created peasant associations.

NOTES

This discussion of pastoralism is based on a study of pastoral nomads in Ethiopia, undertaken for RRC and UNDP (project number UNDP/RRC ETH/81/001) by a team of experts, completed in 1984.

The complete series of reports comprises of four parts:

PART I: Major Findings and Recommendations
PART II: The Physical Resources
PART III: The Socio-Economic Aspects
 A. Social Anthropology
 B. Economy and Livestock Production
PART IV: Development Strategies
Sect. 1: The Frameworks of Development
Sect. 2: Range Development Programme
Sect. 3: Settlement on Irrigated Agriculture
Sect. 4: Settlement on Marine Fishery
Sect. 5: Extension Programme for Hunter- Cultivators

Members of the team were:
Fecadu Gadamu, team leader and social anthropologist,
Girma Brahanu, livestock expert,
Girma Bisrat, range management expert,
Medbib Mamo, land use expert,
Mershya Sahle, irrigation engineer,
Tadesse Yiberta, economist.

20 The Peasant Perspective
Siegfried Pausewang

Since student demonstrations in the 1960s launched the slogan "Land to the tiller", the land question has remained in the focus of political demands. No new government could hope to win public legitimacy after Haile Selassie without a radical land reform. Peasant discontent demanded change, and agricultural stagnation began to be felt as a liability in the business class. In public opinion an awareness was growing that the problems of land tenure and of the depressed peasantry demanded radical measures.

Land reform was an economic as well as a political demand. The expressed opposition from students and other groups was not only anti-feudalist, but demanded rural democracy. There were high expectations of better times to come for peasants. Better living standards, better social conditions, more equity and participation, more influence of peasants both on local and on national affairs were anticipated as consequences of a land reform - not only by the peasants themselves.

To what degree have such hopes come true ? And if they did not materialize, for what reasons could they not be achieved ?

The Land Reform

The land reform in 1975 was the centre-piece of the Ethiopian revolution, and in some respects one of the most radical land reforms ever attempted in Africa.[1] It was, in fact, more than a land reform - in wide areas especially in the south, it was an attempt of the suppressed, exploited, and to a large extent expropriated peasantry to restructure rural society in their own interest.

In those areas where feudal[2] exploitation had been most pronounced and resented, the situation was ripe. Here, peasants got a chance - though only for a short period - to change their own life conditions, to take their own decisions and make improvements through their own work, to take their destiny into their own hands.

There may be some argument about whether peasants were intentionally given a legal mandate for engineering their own development, or whether they just used the chances which a power vacuum in the central government offered for a short interim period. Both the political events and the process of drafting the land reform proclamation in 1974-75, indicate that, in 1974, a law was intended which would empower peasants and give them access to far reaching self-determination and local autonomy. Socialist convictions, political calculations, romantic feelings, and a moral commitment to satisfy popular student demands, may all have contributed to design a land reform law which distributed not only land to the tiller, but also food to the hungry, and power to the peasants.[3] It was only later that political leaders had second thoughts about the governability of a country controlled by independent peasant associations.

There was considerable variation as to how much of this reform was put into practice in the villages. However, in 1976 to 1977, in large parts of the country, peasant associations were rather independent organs of local self-administration. Peasant association chairmen exercised wide authority and acted with a high degree of independence even in their relation to government authorities. Peasants, at least in Sidamo, Shoa, Wollega, Gojam, developed a self-consciousness of considerable standing, faced with urban demands or administrative rigidity. Peasants in Northern Shoa could tell a visiting government official to come back another day with an answer to their demand for better access to salt, matches, everyday consumer goods; only then would they be willing to listen to his advice. Zemetcha students in Sidamo were told to leave rural issues to the peasants who knew best what they needed (Pausewang 1983). There were also areas where the land reform was resisted by peasants. In some villages, peasant-elected leaders acted like landlords and local despots. All in all, however, a distinct, self-conscious peasant identity was germinating and growing fast.

Re-Establishing Central Control

Beginning from 1978, the government started to reorganize rural administration and policy. Problems in urban - rural relations, but probably even more the growing need for state revenue, to finance a growing administration and expensive military campaigns, compelled the government to intervene. The political motivation was to enforce the land reform nationwide, and to initiate the next step towards social reconstruction of rural society. After the government had mobilized peasant militias and solicited support from peasant associations for subduing urban resistance and ending the "red terror" period, it started to use peasant associations to re-establish central control over the villages. The trend towards peasant self-determination was gradually but decisively reversed.

From 1984-86, FAO's "Achefer-Shebadino Study" revealed that peasant independence and self-consciousness had been dramatically restricted. Peasants complained that they felt controlled from above, and that their peasant associations had become the instrument of central control. Peasants felt harassed by leaders who had become independent of peasant support, and complained that they had lost all influence even on local decisions. Also, their economic position had declined. They received little stimulation and felt their initiatives frustrated and their enthusiasm rapidly dwindling (Mulugeta 1987).

A Socialist Agriculture?

Experts agree that Ethiopian agriculture has the potential to feed the population. Ethiopia has little industry and no known natural resources of major economic relevance. The major resource for development is its people. Rural development has to come first, to produce the resources needed for industrialization. But before this can reach a significant scale, a process of self-centred development of agriculture has to become sustainable, to produce the resources needed for its own growth. Such a process depends heavily on peasant work, initiative and enthusiasm, as well as on some investment and know-how from outside.

Government services in rural areas have been expanded substantially since the revolution. Especially in the fields of agricultural extension, health care, and education, services have improved tremendously. However, for a country commanding small resources, and faced with internal and external problems, the possibilities of reaching a large and dispersed rural population are strictly limited. Villagization and collectivization can therefore be seen also as the government's attempt to give the peasants better access to those services.

Through a gradual change in peasant consciousness, the government hopes to win understanding and support for the envisaged socialist transformation of agriculture and rural society, which is seen as the only way out of the hopeless spiral of a growing population with a declining productivity (see the contributions by Dessalegn Rahmato, Stefan Brüne, and Eshetu Chole in this volume). Up to now, however, the attempt shows little sign of success. Instead of being won over to the idea of a socialist rural society, peasants appear estranged and frustrated, and there are indications that they react by retreating into subsistence, as far as possible, as they do in other African countries, albeit for different reasons.

Rural Alternatives?

Western advocates of a free market economy consider economic incentives the main lever through which to appeal to peasants' interest in improving their own economic position, and with it their country's. The problems of such a solution, given Ethiopia's weak position on the world market, are discussed by Fantu Cheru in this volume.

Cohen and Isaksson (1988), in their article on "Food Production Strategy Debates in Revolutionary Ethiopia", categorize rural development strategies in two simple alternatives: *agrarian socialism* - by which they really mean present government policies - or *smallholder agriculture* - which they identify with a free market model of rural development. They assume that all Western donors, in spite of minor differences of opinion over details, essentially agree on the World Bank / IMF approach (see Fantu Cheru).

This simple dualism suits the tendency to categorize as "good" or "bad" pro-West or pro-East policies.[4] But in fact, these moral and ideological labels are often misleading. They disguise rather than clarify problems.[5] The real issues are how to create rural employment, stimulate local responsibility for rural development (ILO 1982), and foster peasant participation in development (FAO 1981). Urban - rural relations play a prominent role in all this, as do international competition, terms of trade, and economic biases (Lipton 1977, Fantu 1989).

A recent suggestion to solve the compounding problems in Ethiopia called for a firm authoritarian leader who jettisoned Marxism and returned to Western standards.[6] Nothing would be more fatal than simply to renounce socialist rural policies but retain paternalistic central authority and jump on the alternative mainstream policy, implementing uncritically a market model tailored by the IMF. Rather than just a free market, it is democracy, the stimulation of local decision making and initiative, that is the key to rural development, as the texts in this volume show. Flexible adaptation to cultural, social, ecological and economic, ethnic and climatic conditions are essential, not simply submission to the laws of the international market.

Most of these issues, and others, have been discussed in this volume. If a conclusion in this context can be drawn, it must be, to quote Fantu Cheru, that 'the only experts on rural development are the peasants themselves'. Without democracy no development is possible. Only the experience, knowledge, and initiative of peasants can build rural development.

A Peasant Option

A few more general lessons can be drawn. Firstly, at the present stage in Ethiopia, progress towards a better standard of living for the large majority of the Ethiopian population can only come from the peasantry. Secondly, free international competition does not stimulate poor peasants, because it rewards exports instead of production for local needs, breeds inequality, and marginalizes the rural majority. Thirdly, without self-determination, participation, and local democracy, the peasantry will not become the leading social force of development.

But peasant democracy does not fall from the skies like rain, just as socialism cannot be received as a gift. Nowhere has a social class developed without controlling economic and political resources. Democracy can only be achieved where a social class is prepared to use its collective power to establish it, as a means to protect its interests. A socialist transformation of society can only be consolidated where a majority perceives it as being in their collective interest.

This should not imply resignation. Nothing can be done before the necessary social forces are developed, but that means, as I see it, that peasants must mobilize their efforts and commitment to rural development precisely because it is in their own interest. Certainly development is in the interest of peasants, if it means more productivity and hence more well-being and food security, more cooperation, more mutual help and solidarity, more self-determination and local democracy.

Which rural policy options can bring such a situation closer ? To demonstrate some of the issues and questions involved, I take as my point of departure the complaints of peasants, as expressed in the Achefer-Shebadino Study. If the argument seems excessive, I hope that it will at least help to accentuate contrasts and make the contours of alternative options visible.

The Market, AMC, and the Peasant

Most peasant complaints concentrated on prices and market conditions, quota deliveries and low prices, compared to offers from private traders. The latter is not astonishing: as long as dual prices exist, peasants will complain about quota deliveries. As long as AMC does not have sufficient capacity to handle all trade and to offer the best prices, a dual market will always develop. Quota deliveries at lower prices will continue to nourish peasant discontent and to discredit AMC in the peasants' eyes (Mulugeta 1987: 137-144). The study therefore suggested finding ways to exploit the interest of small private traders in minimizing transport and administrative costs, while binding them into a system of taxing short distance transports to subsidize the necessary long distance transports.

It would be equally problematic to rely on a totally free market, which would tend to increase differences between rich and poor. A free market will always keep Ethiopian peasants dependent on an international price structure, in which they remain the weakest party, forced to supply cheap goods, to pay the debts of others, and to finance large profits abroad.

However, markets have a known ability to adjust production to needs, which should be exploited. One should not confuse production and needs with supply and demand, but keep the market under strict observation to ensure that needs are matched with buying power, and that the interests of the economically weak are taken care of. Uncontrolled, markets have a tendency to exploit and to aggravate social differences. The biblical "To he who has, it shall be given" is one of the laws of the market.

Markets have a tendency to create local differences. While peasants who produce close to the big markets, especially Addis Ababa, could make huge profits, peasants in remote areas would have to be content with a small fraction of the market price, if they wanted to sell at all. In a country with transportation problems as significant as Ethiopia's, there are good reasons for the one-price system of AMC. The problem with present practice is not the levelling of prices, but the high transportation and administrative costs and the inflexibility of a large organization like AMC. Highly salaried administrators and the enormous costs of keeping a huge fleet of vehicles running, among others, put AMC costs up so high that, instead of unifying prices on a middle level, AMC makes trade more expensive for all peasants, except possibly those in the most remote areas (Pausewang 1986, 1988).

Interference in local markets is another common source of resentment among peasants. Local markets have an essential subsistence function wherever not every single household is able to produce all varieties needed during the year. It is vital to distinguish between a local and a wider market. Local exchange is cooperation in the best sense, it is part of rural solidarity. Disrupting it by accusing peasants who have not fulfilled their quota of "black market sales" is not enforcing AMC functions, it is simply discouraging local production, marketing and cooperation (Mulugeta 1987: 10, 147).

Another peasant complaint is the rigidity with which AMC regulations are applied. Instead of tying up valuable transport equipment on rough roads to collect grain from the most remote service cooperative collection stores, AMC might offer peasants a birr extra for bringing their grain on a donkey to the *woreda* centre, thereby saving on car repairs, running costs, and time, and freeing material and capacity (Mulugeta 1987: 11, 146).

Complaints such as these led the "Achefer-Shebadino Study" to suggest an institution through which peasants could overcome their feeling of helplessness, offering a valve for appeals against arbitrary administrative decisions violating their interests. An ombudsman (after Scandinavian models) responsible for following up peasant complaints, with authority to by-pass administrative hierarchies where necessary and to take up issues of local or general importance at the highest political levels, could contribute much to correct shortcomings in the present administrative set-up. Such an institution would give peasants a chance to be heard, and might rebuild their consciousness of having some rights of their own, increasing their ability to cooperate.

Socialism and Democracy

Socialism is in its essence, in the Ethiopian context, a tradition of mutual help, solidarity, common responsibility, in short, local democracy. People's democracy in Ethiopia must be, first of all, rural democracy, complemented and protected by state authority. For that, peasant interests must have considerable leverage on central decisions, which can only be ensured through strong institutional guarantees in the Constitution of the state.

The primary peasant interest today is individual subsistence. Peasants appreciate cooperation as a means to boost subsistence, but not to overcome it. "Socialism" as it applies to them is not collectivization, but mutual help to secure subsistence. They aspire to widen their subsistence, to supplement it with cooperation, to expand and diversify their consumption, their division of labour. This will, in the end, create conditions conducive to the kind of industrial growth which will supply them with goods and absorb those parts of the population which mechanization will replace. But if they see their diminishing resources extracted and their influence and initiatives curbed, they will have no other course than to reduce their demands and settle on the simplest possible level of subsistence, as a way of escaping, as far as possible, from controls and losses.

Mechanization

Peasant work, not mechanization, is the basis of Ethiopian agriculture. Mechanization cannot be introduced from outside, as a precondition for development or for socialism. So far, the government has not given a consistent answer as to how to avoid massive unemployment if mechanized agriculture ever replaces peasant agriculture, while industrial jobs are scarce. Mechanization is extremely expensive when the machines have to be imported, and the country has to produce export crops to pay for them, especially if the workers the machines replace cannot be productively employed elsewhere. The majority of the rural population would have to continue subsistence agriculture, and serious competition for already scarce land resources would accelerate problems.

Tractors are not in the interest of the peasants. A cooperative which has to sell enough grain to pay for fuel, maintenance, and depreciation of a tractor could hardly feed all its members. As long as alternative jobs are not available, a tractor does not alleviate a peasant's work load and drudgery, but simply deprives him of his means of production, replaces his work, and takes his livelihood. When a tractor eats more resources than twenty peasant families, peasants cannot afford mechanization. It can only come as a result of a long and sustained peasant development. When rural productivity has risen, and industries produce to satisfy growing rural demands, they may absorb so much labour that agriculture can start to replace peasants with tractors. Policies face the challenge of balancing technology that helps to release, apply and expand human energies against the danger of simply replacing those energies.

Cooperation

The large majority of peasants resent producer cooperatives, and do not want to join. They feel they would have to give up their independence, for no advantage. Those who have joined feel dependent on others, both in their work and in their consumption; they feel controlled. Collective work does not offer them a better standard of living, nor an easier work load, nor even more influence. Rather than offering new possibilities to expand their work for a better life, it restricts their initiatives. Interest in work slowly fades, and production goes down.

Ethiopian statistics measure the success of rural transformation in terms of the percentage of cooperative members in the rural population. This practice gives a totally wrong impression, because it simply identifies socialism with the Soviet model of collective production, and with the long term goal of rural mechanization. It overlooks the fact that there are other forms of cooperation practised in Ethiopia, which are more adapted to local culture, and which practice the ideals of solidarity, collective responsibility and equity much better than producer cooperatives can.

Why, then, do politicians insist on collective production? Are they blindly copying Soviet models, or are they interpreting Marx and Lenin to postulate that socialism is only possible through collectivization? Marx confronted bourgeois society by taking the ideals of freedom, equality and brotherhood seriously, applying them also in the economic sphere. At his time, society had reached a stage where industrial production was in fact a collective process: no worker could produce on his own, nor own the tools for his work. Marx's aim was to dissolve the discrepancy between collective production and individual ownership (and hence appropriation). He intended to allow collective control over collective work.

A discrepancy between collective production processes and private ownership does not exist in Ethiopian agriculture at present. Peasants still own the tools for their work, but there is no private ownership of land. The poor are often described as those who do not have their own oxen and plough. Collective work is organized as cooperation of independent individuals for mutual benefit. There are rich traditions of indigenous forms of cooperation, which serve the well-being of the poor, the rural majority. Their interest should be the focus of socialist solidarity in a society consisting of 85 per cent peasants.

Central Control or Local Democracy?

The proper balance between central versus local demand for resources is one of the key topics for development policy. Ultimately, the one who decides on the use of resources, determines the course of development.

Peasants complain frequently about being controlled from above and not having any influence on local decision making. One solution that has been suggested is a return to the situation of 1976, when peasant associations were in effect units of local self-administration and self-determination, and had control over local resources (Pausewang 1988, 1988b). There is, however, a need for central control, to prevent local corruption and the abuse of peasant association office by elected leaders who turn into local despots. Central control also has to guarantee a minimum level of equality between regions and villages, and to assist peasant associations with problems they cannot solve on their own. On the other hand, central authorities need resources to organize services for the rural population, as well as those state functions which local administration cannot take care of. Some extraction of resources is therefore necessary to finance state services. But extraction needs to be kept in line with contribution capacities. It should not be allowed to restrict peasant investment, participation, and initiatives.

Accumulation and re-investment is also needed in agriculture. Rural development depends on an adequate level of resource extraction, which allows a maximum of services with a minimum of negative effects on rural productivity and local democracy. State control in the rural areas needs reorganization to serve the interest of rural development, not to control peasants. Social transformation of rural society must have the aim of securing peasant development.

If it is correct that development has to come from the peasants, then one has to ask: do the peasants have access to the necessary economic and political resources? Are peasant interests represented in the state? Do they, through their participation, control the exercise of central authority over their individual villages? Are they influencing politics, or are they just a pawn in the game of other actors? One cannot just postulate the unity of peasants and workers at the present stage of development. Peasants have no interest in becoming workers - simply because, at this stage, there is no realistic chance that industrial work will, in the foreseeable future, offer them a better living than subsistence agriculture does.

All ideology aside, there is a wide discrepancy between the statement that only peasant agriculture can produce development, and the evidence of declining production and massive peasant complaints. Peasants are well aware that they lack both influence and resources. They choose the "exit option" because they see no way towards improvement of their situation within the economic and administrative framework they are offered at present.

Urban - Rural Relations

We can hardly avoid the conclusion that the hopes of 1975 have not come about. Ethiopia is still an agrarian based society exposed to the harsh winds of the international market. Government has not assumed the role of protector of peasant self-determination and grass-roots democracy. To the contrary, the Ethiopian Government has established firm control both over rural decision making processes and over rural resources. Why have the seedlings of local democracy of 1975 not been allowed to grow? Who opposed, who prevented peasant self-determination? And what is the role of the state in this process?

Urban - rural competition over resources is at the root of conflict. Towns lost resources in the first years of the land reform. Landlords were stripped of their privileges and their large incomes. This reduced urban buying power, created urban unemployment especially in urban service professions. Urban groups were eager to increase the flow of resources from the villages again. The state felt under pressure to stimulate employment, to appease urban discontent. Resources were needed to feed the urban population, and to create public works programmes and social services. The administration demanded more finance to keep the country together, and to expand services in rural and urban areas. The military needed resources to protect the new order against foreign aggression and separatist groups in the country.

As everywhere in Africa, urban interests have more leverage on the government than a scattered peasant majority commands. The combined demands of the urban proletariat, professional interests, the administration and the military gave the state little choice but to increase extraction from agriculture. In addition, the ideological goal of a social transformation of rural society seemed to justify heavy intervention in local decisions and a close control of rural society.

Is Rural Democracy Possible?

Two related questions remain at the end: Is (local) democracy possible with a free market? And is (peasant) democracy possible with a strong state? In an agrarian based developing society, peasant democracy appears hardly compatible with an unmediated integration in the international market. The pressure towards export production, combined with sinking terms of trade for the only export products agriculture can sell, will necessarily create a small group of commercial producers, against whom poor peasants will lose out. Discontent, repression, and mass poverty will result, and peasants will inevitably defend themselves with their only weapon, by "opting out" as much as they can (Fantu 1989).

Only when protected by a strong state can peasants develop an internal market satisfying local needs for food, and local democracy - linked to wider markets, but as little as possible dependent on them. However, peasant democracy under state protection seems hardly possible where the interests of minority urban groups dominate the state. A state protecting peasants is only possible if peasants have a leverage over the state strong enough to neutralize or to counter-balance the influence of other groups, especially urban interests. This is clearly not the case today. Even if some individual top leaders appear to be very concerned about the needs and interests of peasants, the bureaucracy as an institution works as a filter. It enforces a practice in which the interests of peasants carry very little weight, and their voices are seldom heard, if ever. The ignorance about rural life among urban elites and administrators is frightening, and widespread arrogance towards peasants and nomads hardly understandable given the rural roots of most bureaucrats. Such structures can hardly be changed from above, through new laws or a new political will. A change is only possible through a process which strengthens the influence of peasants in the state as well as on lower administrative levels.

The time is ripe: urban groups are beginning to understand that they are killing the goose that lays the golden eggs. Urban prosperity depends on agricultural growth, which demands that extraction is limited to a level which allows rural investments. The state is at a point of exhaustion, and military victory appears impossible without massive additional resources - which can no longer be made available. Agriculture is stagnating, as investment in state farms increases costs faster than returns, while peasant agriculture is disrupted and stripped of resources for re-investment. It is thus in the common interest of all that the pressure on peasant resources is relieved. Many see it absolutely necessary that the war ends and armed conflicts are resolved peacefully, so that military expenditure can be reduced substantially. And a growing number of urban intellectuals now understand that ecological balances are being disturbed, and that an ecological breakdown affects towns just as much as rural areas.

New Alliances?

There is thus a basis for fostering an alliance of peasants with urban groups. It will take some time to grow, and need all support it can get. But short of a new peasant revolution, which is nowhere in sight, there is no other course open than a patient process of strengthening the influence of peasants in the state.[7]

What is needed is peasant self-consciousness and sense of identity, the organization of the political will of peasants, power for the political interests of the rural majority. This cannot be institutionalized through government decision, nor from outside. But it was there in 1976, though it was later curbed by growing state control. Reducing state control now would not necessarily revive the spirit of 1976. But it would help those who might wage the attempt.

One should be careful not to romanticize the situation of 1975 to 1977. Certainly this was no time of peasant prosperity and sunshine, it was a period of struggle and problems, anxieties, and frustration. Nobody would recommend perpetuation of such problems. But it was also a time of hope and of activity in rural areas, it provoked initiatives and inspired enthusiasm among peasants. Referring back to these transitional years should not imply advocacy of the social turmoil and the suffering of that period. We need to understand why, at that time, peasants could expect increased and increasing influence, and mobilize for their own development. We should focus on those particular forces which allowed peasant mobilization and participation; not to erect the peasant paradise, but to stimulate, develop and make the most of their human and economic potential.

Peasants are the weakest group in a political discussion. They are dispersed and face great problems in organizing themselves around their demands, and in putting those demands forcefully. Under Ethiopian conditions, peasants have hardly any possibility of influencing state decisions through a strike.[8] They have few political weapons to hand. Their only effective weapon is the "exit option", which they use with skill. But it is a defensive weapon, not suitable to actively influence decisions.[9]

Although one cannot create peasant consciousness from outside, one can support an alliance of peasants and intellectuals. In the political struggle, peasants need an urban-based voice. In a world of experts, peasants need a counter-expertise to win attention for their interests. Peasants are not without arguments. But they need arguments to be formulated and defended.

Intellectuals can play this role. But one should add a warning that peasants do not need anybody who thinks for them - they need friends who think *with* them. This difference is of utmost importance. It needs a different form of contact and understanding between rural people and urban youths. Peasants need a new form of dialogue, where the urban educated learn from peasants, while they help them discover how to argue in a practical political context. The urban interest in increasing rural production provides a material base for such an alliance. In the longer perspective, the common interest dictates action be taken to preserve and sustain the natural environment and its productive capacity.

If such an alliance were possible, urban intellectuals might eventually assume the role of guardians of decentralized democracy, with the peasants as its bearers.

Outlook

This is a long process, a thorny road. In the meantime, there is no reason to despair. Other forms of organization seem possible to increase peasant influence and create a more conducive climate for rural development. Small steps do not change basic power relations, but they help to improve the situation of peasants - and thereby contribute to their consciousness, their security, their influence.

In the end, one important change will be essential for rural development: the state must be prepared to allow more resources and more influence for the rural people, - and the peasants must be willing and able to re-organize their political identity.

NOTES

1 There was not much land redistributed; but the land reform was radical in the sense that it abolished the landed nobility as an exploitative class. Peasants were freed from almost all obligations stemming from the material and socio-political privileges of the nobility. On average, peasants roughly doubled the food and other resources at their disposal, as all payments of rents, contributions, and even debts to the landlords were abolished. In political terms, peasants were given an opportunity to organize a largely autonomous self-administration, responsible for land distribution, all local courts and even self-defence militias.

Economic exploitation and socio-political suppression varied greatly before the revolution, from areas where the nobility was still part of the local community, to places where representatives of absentee landlords maintained a tight regime of controls and threats. While peasants in some areas were forced to deliver up to three-quarters of their produce, some poorer and more remote areas were hardly affected by such demands.

The land reform did not, therefore, have the same effect, nor the same intensity everywhere. In some areas it was resisted - in others it may have been felt as an unnecessary disturbance. Peasants in large parts especially of the southern Highlands, started a rural revolution even before a land reform law was proclaimed, and felt it as a unique liberation when the law finally legalized their struggle (Pausewang 1983:105-126).

2 There have been long debates about whether one can talk of "feudalism" in Ethiopia or not. Certainly there are characteristic resemblances to the practice of European medieval (and later) nobilities living on the produce of peasants, whom they managed gradually to force into growing dependence and exploitation. There are also traits which clearly distinguish "Ethiopian feudalism" from the European pattern.

The term is here used to characterize the social relations developing as a result of a centralization process in which the local nobility was gradually integrated into the central state administration, but kept their local privileges (Pausewang 1983:33 - 44). The process displays some correspondence to France under Louis XIV or, as far as the newly conquered south is concerned, to the Prussian expansion to the East and its integration into a centralized state.

3 Other scholars, including some of the authors in this volume, argue that the Ethiopian revolution from the beginning intended to restructure the control over the rural population, but never to question it. They see the independence of peasant associations in 1975-77 as an interlude due to a power vacuum, not as an intentional policy.

I agree that this is the outcome, fifteen years later. But my experience in 1976 and knowledge of the processes leading to the land reform make me conclude that the 1974-76 period offered a different social promise.

4 Prominent among such anti-communist simplifiers in Ethiopian studies is Paul B. Henze, an American scholar working for the RAND corporation and the US Defence Secretary. See his discussion of the GOSPLAN (1985) report (Henze 1989).

5 In 1982, ILO sent a "Jobs and Skills Programme in Africa" (JASPA) mission to Ethiopia. Its report (1982), still not officially released, suggested a rural development model for growth with equity, built on ILO's Basic Needs strategy. ILO recommendations focus on employment generation in smallholder agriculture, with local responsibility for development.

In 1985, two members of the ILO team, Keith Griffin and Roger Hay, published an article comparing the productive efficiency of the three systems of agricultural production working in Ethiopia. They concluded that peasant farms were most efficient in absorbing labour, feeding the rural population, and returning profit on capital. In crop yield they might soon be by-passed by state farms, which have better access to fertilizers. Producer cooperatives were seen to have the best potential for accumulation, while state farms were superior in producing marketable surpluses. In conclusion, Griffin and Hay (1985: 64-66) argue that sustained growth with the possibility of increasing equity is best achieved through employing the labour of the rural majority in smallholder production, and releasing their collective ingenuity and their ability to accumulate surpluses through a variety of forms of rural cooperation.

In cooperation with the ILO, FAO (1981) developed principles for local democratic participation and cooperative rural development, as mandated by the 1979 World Conference on Agrarian Reform and Rural Development (WCARRD). Ethiopia supported the conference and its principles, arguing that Ethiopian peasant associations and cooperatives were precisely the sort of homogeneous groups and rural organizations that gave poor peasants the definite influence over their own development which the conference had called for. If this claim reflected government intentions, there must have been other obstacles preventing peasants from using these associations as their tools for local development.

Already in the 1960s and 70s, the French agronomist René Dumont (1962, 1980) criticized African development policies as biased in favour of urban interests and privileged classes. Though he did not develop a specific alternative strategy for Ethiopia, Dumont's works offer important elements, which are reflected in Michael Lipton's (1977) concept of "urban bias" (see also Chambers 1983).

The "Dependency" school of development theory explains that international competition only stimulates development when partners are on an equal level. With large differences in economic capacity, the system produces underdevelopment in the weaker economy. Terms of trade deteriorate, the economy becomes biased towards export production, and cannot develop a national market and national growth.

Fantu Cheru (1989) criticizes the World Bank approach as a reaction to the debt crisis, ensuring that African countries can pay their debts. IMF conditionality is a means to keep developing countries dependent. To Fantu, the only experts on rural development are the peasants themselves. Without democracy there is no development possible, he says. Only the experience, knowledge, and initiative of peasants can build rural development.

6 The last RAND publication by Henze, entitled "Ethiopia in Early 1989: Deepening Crisis" (Santa Monica, California, November 1989), concludes its introduction advising: ..."No one talks of restoration of the monarchy but Ethiopians have little confidence in their ability to operate a democracy. A leader who jettisoned Marxism and led the country with a firm paternalistic, authoritarian hand but with a civilized sense of style and commitment to generally admired Western standards and values would have widespread support." (p. 7)

7 Historical examples from other countries provide useful comparisons. Senghaas shows that the efforts to institute a democratic constitution in Spain in 1812 failed because there was no self-conscious peasantry, and an alliance between large estates and foreign business interests drained resources out of the country. In contrast, the 1814 Constitution in Norway succeeded against heavy odds, because there was an alliance of peasants and urban liberal interests, willing to use international resources, but eager to develop Norway (Senghaas 1982, 1988).

Again, in 1972, in the campaigns preceding the referendum for or against Norwegian membership of the European Community, an alliance between urban intellectuals and a massive rural vote against membership carried the day, and introduced a decade of unusually strong rural influence in Norwegian politics. Peasants could in 1975 muster a parliamentary majority to assert the principle that peasants were entitled to an income equal to that of an average salary of industrial workers, and that the state had a responsibility to guarantee such income (Pausewang 1989). Later governments have not always kept to this commitment in budget allocations, as peasant power did not remain strong enough to enforce it. But the principle, established in a period of political strength, continues to command state support.

8 As they did in Norway in 1975 (Pausewang 1979).

9 There has been an argument about whether peasants have any exit option at all, as they depend both on goods they cannot produce by themselves, and on a state that has achieved a high level of control, and offers them essential services. In an absolute sense, of course, peasants cannot escape into complete isolation. But it still has a considerable effect on a rural economy if peasants decide to do no more than absolutely necessary to satisfy minimal demands, and consciously reduce their involvement in markets and state services, instead of actively using whatever opportunities markets, state, and rural institutions offer. The term "exit option" should be understood as a tendency, including anything from reluctance to cooperate up to passive resistance.

Bibliography

Ethiopian names should never be abreviated or inverted. Alphabetical lists should use the first name. Often, one name is composed of two words: Haile Mariam, for instance, means the power of Mary. A person called Yohannes Haile Mariam is neither Mariam, Y.H nor Yohannes H. Mariam nor Haile M.Y.

Abebe Zegeye, 1989 (Forthcoming) "The Administration of Resettlement in Ethiopia" in *Forced Labour and Migration, Patterns of Movement within Africa*, Oxford

Adams, W.M., 1986 "Traditional Agriculture and Water Use in the Sokota Valley, Nigeria", *Geographical Journal*, Vol.152, p.1

Addis Zemen, 1985 Government owned Amharic daily, Addis Ababa

African Development Bank and Economic Commission for Africa (ADB/ECA), 1988 *Economic Report on Africa*, Abidjan and Addis Ababa

Afshar, Haleh (ed), 1987 *Women, State and Ideology, Studies from Africa and Asia*, London, Macmillan

Aleligne Kefyalew and S. Franzel, 1987 *Initial Results of Informal Survey, Adet Mixed Farming System Zone*, Working Paper No.2/87, Addis Ababa, Institute of Agricultural Research

Alemayehu Mamo and S. Franzel, 1987 *Initial Results of Informal Survey, Sinana Mixed Farming System Zone*, Working Paper No.1/87, Addis Ababa, Institute of Agricultural Research

Alemayehu Lirenso, 1986 "Towards a Rationalization of the Food Grain Marketing Systems in Ethiopia", Paper presented to the National Seminar on Food Strategy in Ethiopia, Alemaya Agricultural University, December

Alemayehu Lirenso, 1987 *Grain Marketing and Pricing in Ethiopia*, Addis Ababa, IDR Research Report No. 28

Alemayehu Lirenso and Dejene Aredo, 1988 *A Socio-Economic Study of Service Co-operative Grain Mill Users*, IDR, Research Report No. 31, Addis Ababa

Alemneh Dejene, 1987 *Peasants, Agrarian Socialism and Rural Development in Ethiopia*, Westview Special Studies on Africa, Westview Press

Ambaye Zekarias, 1966 *Land Tenure in Eritrea (Ethiopia)*, Addis Ababa

Argumenti i Fakti, 1989 (Journal), Moskva, (27)

Avramovic, Dragoslav, 1986 "Specific Production and Trade Features of Primary Commodities", *Primary Commodities, Challenge to Co-operation Among Developing Countries*, Ljubljana, p. 31

Bager, T., 1980 *Marketing Cooperatives and Peasants in Kenya*, Uppsala, SIAS

Balawyder, A., 1980 *Cooperative Movements in Eastern Europe*, London, Macmillan

Banaji, J., 1976 "Summary of Selected Parts of Kautsky's 'The Agrarian Question' ", *Economy and Society*, Vol. 5, No.1

Baran, Paul, 1957 *The Political Economy of Growth*, New York and London

Barber, R., 1984 *An Assessment of the Dominant Soil Degradation Processes in the Ethiopian Highlands*, Highland Reclamation Study, Addis Ababa

Bariagaber, Hadgu, 1979 "Demographic Characteristics of the Rural Population of Ethiopia", *Ethiopian Journal of Development Research*, Vol. 3, No. 2

Bariagaber, Hadgu, 1987 *The Role of Demographic Information in Planning for Urban Growth and Development in Ethiopia*, Seminar on Development Planning and Demographic Analysis, The Case of Ethiopia, DTRC/IDR, Addis Ababa University

Barker, Jonathan, 1985 "Gaps in the Debates about Agriculture in Senegal, Tanzania and Mozambique", *World Development* 13 (1985), 1, pp. 59-76

Bauer, Dan F., 1973 *Land, Leadership and Legitimacy Among the Inderta Tigray of Ethiopia*, New York, Unpublished Ph.D Dissertation

Beckman, Björn, 1982 "Whose State? State and Capitalist Development in Nigeria", *Review of African Political Economy*, 23, pp. 37-51

Befekadu Degefe, 1978 *Investment Policies in Pre-Revolution Ethiopia*, Addis Ababa, IDR

Belshaw, Deryke G.R., 1988 "A Solution for the Food Deficit Areas of Ethiopia, Accelerated Farm Household Systems Development", Addis Ababa, ONCCP, mimeo

Beneria, Lourdes and Gita Sen, 1981 "Accumulation, Reproduction, and Women's Role in Economic Development, Boserup Revisited", *Signs*, Vol. 7 No. 2

Bergmann, Theodor, Peter Gey and Wolfgang Quaisser, 1984 *Sozialistische Agrarpolitik*, Köln

Berihun Teferra, 1988 *An Economic Study of the Villagisation Programme in Ethiopia, The Case of a Village in Selale Awraja of Shewa Region*, Addis Ababa University, Dept. of Economics

Bishop, R., 1984 *Ethiopian Highlands Reclamation Study*, Working Paper 5, An Evaluation of the Ethiopian Resettlement Programme, Addis Ababa, Ministry of Agriculture/FAO

Blaikie, Piers, 1989 "Aspects of Soil Erosion and Land Degradation", Keynote address, Sixth International Soil Conservation Conference, Addis Ababa

Blaikie, Piers, 1985, *The Political Economy of Soil Erosion in Developing Countries*, London and New York

Bondestam, Lars, 1974 "People and Capitalism in the Northeastern Lowlands of Ethiopia", *The Journal of Modern African Studies*, Vol. 12, No. 3

Boserup, Ester, 1965 *The Conditions of Agricultural Growth*, Chicago

Boserup, Ester, 1970 *Women's Role in Economic Development*, London

Boserup, Ester, 1981 *Population and Technological Change*, Chicago, University of Chicago Press

Bradby, Barbara, 1977 "Research Note, The Non-Valorisation of Women's Labour", *Critique of Anthropology*, Vol. 3 Nos. 9/10

Brown, Lester R. and Edward C. Wolf, 1985 *Reversing Africa's Decline*, Worldwatch Paper No. 65

Brown, Jane B., 1989 "Soil Conservation, Forestry and Food Aid in Ethiopia, Some Experiences and Some Current Problems", Paper presented at the Sixth International Soil Conservation Conference, Addis Ababa

Brüne, Stefan, 1983 "Die Äthiopische Agrarreform, Wirtschaftliche und soziale Folgen radikaler Agrarpolitik", *Afrika Spectrum*, 18 (1983), 2, pp. 117-137

Brüne, Stefan, 1988 "Agrarian Development, Famine and Foreign Aid - The Ethiopian Experience", Paper presented to the 10th International Conference of Ethiopian Studies, Paris, August 1988

Bureau, Jaques, 1988 "Ethiopie, De la junte à la république", *Afrique Contemporaine*, 27 (1988) 3 (No. 147), pp. 3-30

Central Planning Supreme Council (later ONCCP), 1982 *Economic Report*, (Amharic) Addis Ababa

Central Planning Supreme Council, 1984 *Assessment of the Six Yearly Plans*, (Amharic) Addis Ababa, December

Chambers, Robert, 1983 *Rural Development, Putting the Last First*, London, Lagos, New York

Chenery et al., 1974 *Redistribution With Growth*, London, Oxford University Press

Clapham, Christopher, 1988 *Transformation and Continuity in Revolutionary Ethiopia*, Cambridge

Clarke, John., 1986 *Resettlement and Rehabilitation, Ethiopia's Campaign against Famine*, London, Harney and Jones

Codippily, Hilarian, 1985 *Ethiopia, International Financial Flows 1967-83*, World Bank, staff working paper, Washington

Cohen, John M. and D. Weintraub, 1975 *Land and Peasant in Imperial Ethiopia, The Social Background of Revolution*, The Netherlands, Van Gorcum and Comp. B.V. Assen Cohen, John M., 1980 "Analyzing the Ethiopian Revolution, A Cautionary Tale", *Journal of Modern African Studies* 18 (1980), 4, pp. 685-691 Cohen, John M., 1987 *Integrated Rural Development, The Ethiopian Experience and the Debate*, Uppsala, Scandinavian Institute of African Studies

Cohen, John and Nils-Ivar Isaksson, 1987 *Villagization in the Arsi Region of Ethiopia*, Uppsala, Swedish University of Applied Sciences

Cohen, John and Nils-Ivar Isaksson, 1988 "Food Production Strategy Debates in Revolutionary Ethiopia" in *World Development* 16 (1988) 3, pp. 323-348

Colaris, Samuel J. and Yibrah Hagos, 1985 *Resettlement Strategy Proposals*, Addis Ababa, Highland Reclamation Study

Colaris, Samuel, 1985 *Ethiopian Highlands Reclamation Study, Resettlement Strategy Proposals*, Addis Ababa, Ministry of Agriculture, Addis Ababa, Land Use Planning and Regulatory Department/FAO

Colklough, Christopher, 1983 "Are African Governments as Unproductive as the Accelerated Development Report Implies ?", *IDS Bulletin*, Vol. 14, No. 2, pp. 24-29

Constable, M., 1985 *Resources for Rural Development in Ethiopia*, Ethiopian Highland Reclamation Study, Working Paper 24, Addis Ababa

Constable, M. and Belshaw, D., 1985 *A Summary of Major Findings and Recommendations from the Ethiopian Highlands Reclamation Study*, Addis Ababa, Ministry of Agriculture, Addis Ababa, Land Use Planning and Regulatory Department/FAO

Cornia, G.A., 1985 "Farm Size, Land Yields and the Agricultural Production Function, An Analysis of Fifteen Developing Countries", *World Development*, Vol.13, No. 4

Council of Ministers (PDRE), 1988 (a) *Activities of the Resettlement Source Areas, Study Report*, (Amharic) Addis Ababa, Megabit, 1980 EC

Council of Ministers (PDRE), 1988 (b) *Resettlement in Post-Revolution Ethiopia, Results, Problems and Future Prospects*, (Amharic) Addis Ababa, National Committee for Natural Disaster Rehabilitation, Host Regions Study Committee, Miyazya, 1980 EC

Croll, Elizabeth, 1981 "Women in Rural Production and reproduction in the Soviet Union, China, Cuba and Tanzania", *Signs*, Vol.7 No. 2

CSO (Central Statistical Office), 1964 *Selected Data on Population of Ethiopia*, Document No. 2, Addis Ababa

CSO, 1971 *The Population of Ethiopia*, Statistical Bulletin No. 6, Addis Ababa

CSO, 1974 *The Demography of Ethiopia*, Statistical Bulletin No. 6, Addis Ababa

CSO, 1975 *Statistical Abstract*, 1975, 1978, 1980

CSO, 1975 *Results of Urban Survey Second Round, Tables of Demographic Data for Ninety One Towns*, Statistical Bulletin No. 12, Addis Ababa

CSO, 1984 *Ethiopia 1984, Population and Housing Census Preliminary Report*, Addis Ababa

CSO, 1984 *Time Series Data on Area, Production Yield of Principal Crops by Region 1979/80 - 1983/84*, Addis Ababa, December

CSO, 1985 (a) *Population Situation in Ethiopia, 1990-1984*, Addis Ababa

CSO, 1985 (b) *Report on the Results of the 1981 Demographic Survey*, Statistical Bulletin No. 46, Addis Ababa

CSO, 1986 *Agricultural Sample Survey 1984/85*, Addis Ababa, Central Statistical Office

CSO, 1986 *Area by Region, Awraja, Woreda*, Addis Ababa, Statistical Bulletin 49.

CSO, 1987 *Agricultural Sample Survey 1985/86*, Addis Ababa

CSO, 1987 *Peoples Demographic Republic of Ethiopia, Facts and Figures*, Addis Ababa

CSO, 1988 *Population Projection of Ethiopia, Total and Sectoral*, Population Studies Series No. 2, Addis Ababa

CSO, 1988 *Population Situation in Ethiopia - Past, Present, and Future*, Population Studies Series No. 1, Addis Ababa

Curtis, Donald, Michael Hubbard and Andrew Shaperd, 1988 *Preventing Famine, Policies and Prospects for Africa*, London, New York

Daniel Gamachu, 1988 "Environment ad Development in Ethiopia", in A. Penrose, *Beyond Famine, An Examination of the Issues Behind Famine in Ethiopia*, Geneva

David Wolde Giorgis, 1989 *Red Tears. War, Famine, and Revolution in Ethiopia*, Trenton

Davidson, John, 1988 *Ethiopia, Preparatory Assistance to Research for Afforestation and Conservation*, Addis Ababa, FAO

Davies, R.W., 1980 *The Socialist Offensive, The Collectivization of Soviet Agriculture 1929-1930*, London, MacMillan

Department of Natural Resources Development and Conservation, 1988 *1989 Plan for Existing Settlements*, (Amharic) Addis Ababa, Sene 1980 Dessalegn Rahmato, 1984 *Agrarian Reform in Ethiopia*, Trenton, NJ, Red Sea Press

Dessalegn Rahmato, 1986 "Moral Crusaders and Incipient Capitalists. Mechanized Agriculture and its Critics in Ethiopia", *Proceedings of the Third Annual Seminar of the Department of History*, Addis Ababa University

Dessalegn Rahmato, 1986 "Some Notes on Settlement and Resettlement in Metekel Awraja", *Proceedings of the Ninth International Congress of Ethiopian Studies*, Moscow, Vol. 1, pp. 116-134

Dessalegn Rahmato, 1987 *Famine and Survival Strategies, A Case Study from Northeast Ethiopia*, Food and Famine Monograph Series, No.1, Addis Ababa, Institute of Development Research

Dessalegn Rahmato, 1987 *Settlement and Environment in Wollo. Considerations for Food Security Planning*, DTRC/IDR, Addis Ababa, Addis Ababa University

Dessalegn Rahmato, 1988 "Some Notes on Settlement and Resettlement in Mettekel Awraja (Gojjam Province)", *Proceedings of the Ninth International Congress of Ethiopian Studies*, Vol. 1, Moscow, Nauka Publishers

Dumont, René, 1962 *L'Afrique noire est mal partie*, Paris

Dumont, René, 1980 *L'Afrique Etranglé*, Paris

ECA (Economic Commission for Africa), see UNECA

Eicher, Carl and Witt, eds., 1964 *Agriculture in Economic Development*, New York, McGraw-Hill

Ellis, Gene, 1976 "The Feudal Pardigm as a Hindrance to the Understanding of Ethiopia", *Journal of Modern African Studies*, Vol. 14, No. 22

Eshetu Chole, 1986 "Constraints to Industrial Development in Ethiopia", *Proceedings of the Ninth International Congress of Ethiopian Studies*, Moscow, Vol. 1, pp. 151-165

Eshetu Chole, 1988 The Ethiopian Economy, An Overviewin, *Beyond the Famine, An Examination of the Issues Behind Famine in Ethiopia*, Geneva, pp. 27-54

Eshetu Chole and Teshome Mulat, 1988 "Land Settlement in Ethiopia, A Review of Developments" in A. Oberai (ed.,) *Land Settlement Policies and Population Distribution in Developing Countries*, New York, Praeger

ESP (Etiopia Serategnoch Party), see WPE

Fagen, R. et al., 1979 *Transition and Development, Problems of Third World Socialism*, New York, Monthly Review Press

Fantu Cheru, 1989 *The Silent Revolution in Africa. Debt, Development and Democracy*, London, Zed Books

FAO (Food and Agriculture Organisation of the UN), 1981 *The Peasant's Charter. Declaration of Principles and Programme of Action*, Rome

FAO / UNDP, 1984 *Ethiopia, Land Use, Production Regions and Farming Systems Inventory*, Rome

FAO, 1986 *Ethiopian Highland Reclamation Study, Ethiopia. Final Report*, Rome, 2 vols.

FAO / UNDP, 1988 *Master Land Use Plan*, Rome

FAO, 1988 *Report of the Mission to Ethiopia on Tropical Forestry Action Plan*, Rome

Faught, W.A., 1987 "An Appraisal of Ethiopia's Agricultural Prospects", Memorandum of Analysis, USAID, Addis Ababa

Fellows, Ruth, 1987 "Background Information on the Status of Women in Ethiopia", mimeo prepared for the Canadian Embassy, Addis Ababa

Fitzgerald, E.V.K., 1985 "The Problem of Balance in the Peripheral Socialist Economy, A Conceptual Note", *World Development* 13 (1985), 1, pp. 5-14

Francisco, R. et al., 1979 *The Political Economy of Collectivized Agriculture, Comparative Study of Communist and Non-Communist Systems*, New York, Pergamon Press

Galperin, Georgi, 1978 *Ethiopia. Population, Resources, Economy*, Moscow

Galperin, Georgi, 1986 "Some Notes on Population Migrations in Ethiopia Before and in the Course of the Revolution", *Proceedings of the Ninth International Congress of Ethiopian Studies*, Moscow, Vol. 1, pp. 176-185

GATT 1985 *International Trade, 1984-85*, Geneva

Getachew Asamenew et al., 1988 "Economic Evaluation of Improved Vertisol Drainage for Food Crop Production in the Ethiopian Highlands", in S.C.Jutzi et al., *Management of Vertisols in Sub-Saharan Africa*, Addis Ababa (ILCA)

Ghose, Ajit Kumar, 1985 "Transforming Feudal Agriculture, Agrarian Change in Ethiopia since 1974", *Journal of Development Studies 22 (1985)*, 1, pp. 127-149

Gill, Peter, 1986 *A Year in the Death of Africa. Politics, Bureaucracy and the Famine*, London

Glover, D., 1984 "Contract Farming and Smallholder Outgrower Schemes in Less-Developed Countries", *World Development*, Vol.12, Nos. 11/12

Goshe, A.K., 1985 "Transforming Feudal Agriculture, Agrarian Change in Ethiopia Since 1974", A. Saith (ed.)

GOSPLAN, 1985 *Considerations on the Economic Policy of Ethiopia for the Next Few Years*, Unpublished paper, Addis Ababa, National Commission for Central Planning, NCCP

Griffin, Keith and Roger Hay, 1985 "Problems of Agricultural Development in Socialist Ethiopia, An Overview and a Suggested Strategy", *The Journal of Peasant Studies*, Vol. 13, No. 1, p. 37-66

Hagmann, Gunnar, 1988 *From Disaster Relief to Development*, Geneva

Haile Yesus Abegaz, 1983 *The Organisation of State Farms in Ethiopia after the Land Reform of 1975*, Stockholm

Hallet, Graham, 1981 *The Economics of Agricultural Policy*, Oxford

Hallpike, R.R., 1970 "Konso Agriculture", *Journal of Ethiopian Studies*, Vol. VIII, No.I

Harbeson, John W., 1988 *The Ethiopian Transformation. The Quest for the Post-Imperial State*, Boulder

Hareide, Dag, 1986 *Report on the New Resettlements in Ethiopia 1984-86*, Addis Ababa, United Nations Office for Emergency Operations in Ethiopia

Hart, K., 1982 *The Political Economy of West African Agriculture*, London, Cambridge University Press

Henrickson, Barry et al., 1983 *Provisional Soil Depth map of Ethiopia*, Land Use Planning and Regulatory Department, Addis Ababa

Henze, Paul, 1989 *Ethiopia in Early 1989, Deepening Crisis*, Santa Monica, RAND Corp.

Henze, Paul B. 1989 *Ethiopia, Crisis of a Marxist Economy. Analysis and Text of a Soviet Report*, RAND, National Defence Research Institute, April 1989, Santa Monica, California

Hirut Terefe and Lakew Woldetekle, 1986 *Study of the Situation of Women in Ethiopia*, IDR, Research Project No. 23, Addis Ababa

Hoben, Allen, 1973 *Land Tenure Among the Amhara of Ethiopia, The Dynamics of Cognatic Descent*, Chicago, The University of Chicago Press

Holmberg, Johan, 1972 "The Credit Programme of the Chilalo Agricultural Development in Ethiopia (AID)", *Spring Review of Small Farmer Credit*, Vol. VIII, No. SR 108 USAID

Holmberg, Johan, 1977 *Grain Marketing and Land Reform, An Analysis of the Marketing and Pricing of Food Grains in 1976 after Land Reform*, Uppsala, Scandinavian Institute of African Studies Research Report No. 41

Horvath, P.J., 1974 "The Process of Urban Agglomeration in Ethiopia", in G.J. Gill (ed.) *Readings on the Ethiopian Economy*, Haile Sellasie I University

Hough, Jerry F., 1980 *Soviet Leadership in Transition*, Washington D.C., Brookings Institute

Huntingford, G.W.B., 1965 *The Land Charters of Ethiopia*, Addis Ababa

Hurni, Hans, 1985 "Erosion-Productivity-Conservation systems in Ethiopia", Paper presented at the IV International Conference on Soil Conservation, Maracay, Venezuela

Hurni, Hans, 1986 "Degradation and Conservation of the Soil Resource in the Ethiopian Highlands", Paper presented at First International Workshop on African Mountains and Highlands, Addis Ababa

Hurni, Hans, 1988 "Ecological Issues in the Creation of Famines in Ethiopia", Paper presented at the National Conference on a Desaster Prevention and Preparedness Strategy for Ethiopia, Addis Ababa

Hyden, Göran, 1980 *Beyond Ujamma in Tanzania, Underdevelopment and the Uncaptured Peasantry*, Berkeley and Los Angeles, University of California

IAR (Institute of Agricultural Research), See under Aleligne and Franzel, Alemayehu and Franzel, and Legesse Dadi

IEG (Imperial Ethiopian Government), 1957 *First Five Year Plan (1957-1961)*

IEG, 1963 *Second Five Year Plan (1963-1967)*

IEG, 1968 *Third Five Year Development Plan (1968-1973)*

ILO (International Labour Organisation of the UN), 1982 *Socialism from the Grass-Roots, Accumulation, Employment and Equity in Ethiopia*, Addis Ababa, ILO/JASPA

IMF (International Monetary Fund), 1987 *Ethiopia - Recent Economic Developments* (SM/87/288; Dec.9,1987)

IUCN (International Union for the Conservation of Nature and Natural Resources), 1986 *Ethiopia, Land Use Planning and Natural Resource Conservation*, Mission Report, Gland

Jackson, R.T. et al., 1969 *Report of the Oxford University Expedition to the Gamu Highlands*, Unpublished Report, School of Geography, Oxford University

Jansson, Kurt, Michael Harris and Angela Penrose, 1987 *The Ethiopian Famine*, London, Zed Books

Jean, Francois, 1986 *Ethiopie - Du bon usage de la famine*, Paris

Johnston, Bruce and John W. Mellor, 1961 "The Role of Agriculture in Economic Development", *American Economic Review*

Jorgenson, D.W., 1961 "The Development of a Dual Economy", *Economic Journal*, 71

Kautsky, Karl, see under Banaji

Kemp, C. et al., 1987 *People in Plantations, Means or Ends*, IDS Bulletin, Vol. 18, No. 2

Kirsch-Göricke-Wörz, 1989 *Agricultural Revolution and Peasant Emancipation in Ethiopia - A Missed Opportunity*, Saarbrücken / Fort Lauerdale

Kjekshus, Helge, 1977 "The Tanzanian Villagization Policy, Implementational Lessons and Ecological Dimensions", *Canadian Journal of African Studies*, Vol. 11, No.2, pp. 269-282

Koehn, Peter H., 1980 "Ethiopia, Famine, Food Production, and Changes in the Legal Order", in, *African Studies Review* 22 (1980), 4, pp. 685-699

Langdon, Steven, 1985 *Multinationals in the Political Economy of Kenya*, New York

Legesse Dadi et al., 1987 *Bako Mixed Farming System Diagnostic Survey Report. Welega and Shewa Regions*, Report No.1, Addis Ababa, Institute of Agricultural Research

Lele, Uma, 1976 *The Design of Rural Development - Lessons from Africa*, New York

Lewin, M., 1968 *Russian Peasants and Soviety Power, A Study of Collectivization*, London, Allen and Unwin

Lewis, W.A., 1954 "Economic Development with Unlimited Supplies of Labour", *Manchester School of Economic and Social Studies*, 22 (2)

Lipton, Michael, 1977 *Why Poor People Stay Poor. A Study of Urban Bias in World Development*, London Mahteme Selassie Wolde Meskel, 1957 "The Land System in Ethiopia", *Ethiopia Observer*, Vol. 1

Little, I.M.D., 1982 *Economic Development, Theory, Policy and International Relations*, New York, Basic Books

Mann, H.J., 1965 *Land Tenure in Chore (Shoa)*, Addis Ababa, HSIU

Markakis, John, 1974 *Ethiopia. Anatomy of a Traditional Polity*, Oxford, Clarendon Press

Martin, E., 1970 *Development Assistance, Effort and Policies of the Members of the Development Assistance Committee*, OECD, Paris

McCall, M., 1985 "Environmental and Agricultural Impacts of Tanzania's Villagization Programme" in *Population and Development Projects in Africa*, Clarke et al (eds.) pp. 123-140

McCann, James, 1986 "Toward a History of Modern Highland Agriculture in Ethiopia, The Sources", *Proceedings of the Ninth International Congress of Ethiopian Studies*, Moscow, Vol. 6, pp. 149-166

McCann, James, 1988 "Famine, Poverty and Conjuncture, A Historical Typology of Famine and Rural Vulnerability in Ethiopia"

McNamara, Robert, 1973 "Address to the Board of Governors of the World Bank", Washington

Mesfin Wolde Mariam 1984 *Rural Vulnerability to Famine in Ethiopia, 1958 - 1977*, Addis Ababa

Ministry of Agriculture, 1970 *A Master Plan for the Extension and Project Implementation Department*, Addis Ababa

Ministry of Agriculture, 1973 *Findings of a Market Structures Survey and Analysis*, Addis Ababa

Ministry of Agriculture, 1984 *Ethiopia, Livestock Sub-Sector Review*, February 1984

Ministry of Agriculture 1984 *The Degradation of Resources and an Evaluation of Actions to Combat it*, Ethiopian Highlands Reclamation Study, Working Paper 19, Addis Ababa, Ministry of Agriculture, 1984 (a) *General Agricultural Survey Preliminary Report 1984/85*, Vol.1, Addis Ababa, Ministry of Agriculture, October 1984

Ministry of Agriculture, 1984 (b) *Gibrinnachin* (Amharic), Addis Ababa, September

Ministry of Agriculture, 1985 *General Agricultural Survey, Producers Cooperatives Preliminary Report 1983/84*, Addis Ababa, October

Ministry of Agriculture, 1986 *The Villagization Guidelines*, (Amharic) Addis Ababa, January

Ministry of Agriculture, 1989 (a) *Production Assessment Report from 77-78 to 80-81 EC* (Amharic) Addis Ababa, Resettlement Coordination Office, Yekkatit 1981

Ministry of Agriculture, 1989 (b) *Assessment Report of Agricultural Development Work in Resettlement Areas during 1977-81 EC* Addis Ababa, Resettlement Coordination Office, Meggabit 1981

Ministry of Agriculture, 1989 (c) *Study Report Concerning Land Fragmentation and Reallocation*, (Amharic) Addis Ababa, Land Use Planning and Regulatory Department, Sene 1981

Ministry of Foreign Trade, 1987 *An Evaluation Report on EOPEC*, Addis Ababa (Amharic)

Ministry of Health, 1985 *Primary Health Care Review*, Addis Ababa

Ministry of Land Reform and Administration *Reports on Land Surveys, 1967, 1968, 1969*, Addis Ababa

Mittelman, James, 1984 *Underdevelopment and the Transition to Socialism, Mozambique and Tanzania*, New York, Academic Press

Molyneux, Maxine, 1981 "Socialist Societies Old and New, Progress Towards Women's Emancipation", *Feminist Review*, Vol. 8

MSFD (Ministry of State Farm Development), 1982 Background Paper, ILO/JASPA Advisory Mission to Ethiopia, 15 August - 11 September

MSFD, 1984 (a) *Ministry of State Farms, Its Role, Organization, Present and Future Activities*, Addis Ababa

MSFD, 1984 (b) *State Farm Development*, (Amharic), Addis Ababa

MSFD, 1986 *Towards a Strategy for the Development of State Farms*, Vol.I, Main Report, Vol II, Production of Crops, Vol. III, Livestock Production, Vol. IV, Soils, Land Use, Irrigation and Mechanization, Vol. V, Agro-Industries, Addis Ababa

Mulugeta Dejenu et al., 1987 *Agrarian Reform and Rural Development, Achefer - Shebadino Study*, Addis Ababa

Myrdal, Gunnar, 1966 "Paths of Development", *New Left Review*, xxxvi

Nadel, S., 1946 "Land Tenure in the Eritrean Plateau", *Africa*, Vol. 16, Nos. 1 and 16

National Bank of Ethiopia, 1986 (a) *Annual Report 1985/86*,

National Bank of Ethiopia, 1985/86 (b) *Quarterly Bulletin*, Vol. 1 No. 4, Addis Ababa

Negarit Gazeta Proclamation Nos. 31/1975, 54-76/1975, 156/1978, 3/1979, 223/1982

Nekby, Bengt, 1971 *CADU, An Ethiopian Experience in Developing Peasant Farming*, Stockholm, Prisma Publisher

Nicholls, William H., 1964 "The Place of Agriculture in Economic Development", in Carl Eicher and Lawrence Witt (eds), *Agriculture in Economic Development*, New York

Nurske, Ragnar, 1970 "The Conflict between Balanced Growth and International Specialisation", in Gerald M. Meier, *Leading Issues in Economic Development*, Oxford

NVCC (National Villagisation Coordination Committee), 1987 (a) *Rural Transformation*, Addis Ababa

NVCC, 1987 (b) *Mender*, (Amharic) Addis Ababa, May 1987

NVCC, 1987 (c) *Villagization Plan Performance Report*, (Amharic)

OAU (Organisation of African Unity), 1985 *Africa's Priority Programme for Economic Recovery, 1986-1990*, adopted by the Heads of State and Governments of the Organisation of African Unity in July 1985, Addis Ababa

ONCCP (Office of the National Commission for Central Planning), 1980 *Study on Grain Price Determination* (revised), Addis Ababa, in Amharic

ONCCP, 1981 *Initial Targets and Preparation Guidelines for the First Five Year (1982-1986) Development Plan and the 1982 Annual Plan*, Addis Ababa, in Amharic

ONCCP, 1984 *Ten Years Perspective Plan 1984-85 - 1993-94*, Addis Ababa

ONCCP, 1984 (a) *Ten Year Perspective Development Plans Agriculture, Natural Resources Protection and Development Plan*, Addis Ababa, September

ONCCP, 1984 (b) *Action Programme Prepared to Address Problems Arising from the Drought*, (Amharic) Addis Ababa, Hidar 1977 EC

ONCCP, 1984 (c) *Assessment of the Six Year Plan Implementation 1971-76 EC* (Amharic) Addis Ababa, Tahsas 1977

ONCCP, 1985 *Considerations on the Economic Policy of Ethiopia for the Next Few Years*, Report prepared by a team of Soviet Consulting Advisers attached to ONCCP, Addis Ababa, September, (see GOSPLAN)

ONCCP, 1987 *Three-Year Development Plan*, (1986/88-1988/89)

Ottaway, Marina and David, 1978 *Ethiopia, Empire in Revolution*, New York, African Publishing Company

Pankhurst, Alula, 1988 (a) "Social Dimensions of Famine in Ethiopia, Exchange, Migration and Integration", *Proceedings of the Ninth International Congress of Ethiopian Studies*, Vol. 2, Moscow, Nauka Publishers

Pankhurst, Alula, 1988 (b) *Resettlement in Ethiopia, A Background Paper*, Unpublished Report, Addis Ababa

Pankhurst, Alula, 1988 (c) *Social Dynamics of Resettlement, A Village Perspective*, Unpublished Report, Addis Ababa

Pankhurst, Alula, 1988 (d) *Response to Resettlement, Household, Marriage and Divorce*, Paper presented at the Tenth International Conference of Ethiopian Studies, Paris

Pankhurst, Alula and Hezekiel Gebissa, 1986 *Report on a Study Tour of Settlement Schemes in Wollega*, 12 October-9 November, Unpublished Report, Addis Ababa

Pankhurst, Richard, 1966 *State and Land in Ethiopian History*, Addis Ababa, HSIU

Pankhurst, Rita, 1981 "Women in Ethiopia Today", *Africa Today*, Vol. 28, No. 4

Paoukov, Vladislav and Grigori Polyakov, 1986 "Etiopia, teoria i praktika cooperatsii" (Ethiopia, Theory and practice of cooperation), *Asia i Afrika Segodnia*, (journal), 12

Pausewang, Siegfried, 1979 Entwicklung der Agrarverhltnisse und Agrarpolitik in Norwegen, in *Leviathan* 2/79, pp.253-69

Pausewang, Siegfried, 1983 *Peasants, Land and Society, A Social History of Land Reform in Ethiopia*, München, Weltforum Verlag

Pausewang, Siegfried, 1986 "Peasants, Organisations, Markets - Ten Years After the Land Reform", *Proceedings of the Ninth International Congress of Ethiopian Studies*, Moscow, Vol. 2, pp. 81-92

Pausewang, Siegfried, 1988 "Alternatives in Rural Development in Ethiopia", Paper prepared for the Xth International Conference of Ethiopian Studies, Paris

Pearson, Lester B., 1969 *Partners in Development, Report of the Commission on International Development*, New York, Praeger

People's Democratic Republic of Ethiopia, 1987 "Revised Draft Constitution of the People's Democratic Republic of Ethiopia", Addis Ababa, *Ethiopian Herald*, 30 January

PMAC (Provisional Military Administrative Council), 1975 (a) *Programme of the National Democratic Revolution*, Addis Ababa

PMAC, 1975 (b) *Declaration on Economic Policy of Ethiopia*, Addis Ababa

PMAC, 1979 *Peasant Producer Cooperatives*, Addis Ababa

PMAC, 1981 *Directives for the Formation of Farmer's Producers Cooperatives*, (Amharic) Addis Ababa

PMAC, 1984 *The Ten-Year Perspective Plan*, (1984/85-1993/94)

Poluha, Eva, 1980 "A Study of Two Ethiopian Woredas on the Economic Activities of Peasant Women and their Role in Rural Development", (unpublished paper)

Poluha, Eva, 1987 "The Current Situation of Women in Ethiopia", Report to the World Bank

Polyakov, Grigori 1982 "Postroieno pri ekonomicheskom i technicheskom sodeistvii Sovietskogo Soyuza" (Constructed with economic and technical assistance from the Soviet Union), *Mejdunarodnie Otnosjeniya*, (periodical), Moskva 1982

Polyakov, Grigori, 1987 "Ekonomitseskoie Sotrudnitsestvo stran - tslenov SEV se Narodnoi Demokratitseskoi Republikoi Etiopii v obleskogo hosjaistva" (Economic cooperation of COMECON member countries with the People's Democratic Republic of Ethiopia), *Mejdunarodnii Selskohozaistvienii Jurnal* (International Agricultural Journal), 6, 1987, Moskva

Polyakov, Grigori, 1988 "V/O Selchospromexport - razvitiu kluchevoi otrasli i eksporta Etiopii" (V/O Selchozpromexport - for the development of the key economic branch and the export of Ethiopia), *Sovietski Eksport* (journal), Moskva, 5, 1988

Polyakov, Grigori 1989 "Sto kupim v Afrike?" (What shall we buy in Africa?) *Mejdunarodnaia Jiznie* (International Affairs), 9, 1989, Moskva

Population and Development Planning Division, ONCCP, 1989 *Rural Resettlement in Post-Revolution Ethiopia, Problems and Prospects*, Paper prepared for the conference on Population Issues in Ethiopia's National Development, July 20-22

Progress Publishers, 1986 *Ten Years of the Ethiopian Revolution*, Moscow

Provisional Military Government of Socialist Ethiopia, 1974 *An Order to Establish a Relief and Rehabilitation Commission for Areas Affected by Natural Disaster*, 29 August, Negarit Gazeta, Addis Ababa

Provisional Military Government of Socialist Ethiopia, 1976 *Proclamation to Provide for the Establishment of a Settlement Authority, Proclamation Proclamation 78 of 1976*, Negarit Gazeta, Addis Ababa

Provisional Military Government of Socialist Ethiopia, 1979 *A Proclamation to Establish a Relief and Rehabilitation Commission, Proclamation 173 of 1979*, Negarit Gazeta, Addis Ababa

Ranis, G. and J.C.H. Fei, 1961 "A Theory of Economic Development", *American Economic Review*, 51(4)

Ranis, G. and J.C.H. Fei, 1984 *Development of the Labour Surplus Economy, Theory and Policy*, Homewood, Richard D. Irwin

Roberts, Pepe, 1987 "Bearers of Labour, Gender Divisions and Development in Africa", Paper presented to the African Futures Conference, Centre for African Studies, Edinburgh University

Robertson, Alan, 1989 "A Realistic Approach to Forage Development in the Ethiopian Highlands", Paper presented to the Third National Livestock Conference, Addis Ababa

Robinson and Yemazaki, 1986 "Agriculture, Population, and Economic Planning in Ethiopia, 1953-1980", *Journal of Developing Areas*, 20 April

Rosaldo, Michele and Louise Lamphere (eds), 1974 *Women, Culture and Society*, Stanford

RRC (Relief and Rehabilitation Commission), 1981 *Settlement Policy*, Addis Ababa, RRC

RRC, 1983 *Directives for Discussion*, (Amharic) Unpublished ms, 1975 EC Addis Ababa

RRC, 1984 *Rehabilitation and Programmes*, Addis Ababa

RRC, 1985 *The Challenges of Drought, Ethiopia's Decade of Struggle in Relief and Rehabilitation*, Addis Ababa

RRC / Dag Hareide, 1989 *Vulnerability Profile for Wollo, Facts and Figures*, Addis Ababa

Saith, A., 1985 "The Distributional Dimensions of Revolutionary Transition; Ethiopia", in A. Saith (ed.), *The Agrarian Question in Socialist Transition*, London, Frank Cass

Sandbrook, Richard, 1985 *The Politics of Africa's Economic Stagnation*, Cambridge

Saul, John, 1985 *A Difficult Road, The Transition to Socialism in Mozambique*, New York, Monthly Review Press

Schatz, Sayre, 1987 "Laissez-Faireism for Africa?", *The Journal of Modern African Studies*, 25, I, p. 134

Sen, Amartya, 1981 *Poverty and Famines, An Essay on Entitlement and Deprivation*, Oxford

Sen, Amartya, 1986 *Food, Economics and Entitlement*, United Nations University

Senghaas, Dieter, 1982 *Von Europa lernen, Entwicklungsgeschichtliche Betrachtungen*, Frankfurt

Senghaas, Dieter, 1988 *Konfliktformationen im internationalen System*, Frankfurt

Shewa Regional VCC (Villagisation Coordinating Committee), 1986 *Villagization Guidelines Study for Ensete Growing Awrajas of Shewa*, (Amharic) Addis Ababa

Shewa Regional VCC, 1986 *Performance and Problems of Villagization Programme in Shewa Region During 1985/86*, (Amharic) Nazaret

Shiferaw Bekele, 1988 "An Empirical Account of Resettlement in Ethiopia (1975-1985)", *Proceedings of the Ninth International Congress of Ethiopian Studies*, Moscow, Vol, 2, pp. 127-142

Sileshi Sisay, 1982 "Swedish Development Aid Policy, A Discussion with Reference to Ethiopia", *Public Administration and Development*, Vol. 2

Simpson, Gail., 1976 "Socio-Political Aspects of Settlement Schemes in Ethiopia and their Contribution to Development", *Land Reform, Land Settlements and Cooperatives*, 2

Simpson, Gail., 1975 *A Preliminary Survey of Settlement Projects in Ethiopia*, Addis Ababa, Institute of Development Research, Report 21

Sivini, Giordano., 1986 "Famine and the Resettlement Program in Ethiopia", *Africa* (Rome), No. 2

Sokolov, V.V. 1985, see GOSPLAN

Sovremienaia Etiopia 1988 (Modern Ethiopia), Moscow, Nauka

Ståhl, Michael, 1973 *Contradictions in Agricultural Development, A Study of Three Minimum Package Projects in Southern Ethiopia*, Uppsala, Scandinavian Institute of African Studies, Research Report No. 14

Ståhl, Michael, 1974 *Ethiopia, Political Contradictions in Agricultural Development*, Uppsala

Starikov, Yevgeni, 1989 "Marginali, ili razmishlenie na staruyu tjemu,'Sto ce namie proishodiet?'" (Marginals, or discussion on the old topic "What is happening with us?") *Zwiesda*, (journal), 10, 1989, Moskva

State Farms Development Authority, 1978 *State Farms Development Authority I*, Addis Ababa, March

Tadesse Kidane Mariam, 1989 *Ethiopia's Population Distribution in Relation to Resources and the Environment*, Paper prepared for the national Conference on "Population Issues in Ethiopia's National Development", Addis Ababa, ONCCP

Tahal Consulting Engineers Ltd., 1988(a) *Ethiopia, Conservation Based Farming Systems Trial Programme, Preparation Study*, Tel Aviv

Tahal Consulting, 1988(b) *Ethiopia, Study of Traditional Conservation Practices*, Tel Aviv

Taye Mengistae and Beyene Solomon, 1982 *A Study of Land Reform in Ethiopia*, (Mimeo) Addis Ababa, Addis Ababa University

Tegegne Teka, 1984 *Cooperatives and national Development, the Ethiopian Experience*, IDR-Working Paper No. 18, Addis Ababa

Tegegne Teka, 1988 "The State and Rural Cooperatives in Ethiopia", *Cooperatives Revisited*, edited by H. Hedlund, Uppsala, Scandinavian Institute of African Studies

Tenassie Nichola, 1988 "The Agricultural Sector in Ethiopia, Organisation, Policies and Prospects", in *Beyond the Famine, An Examination of the Issues Behind the Famine in Ethiopia, Geneva, 97-141*

Tesfai Tekle, 1975 *The Evolution of Rural Development and Income Distribution*, African Rural Employment Research Network Paper No. 12

Tesfaye Teclu, 1979 *Socio-Economic Conditions in Shashemane, Bedota, Dangla*, IDR Report, Nos. 26-28

Tesfayesus Mehari, 1988 *Applicability of Fertility Estimation Techniques on Ethiopian Data*, Paper prepared for the African Population Conference in Dakar

The Ethiopian Herald, 1987 "Overcoming Drawbacks of Scattered Settlement", July 29

Thodey, A.R., 1969 *Marketing of Grains and Pulses in Ethiopia*, Stanford

Tsehai Berhane Selassie, 1984 *In Search of Ethiopian Women*, London, *Change* Report No. 11

Weissleder, Wolfgang, 1965 *The Political Ecology of Amhara Domination*, Chicago, Illinois

Weissleder, Wolfgang, 1974 "Amhara Marriage. The Stability of Divorce", *Canadian Review of Sociology and Anthropology*, Vol.11,Part 1

UN (United Nations), 1983 *Demographic Indicators of Countries, Estimates and Projections as Assessed in 1983*, N.Y.

UN, 1984 *The Balance of Payments Problems of Developing Africa, A Reassessment*, Socio-Economic Planning Division, New York

UN, 1984 (a) *Population Policy Compendium*, New York

UN, 1985 *The History of UNCTAD, 1964-1984*, New York

UN 1986 *Compendium of Statistics and Indicators on the Situation of Women*, New York

UN, 1987 (a) *United Nations Programme of Action for African Economic Recovery and Development, 1986-1990*, Report of the Secretary-General, Doc. A/42/560, New York

UN, 1987 (b) *Africa, One Year Later*, New York

UN, 1988 *Financing Africa's Recovery*, New York

UN, 1989 *World Population Prospects 1988*, New York

UNECA (United Nations Economic Commission for Africa), 1986 *Africa's Economic Recovery, Growth and Development, Proposals for UNCTAD VII*, Document E/ECA/TRADE/54, Addis Ababa

UNECA, 1987 *Survey of Economic and Social Conditions in Africa, 1986-1988*, document E/ECA/CM.13/3, Addis Ababa

UNECA 1989 *African Alternative Framework to Structural Adjustment Programmes for Socio-economic Recovery and Transformation*, Addis Ababa

UNICEF (United Nations Children's Fund), 1988 *Integrated Rehabilitation Project Baseline Survey*, Addis Ababa

UNRISD (United Nations Research Institute for Social Development), 1975 *Rural Cooperatives as Agents of Change*, Geneva,UNRISD

Wadekin, Karl-Eugen, 1982 *Agrarian Policies in Communist Europe*, The Hague

White, Christine, and Gordon White, (eds.), 1982 *Agriculture, the Peasantry and Socialist Development*, IDS Bulletin, September

White, Gordon et al., 1983 *Revolutionary Socialist Development in the Third World*, Brighton, Wheatsheaf Books

Winternitz, Helen, 1981 "Ethiopia Turns Tentatively to West Out of Need for Development", *Sun*, August 31

Wood, Adrian P., 1977 *Resettlement in Illubabor Province, Ethiopa*, Ph.D. thesis, University of Liverpool

Wood, Adrian P., 1982 "Spontaneous Agricultural Resettlement in Ethiopia", *Redistribution of Population in Africa*, Clarke and Kosinski (eds.), London, Heinemann

Wood, Adrian P., 1983 "Rural Development and National Integration in Ethiopia", *African Affairs*, Vol.82, No.329

Wood, Adrian P., 1985 "Population Redistribution and Agricultural Settlement Schemes in Ethiopia, 1958-80," *Population and Development Projects in Africa*, Clarke, Khogali and Kosinski (eds.), Cambridge, Cambridge University Press

Wood, Adrian P., 1987 "The State, Soil Erosion and Environmental Conservation in Ethiopia", Paper presented at the Institute of British Geographers, Developing Areas Study Group Meeting on Environmental Crisis in Developing Countries

World Bank, 1981 *Accelerated Development in Sub-Saharan Africa, An Agenda for Action*, Washington D.C.

World Bank, 1984 *Ethiopia, Issues and Options in the Energy Sector*, Washington D.C.

World Bank, 1985 *Ethiopia and the World Bank*, Washington D.C.

World Bank, 1986 *Poverty and Hunger, A World Bank Policy Study*, Washington D.C.

World Bank, 1986 *Financing Adjustment with Growth in Sub-Saharan Africa*, Washington D.C.

World Bank, 1986 *World Development Report 1986*, Washington D.C.

World Bank, 1987 (a) *Ethiopia, Recent Economic Developments and Prospects for Recovery and Growth*, Washington, D.C.

World Bank, 1987 (b) *Ethiopia, An Export Action Programme*, Washington D.C.

World Bank, 1988 *Ethiopia, Public Investment Program Review*, Washington D.C.

World Bank, 1988 *World Development Report 1988*, New York

World Bank, 1989 *Sub-Saharan Africa:From Crisis to Sustainable Growth. A Long-Term Perspective Study*, Washington

WPE (Workers Party of Ethiopia), 1984 *Programme of the Party*, Workers Party of Ethiopia, Addis Ababa, September

WPE, 1988 *Central Report of the General Secretary of the Workers Party of Ethiopia to the Ninth Plenum of the Central Committee*, Addis Ababa

Yanov, Alexander, 1989 "Sovietskaia vnietsjnaia politica na criticjeskom etape perestroike" (Soviet International policy at a critical stage of perestroika), *Mejdunarodnaia Jiznie* (International Affairs), Moskva, 9, 1989, pp. 46-57

Yemane Kidane and Demissie Gebre Michael, 1985 *The Food and Nutrition Situation in Ethiopia*, Proceedings of Inter-Country Seminar on "Integration of Nutrition into Agricultural and Rural Development Projects", Kenya

Yerazwork Admasie, 1988 *Impact and Sustainability Study of WFP-Assisted Project ETH 2488/II Rehabilitation of Forest, Grazing and Agricultural Lands*, Addis Ababa, WFP

Young, Kate, Carol Wolkowith and Roslyn Mccullagh (ed.), 1984 *Of Marriage and the Market. Women's Subordination Internationally and its Lessons*, London

Glossary

Amharic words and terms used in the texts

Abdara	spirit associated with a specific area
Abuna	bishop
Abyssinian	person from Ethiopia
Aganinta	spirit of a particular type; the devil
Ager	country
Amhara	ethnic group which was since the medieval period the bearer of the Abyssinian tradition; member of the Amhara ethnic group
Amharigna	language of the Amhara
Angel-libs	a special neck-scarf used in spirit ceremonies
Arrash	ploughman, cultivator, peasant
Ato	Mr.
Awraja	administrative district
Aynet'elaa	spirit of a particular type; a spell cast upon a person
Balabat	lowest chief in the functional hierarchy in feudal Southern Ethiopia; landlord
Begi	(also *Bega*) linguistic group in Ethiopia
Belg	small rainy season (April - May)
Beni	(*Beni Amir*) linguistic group
Birr	Ethiopian currency
Borana	(also *Borena*) linguistic group, sub-group of the Oromo
Bota	place, spot
Buda	evil eye; also used for a person capable of controlling the spell of the evil eye
Ch'elea	spirit of particular type; beeds worn round the neck, used as a ritual object
Corvée labour	forced labour; labour in lieu of tax
Cremt	Long rainy season (July - Sept/Oct.)
Debbo	collective labour performed in return
Debre	fortress, mountain
Deisa	land distribution system in Tigrean areas - based on redistribution in regular intervals within the village community
Demoz	salary
Derg	committee, junta
Dorze	ethnic group in South Ethiopia, known for their weaving skill
Ekul	half (*ekul arrash* = a tenant being obliged to deliver half of his produce to the landlord)

Ekuna	(also *Kuna*) a measure, originally a basket
Enset	root crop in Southern Ethiopia in middle elevations; "false banana". The enset tree offers a flour rich in starch, allowing to feed large populations on a small area
Eritrean	a person from Eritrea
Ethiopian	a person from Ethiopia
Felasha	Ethiopian Jews; usually considered a separate ethnic group in Northern Ethiopia, though the distinctive feature is religion rather than ethnicity. In traditional society, the felasha were excluded from the community of rist holders, and therefore forced to constitute a separate community
Gada	age cycle; age group; socio-political organisation of the Oromo
Galla	amharic term for the Oromo ethnic group, (today having generally a pejorative connotation)
Gawithick	garment worn around the shoulder
Gebar	(also *gabar*) tax payer, (originally "contributor"; note the shift of meaning explained in chapter 3)
Gebarewotch	plural form of *gebar*
Gendia	livestock disease
Gettem	poetry
Ginna	spirit of a particular type
Glasnost	(from Russian) openness; term used by Gorbachov to mark a process of democratising the USSR
Gult	fief; land given in lieu of a salary; also the area given to a nobleman to administer, against a right to tax peasants. (All gult rights were abolished in the 1975 land *reform*)
Gurage	ethnic group in southern Shoa, closely related to the Amhara/Tigre, known as traders and for their economic activities
Habesha	(also *habesh*) "proper" Ethiopian The word distinguishes the people from the traditional Abyssinian Empire and their culture and way of life from other (African and European) ethnicities and cultures
Hadiya	ethnic group in Southern Shoa (Hadiya and Kambata Awraja)
Ijjige	collective work arrangement in agriculture
Injera	(also *enjera*) bread or pancake made of teff; main food in Northern Ethiopia
Irboa	fourth (*irbo arrash* a tenant obliged to deliver one fourth of his produce to the landlord)
Kalu	ritual expert of the Oromo

Kebede	urban ward; lowest administrative unit in towns; the term is also used for rural kebele (peasant associations)
Kolkhoze	(from Russian), collective farm
Konso	ethnic group in Gemu Gofa, known for their intensive terracing agriculture
Kulak	(from Russian), rich peasant, commercial farmer (implicitly those farmers who exploit rural economic opportunities at the expense of the poorer majority of peasants)
Kuna	(also *Ekuna*) a measure, originally a basket
Kuta	garment worn around the shoulder
Limat	development
Mahber	association (e.g. Gebrewotch mahber, peasant association)
Malba	first stage of producer cooperative; malba is a newly created word
Mecha	ethnic subgroup of the Oromo
Medebegna	regular
Meher	Spring
Meret	land
Neftegna	a man with a gun; in southern Ethiopia a common name for the landlords and settlers of northern origin, rural exploiters
Neug	oil seeds
Oromifa	(also *Oromigna*) language of the Oromo ethnic group
Oromo	largest ethnic group in Ethiopia, mainly residing in the South
Perestroika	(russian) restructuring; term used by Gorbachew for the economic reform programme in the USSR
Rist	inherited right to land (and community participation). (Rist rights were inherited through descent from mothers and fathers line; they did not give inheritance rights on a particular plot of land, but on membership in a common forefather's community, and in it on provision of livelihood, through a share in the common land. The land reform of 1975 replaced rist rights by a common right to land for cultivation)
Riste-gult	inheritable gult rights (abolished in the 1975 land reform)
Ristegna	a person having rist rights; person holding land in consequence of his inherited rights
Saho	ethnic group in the Red Sea area in Eritrea
Schistosomiasis	bilharzia
Selassie	Trinity (usual in names in combination with another word. Haile Selassie = the power of the trinity)

Shamma	garment worn around the shoulder
Shehena	land distribution system in Tigrean areas - based on regular redistribution within the village community
Sidama	ethnic group in Sidamo
Sigsega	settlement in already settled areas, integrated settlement
Siso	one third (*siso arras*h a tenant having to deliver one third of his crop to the landlord).
Somali	ethnic group in South East Ethiopia; ethnically related to the Somali in the neighbouring state
Tabot	Ark of the Covenant; the ten commandments
Teff	small- seeded grain, endemic to Ethiopia; staple crop of Northern Ethiopia
Tigray	ethnic group in the North; also language group
Tigrigna	language of the Tigre
Timbuho	tobacco
Trypanosomiasis	animal disease
Villagization	English term for the programme of bringing Ethiopian peasants together in large, planned villages
Weland	third stage of collective agriculture
Welba	second stage of collective agriculture
Wikabi	spirit, also Wik'abi
Wolaita	ethnic group in Sidamo
Wonfel	collective labour in agriculture
Woreda	administrative unit in rural Ethiopia; smallest unit above village or peasant association; since 1989 dissolved
Zar	evil spirit
Zemetcha	campaign
Zuria	encirclement; environment; region

Acronyms

ADB	African Development Bank
ADDP	Ada District Development Project
AMC	Agricultural Marketing Corporation
APPER	Africa's Priority Programme for Economic Recovery, 1986-1990
ARDU	Ada Rural Development Unit
BARDU	Bale Rural Development Unit
C.i.f.	Cost, insurance and freight (price includes transport)
CADU	Chilalo Agricultural Development Unit
CMC	Coffee Marketing Board
CoM	Council of Ministers
CPSC	Communist Party of Socialist China
CPSC	Central Planning Supreme Council
CPSU	Communist Party of the Soviet Union
CRDA	Christian Relief and Development Association
CSA	Central Statistical Authority
CSO	Central Statistical Office (in 1989 renamed CSA)
ECA	Economic Commission for Africa (of the UN)
EOPEC	Ethiopian Oilseeds and Pulses Export Corporation
EPPG	Emergency Programme Planning Group
ESP	Etiopia Serategnotch Party : Workers Party of Ethiopia (WEP)
F.O.B.	Free on board (buyer pays freight in addition to price)
GATT	General Agreement on Tariffs and Trade
GDP	Gross Domestic Product
GOSPLAN	Soviet planning authority
HPC	High Potential Cereal Highland Zone
HPP	High Potential Perennial Highland Zone
HSMC	Hides and Skins Marketing Corporation
IAR	Institute of Agricultural Research
IBRD	International Bank for Reconstruction and Development (World Bank)
ICA	International Commodity Agreement
IEG	Imperial Ethiopian Government
IFAD	International Fund for Agricultural Development
ILO	International Labour Organisation (of the UN)
IMF	International Monetary Fund
IPC	Integrated Programme for Commodities
IRD	Integrated Rural Development

JASPA	Jobs and Skills Programme for Africa (of ILO)
JIRDU	Jijigga Range Development Unit
LDC	Least Developed Countries
LLDC	Last (of the) Least Developed Countries
LPC	Low Potential Cereal Highland Zone
LSC	Leather and Shoes Corporation
LUPRD	Land Use Planning and Regulatory Department
MoA	Ministry of Agriculture (also written as MOA)
MPP	Minimum Package Programme
MSFD	Ministry of State Farm Development
MT	Metric tons
MTS	Machine and Tractor Station
NDR	National Democratic Revolution
NERDU	North Eastern Range Development Unit
NGO	Non-Governmental Organisation
NRDC	National Rural Development Council
NVCC	National Villagisation Coordination Committee
ONCCP	Office of the National Comittee for Central Planning
PA	Peasant Association
PADEP	Peasant Agriculture Development Extension Programme
PC	Producer Cooperative
PDRE	People's Democratic Republic of Ethiopia
PMAC	Provisional Military Administrative Council
REWA	Revolutionary Ethiopian Women's Association
REYA	Revolutionary Ethiopian Youth Association
RRC	Relief and Rehabilitation Commission
SIDA	Swedish International Development Agency
SORDU	Southern Rangelands Development Unit
TYPP	Ten Year Perspective Plan (1984/85 - 1993/94)
UN	United Nations
UNCTAD	United Nations Conference on Trade and Development
UNDP	United Nations Development Programme
UNECA	United Nations Economic Commission for Africa
UNPAAERD	United Nations Programme of Action for African-Economic Recovery and Development, 1986-1990
VCC	Villagisation Coordination Committee
VVC	Village level Villagisation Committee
WADU	Wolamo Agricultural Development Unit
WCARRD	World Conference on Agrarian Reform and Rural Development
WFP	World Food Programme
WPE	Workers Party of Ethiopia
WWII	World War II

Geographical Names in Ethiopia

(Because of different transliterations, many place names occur in different spelling. Where possible, both forms are listed: (conv) indicates the conventional, but incorrect forms, (c) the more correct transliteration.)

Abadir — Place east of Addis Ababa

Abbai — Blue Nile River in Ethiopia

Abyssinia — Old name for Ethiopia; the old state (not including all of the recent geographical entity of Ethiopia)

Achefer — Sub-district (woreda) in Gojam

Ada — Fertile teff growing area south of Addis Ababa

Addis Ababa — Capital of Ethiopia

Adola — District in Sidamo

Adowa — Town in Northern Ethiopia, (also *Adua*), battleground of the 1896 victory over Italian troops

Agaro — Town in Kaffa

Akaki — Industrial suburbs south of Addis Ababa

Ambo — Town in Western Shoa

Amhara Sayent — Place in Wollo

Arba Minch — Capital in Gemu Gofa

Arsi — Region (former province*) (also *Arssi*, *Arussi*)

Arussi — see *Arsi*

Aseb — Town at the Red Sea coast (also *Assab*)

Asmara — Capital of Eritrea

Asosa — Town and district in Western Wolega

Assab — Town at the Red Sea coast (conv) (also *Aseb*)

Assela — Capital of Arsi

Awasa — Capital of Sidamo

Awash — River in Eastern Ethiopia, ending in the Danakil desert.

Axum — Town in Tigre, capital of the old Abyssinian Empire (4th century)

Bahr Dar — Town at Lake Tana (also *Bahar Dar*, *Baher Dar*)

Bale — Region (former province*) in Southern Ethiopia

Baro — River in Western Ethiopia (Illubabor)

Begemder — Former region/province* in Ethiopia, later renamed Gonder region. (also *Begemdir*)

Borana — Area in Southern Ethiopia (also *Borena*)

Butajira	Town in Soddo Gurage - Southern Shoa
Chebo	Region in Gurage; Oromo section in Gurage area (Ch'ebo)
Chercher	Region in South Eastern Shoa
Chewa	Region, former province* in central Ethiopia, also *Shoa* (conv), *Shewa*
Chilalo	Area in Arsi, around Assela
Dalocha	District in Gamu Gofa
Dawa	River in Southern Ethiopia
Debre Sina	Town in Eastern Shoa
Debre Zeyt	Town in Shoa, ca. 60 km south of Addis Ababa
Debre Berhan	Town in Eastern Shoa
Debre Markos	Capital of Gojam
Dedessa	River in Western Ethiopia (Wollega) - (also *Dedesa*, *Didessa*)
Dessie	Capital of Wollo
Dinder Shinfu	River plains in Western Ethiopia
Dindo	River in Western Ethiopia
Dire Dawa	Town in South East Ethiopia
Eritrea	Region in North and Northwest Ethiopia, until 1945 Italian colony, since 1952 in federation with Ethiopia, since 1962 annexed as a province of Ethiopia.
Ethiopia	"Modern" name of the (enlarged) Empire after the conquest of the South; the two terms "Abyssinia" and "Ethiopia" overlap in time, but Ethiopia comprises areas which did not belong to Abyssinia.
Gambela	Town and district (awraja) in Western Ethiopia (Illubabor)
Gamu Gofa	Region, former province* (also *Gemu Gofa*)
Genale	River in Southern Ethiopia
Gilo	River in Gambela area, Western Ethiopia
Goba	Capital in Bale
Gojam	Region in Ethiopia, former province* (also *Gojjam*)
Gondar	Town and region in Northwest Ethiopia, after 1980 also name for the province* of Begemdir (also *Gonder* (c).)
Gore	Capital of Illubabor
Gura Ferda	Place name
Gurage	Region (and ethnic group) in Southern Shoa
Haikotch	Place in Soddo Gurage - Southern Shoa
Harar	Town in Eastern Ethiopia; capital of Hararge (conv) (also *Harer*, *Harrar*)
Hararge	

	Region, former province*, in Eastern Ethiopia (also *Hararghe*)
Illubabor	Region, former province*, in Western Ethiopia
Jarsso	Subdistrict, (also *Jareso*)
Jibat	Subdistrict in Northern Shoa
Jijiga	Town in Ogaden, South East Ethiopia, (c), also *Jigjiga* (conv).
Jima	Town in Western Ethiopia, capital of Kaffa (c), also *Jimma* (conv).
Jimma	Town in Western Ethiopia, capital of Kaffa
Kaffa	Region in Western Ethiopia, former province* (conv), also *Kefa*, *Keffa*.
Kefa	Region in Western Ethiopia, former province* (c), also *Keffa*, *Kaffa* (conv).
Kelafo	Place in Arsi
Kembata	Area in Southern Shoa, Hadiya- Kembata Awraja (also *Kambata*).
Konso	Region (and ethnic group) in Gemu Gofa, South West Ethiopia
Mecha	Area in Western Shoa, home area of the Mecha Oromo
Mekele	Town in Tigre, capital of province of Tigre (conv) (also *Makele*, Mekale)
Menagesha	Area in Central Shoa, around Addis Ababa
Menz	Area in Northern Shoa; origin of the Shoa Amhara kingdom (also *Manz*)
Metekel	District (Awraja) in Western Gojam
Metemma	District in Gonder region
Nazareth	Town in Southern Shoa (conv) (also *Nazaret*, *Nazret*)
Nekemte	Capital of Wollega (conv), also *Nekemt*, *Lekemt*.
Ogaden	Region in South East Ethiopia
Omo	River in Southwestern Ethiopia
Saho	Region and ethnic group in Eritrea, Red Sea coast
Sayent	*Amhara Sayent:* Place in Wollo
Shashemane	Town in Southern Shoa
Shebadino	Subdistrict (woreda) in Sidamo
Shebelle	*Wabe Shebelle* River in Southern Ethiopia (Bale)
Shoa	Region, former province in central Ethiopia, around Addis Ababa* (conv). (also *Shewa*, *Chowa*)
Sidamo	Region, former province* in Southern Ethiopia. (Also an ethnic group.)
Soddo	Town in Southern Ethiopia

Somali	Area (and ethnic group) in South East Ethiopia
Somalia	Neighbouring state in the South
Tana	Lake in North-western Ethiopia
Tana-beles	River in Metekel
Tekaze	River in Western Ethiopia
Tendaho	Place in the Awash valley, site of large irrigated cotton plantations
Tigrai	Area (and ethnic group) in the North
Tigre	Region (and ethnic group) in Northern Ethiopia, former province* of Tigre
Wabe Shebelle	River in Southern Ethiopia (Bale). Also *Wabi Shebelle*.
Wadla Delanta	District in Wollo
Wellega	Region in Western Ethiopia, former province* (c), also *Wollega* (conv), *Welegga*.
Wello	Region, former province*, in Eastern Ethiopia (c), also *Wollo* (conv), *Welo*
Wolaita	Area (and ethnic group) in Sidamo
Wondo	Place in Sidamo
Wondo Genet	Place in Southern Shoa
Yeju	Place in Wollo
Yirgalem	Town in Southern Ethiopia, until 1960 capital of Sidamo

*In 1989-90, the administrative structure was changed in Ethiopia, the former 14 provinces - after 1975 called administrative regions - were replaced by 25 administrative regions and 5 autonomous regions.

Index

administration 5, 30, 32, 35, 41, 42, 46, 54, 62, 69, 112, 147, 173, 214, 217, 218, 220, 221, 222

agrarian crisis 3, 16, 26, 30, 69, 75, 122, 124, 156, 213, 222

basic needs 4, 6, 13, 71, 78, 80, 84, 86, 87, 93, 101, 108, 144, 214

bureaucracy, civil service 30, 32, 34, 71, 79, 83, 108, 118, 129, 214, 222

centralisation 5, 30, **40-45**, 51, 170, 214, 218, **220-22**

cereals, grain, crops 25, 103, 106, 130, 140, 142, 144, 164, 167, 175, 184, 191, 205-06

collective agriculture 3, 8, 16, 24, 25, 884, 90, 108, 136, 142, **179**, 180, 215, 219, 220

collective decisions 7, 39, 62, 65, 70, 71, 89, 215, 218, **219**

colonialism 5, 42, 174

communications 9, 10, 19, 26, 33, 54, 71, 174, 203, 205, 209, 217

community rights, responsib. **38-42**, **45-47**, 62, 66, **67**, 100, 213, 216

conservation 10, 55, 78, 98, 103, **164-73**, 178, 185, 189, **192-98**

consumption 12, 33, 58, 65, 79, 112, 118, 160, 164, 187, 216, 218, 219

control 9, 13, 27, 35, 65, 72, **73**, 75, 84, 105, 124, 128, 136, 145, 180, **214-15**, 219, **220**, **223**

cooperation 4, 5, 8, 11, 42, 63, 66, 79, 80, 82, 86, 101, **217-23**, 225

corruption 4, 44, 71, 127, 220

crafts 103, 139

cultural background, context 4, 7, 11, 13, **39**, 40, 42, **47**, 65, 87, **150-52**, **154-55**, 173, 207

debt 6, 10, 24, 45, **72-78**, 81, **82**, 166, 191, 217, 224, 226

decentralisation 7, 82, **172-3**, 214, 218, **220-22**

democracy 4, 6, 12, 13, 14, 44, 58, 59, 65, 70, 78, 83, 87, 108, 119, 132, 140-42, 149-50, 152, 166, 172, 176, 205, 207, 208, 213, **216-20**, **220-21**, **222-24**

drought 3, 9, 11, 52, 62, 65, 75, 81, 104, 106, 127, 163, 165, 168, 174, 199, 211

dual economy, duality 9, 27, **33**, 119, 207-8, 215, 217

ecology 4, 6, 7, 9, 10, 11, 14, 19, 72, 75, 103, 105, 118, 121, 124, 130, 135, 147, 156, **160-63**, **164-73**, **174-86**, **187-95**, **223**, **224**

education 4, 6, 7, 8, 59, 64, 68, 125, 148, 207, 209, 211

efficiency 13, 24, 63, 69, 83, 103, 108, 135, 207

employment 3, 12, 13, 34, 35, 50, 59, 61-64, 68, 73, 89, 103, 106, 160, 216, 219, 221

energy 160

equity, equality 4, 21, 22, 32, 39, 40, 46, 58, 59, 63, **66**, 71, **72**, 76, 94, 111, **145-47**, 166, 168-69, **171**, 213, 216, **219**, 220, 225

erosion 10, 75, 101, 103, 135, 147, **160-63**, 175, 177, **180-82**, **187-89**, **191-92**

ethnic differences 5, 32, 124

exit option 13, 27, **124**, 215, 218, **223**, **226**

export production 3, 6, 12, 16, 17, 19, 24, 50, 70, **71-75**, 81, 91, 97, 103, 106, 112, 216, 219, **222**

extraction of resources 7, 8, 33, 34, **35**, 40, **41**, 42, 43, 47, **89-99**, 112, 119, 147, 213, 218, 220-22

fallow 165, 170

family 5, 8, 21, 22, 24, 26, 27, 38, 39, 43, **58-61**, **65**, 101, 122, 127, 128, 160, 163, 166

famine 10, 11, 19, 22, 26, 27, 52, 62, 65, 69, 80, 82, 117, 121, 124, 127, 164, 168, 174, 177, 189, **199-204**

feudalism 5, 21, 27, 30, 31, 40-46, 168, 170, 174, 185, 213, 221

food security 3, 6, 11, 13, 19, 26, 27, 52, **72**, 80, 104, 119, 165, 168, 183, 189, 200, 203, 214, 216, **217**, 222, **224-25**

food production 3, 6, 7, 13, 16, 19, 22, 24, 25, 26, 33, 43, 52, 65, 78, 84, **99**, 103, **106**, 118, 135, 162, 183, 198, 199, 215, 219

foreign exchange 25, **72-73**, **97-99**, **106**, 114, 138

forest, forest resources 136, 140, 147-48, 162, 165, 167, 169, 172, 175, **177-84**, **187**

fragmentation of holdings 41, 100, 101, 103, **171**, 177

garden crops 103, 112, 135

glasnost 3, 70, **83-85**,

government policies 3, 15, 34, 35, **49-55**, 135, 166, 170, 214, 221-22

growth 6, 19, 27, 30, 34, 51, **69**, 89, 101

health 4, 6, 7, 8, 12, 26, 125, 126, 129, 135, 148-49, **158-60**, 180, 203, 211

history 5, , 30, 38, 40, 49, 171, 173

household 31, 34, 39, 58, **59**, 62-64, **65-68**, 100, 121, 125-8, 135, 139, 144-52, 167, 175-6, 191, 218

human rights 58, 65, 67, 72, 84, 215, 218

human relations 4, 58, 67, 72, 86, 215, 219, 223

IMF 3, **69-78**, 116, 215, 216

income 13, 50, 58, 63-67, 70, 74, 84, 100, 112, 119, 167

indigenous knowledge 4, 11, 103, 172-73, 194-5, **216**, 223-26

intercropping, crop rotation 164, 181

international market 4, 6, 44-45, **72-78**, 107, 108, 113, 215, **216**, 217, **221**, **222**, 226

investment 6, 7, 8, 12, 44, 52, 83, 171, 215

labour, work 13, 19, 25, 30, 31, 33, 39, 41, 58, 61, 64, 67, **89**, 90, 100, 105, 107, 117, 124, 128, 129, 138, 148, 167, 173, 179, 208, 215, 218, 219, 221

land tenure, land ownership 2, 3, 4, 519, 27, 30, **38-47**, 59, 63, 78, 100, **146**, 169, 213

land reform 3, , 16, 21, 22, 27, **35**, **38**, **45-47**, 50, 63, 65, 100, 121, 158, 171, 213, 214, 222, 224

land use 26, 27, 47, 70, 78, 103, 106, 114, 117, 124, 135, 139, 160, 166, 171-73, **182**, 187, 189, 191, 192, **196**, **208-29**

leadership 21, 39, 46, 147, 214, 220, 222

lease 31, 32, 100, 173

legislation 4, 7, 21, **44**, 67, 116, 164, 210, 211, 213

livestock 17, 112, 113, 130, 140, **144-45**, 152, 166-68, 175, 178, 185, 189, **205-210**

living standard 3, 11, 12, 13, 21, 31, 61, 62, 144, 166, 168, 187, 198, 206, 213, 216, 219, 221

local democracy 3, 4, 7, 46, 70, 71, 122, 127, 132, 135, 141, 172, **213-24**

local institutions 4, 5, 21, 34, 39, 55, 68, 70, 127, 135, 138, 141, 147, 176, 192, 210, 214, **218**

local initiative 4, 7, 9, 13, 46, 84, 87, 103, 104, 132, 142, 170, 172, 194, 210, **213-24**

local market 4, 8, 14, 113, 119, 129, 211, 214, 217, **218-20**, **222**

local planning 3, 9, 61, 70, 103, 132, 135, 139, 141, 213-14, 216, **220**

management 24, 71, 104, 179, 187-98, **202**, 217

manure 144, 165, 188

market economy 3, 6, 8, 14, **69**, 75-84, 112, 119, 191, 215, **222**

market production 50, 51, 63, 65, 92, 107, 130, 162

marketing 8, 9, 24, 33, 46, 51, 58, 62, 67, 72, 92, 103, 107, **111-118**, 147, 217

marketing system 3, 4, 8, 9, 33, 64, 67, **69-78**, 84, **92-96**, 108, 112, 115, 117, 119, 171, 203, 215, 216, 217

marriage 58, **59-60**, 64, 145, 146, 149

mechanisation 3, 24, 51, **80**, 82, 106, 122, 125, 130, 132, 170, **179-80**, 182, 183, 211, **219**

middle class 33, 34, 221, **223-24**

migration 65, 121-33, **156-58**, 169, 171, 203

military 2, 5, 7, 30, 147, 174, 214, 221-22

minorities 58, 87, **124**, 139, 166, 205-209, 222

mobility 40, **41**, 141, 174, 295, 208, 209, 211

mutual aid 4, 8, 62, 151, **217-220**

natural resources 3, 9, 10, 11, 14, 140, 146, 164-68, **187-198**, 215

participation 11, 14, 58, **65-68**, 71, 98, 141, **142**, 173, 194, 205, 207, **213**, **216**, **220**, **222-24**, 225

pastoralists 11, 58, 121, 127, 139, 169, **205-211**, 222

pasture 160, 175, 178, 189, 211

peasant association 3, 7, 13, 21, 39, 45, 46, 51, 63, 85, 100, 147, 180, 185, 220

peasant interest 5, 11, 28, 71, 82, 84, 87, 117, 141-42, 166, 185, 192, 213, 215, **216**, **218**, **220-24**

peasant - state relations 6, 7, 9, 10, 12, 13, 22, 71, 80, 84, 101, 135, 141, 144, **147-49**, 152, 185, 213, 214, **221-24**

perennial crops 103, 112, 139-40, 167, 181, 197

perestroika 3, 6, 79, 80, **83-85**,

plough oxen 17, 31, **101**, 105, 125, 127, 128, 130, 182, 189, 220

population growth 3, 9, 10, 11, 17, 19, 33, 34, 40, 51, 62, 118, 121, **149**, **156-163**, 164, 165, 174, 178, 191, 215

poultry, small animals 145, 180

poverty 10, 12, 17, 32, 79, 101, 108, 162, **164-73**, 198, 200, 217, 220, 222

power 30, 31, 32, 40, 41, 43, 51, 63, 65, **66**, **71**, 72, **78**, 145, 147, 166, 174, 203, **213-14**, 216, 223

prices 9, 12, 16, 24, 27, 33, 35, 46, 51, 62, **69-78**, 82, **92-96**, **111-118**, 124, 131, 191, 195, 217

private 16, 22, 24, 27, 31, **44**, 63, **71**, 72, 80, 101, 107, 112, 113, 125, 131, 169, 170, **217**

producer cooperatives 8, 16, 22, 23, 24, 25, 51, 63, 65, 70, 80, 84, 91, **100-108**, 124, 125, 132, 138, 147, 171, 181, 219

production 6, 7, 8, 10, 12, 13, 16, **20**, 21, 22, 24, 25, 27, 31, 41, 42, 46, 49, 51, 58, 63, 66, 100, 117, 119, 132, 135, 147, 163, 166-67, 184, 187, 189, 207, 217, 218, 221, 222

productivity 3, 4, 5, 6, 13, 21, 25, 34, 49, 58, **61-63**, 69, 92, 101, 107, 117, 121, 160, 162, 169, 196, 211, 215, 216, 220 quota 1, 10, 62, 84, **93**, 114, **116-7**, 171, 177, **217**

redistribution 2, 6, 7, 8, 32, 38, 39, 40, 43, **45-46**,

refugees 26, 174, 176

relief 10, 22, 26, 122, 174, 176, 183, 193, **199-203**, 211

religion 4, 39, 41, 42, 58, **129**, **150-52**, **154-55**, 207

resettlement 3, 9, 10, 16, 26, 43, 64, 65, **121-133**, 160, **174-86**

rural development 6, 12, **49-56**, 103, 135, 142, 144, 150, **156-63**, 166, 168-73, 187-98, 199, **200-204**, 205-211, **215**, 216, 219, **220**, 223

rural policies 16, 19, 25, 27, 28, 34, 36, **49-56**, **70**, 75, 80-85, **89-99**, 100, 101, **108**, 111, 119, 135, 199-203, 214, 219

rural resources 3, 4, 6, 9, 10, 12, 14, 19, 21, 24, 34, 35, 38, 39, 41, 58, 67, 124, 135, 167, 177, 208-09, 215, **220-22**

self-consciousness 59, 65, 66, 67, 172, **214**, **218**, **223-24**

self-determination 11, 12, 66, 214-15, 216, 217, 218, 219, 220, 221, 222-224

self-reliance 6, **69**, 75, 84, 103, 173, 213, 215, 217

self-sufficiency 3, 6, 13, 26, 27, 28, 39, 52, 104, 122, 127, 130, 184

service cooperatives 3, 7, 13, 16, 55, 70, 116, 118, 125, 147

services 8, 9, 11, 26, 124, 136, 139, **142**, 147, 163, 205, 208, 209, 215, 221

smallholders 8, 17, 22, 24, 25, 27, 32, 34, 36, 50, 55, **100-108**, 170, 215

social conflict 5, 22, 27, 141, 164, 214, 216, 217

social security 8, 12, 34, 38, 45, 140, 166, 178, 192, 213, 224

socialist agriculture 3, 6, 14, 16, 24, 35, 51, 70, 80, 101, 102, 107, 171, **215**, 222

soil fertility 10, 19, 101, 140, 175, **179-84**, **187-88**

solidarity 4, 7, 8, 81, 209, **217-220**

state intervention 9, 12, 16, 47, **69**, **72**, 101, 125, 128, **135-42**, 164, 166, **214**, 221-22

state farms 3, 8, 13, 16, 22, 23, 24, 25, 63, 70, 79, 81, 91, 99, **100-108**, 112, 124, 222

status 32, 58, **59**, 65-67, 144, 209

storage 33, 82, 140, **203**, 211

structural adjustment 6, **69**, **73-78**

subsidy 8, 70-71, 73, 77, 79, 82, 104, 111, 114, 217

subsistence 4, 8, 11, 13, 17, 23, 31, 32, 50, 64, 71, 89, 147, 164, 189, 215, **218**, 219, 221

surplus 8, 12, 13, 24, 32, 52, 81, **89-99**, 105, 117-9, 135, 166, 182

taxation 6, 7, 8, 10, 13, 27, 30, 33, 43, 44, 45, 46, 82, **89-92**, 114, 117, 129, 147, 178, 217

technology 4, 7, 13, 17, 22, 27, 34, 51, 54, 55, 71, **80**, **82**, **85**, **86**, 102, 103, **105-7**, 124, 129, **130**, 139, 160, 164, 167, 170, 179, 182, 207, 219

tenants 21, 30, 31, 34, **44**, 63, 100, 170

terms of trade 6, 27, **33**, **34**, **35**, 72, 73, 76, 77, **95-96**, 98, 118, 166, 216, **222**

urban society 5, 30, 32, 147, 149

urban-rural relations 5, 27, **30-36**, 38, 40, 43, 46, **92**, **112**, 138, 158, 166, **214**, 216, **221-23**, 225

usufruct 30, 32, 38, **100**

villagisation 3, 9, 16, 26, 65, 102, **135-42**, **151**, 215

vulnerability 10, 11, 19, 27, 167, **168-70**, **200-01**, 204

war 2, 3, 12, 62, 65, 108, 117, 222

women 4, 5, 9, 55, **58-68**, 129, **144-52**

wool 144-46, 152

World Bank 3, 6, 22, 26, 50, 55, **69-78**, 116, 215

yield 25, 122, 130, 132, 146, 175, 180, 183